NORTH AMERICAN
CLONE
BREWS

NORTH AMERICAN CLONE BREWS

Homebrew Recipes for Your Favorite American & Canadian Beers

Scott R. Russell

Storey Publishing

The mission of Storey Publishing is to serve our customers by publishing practical information that encourages personal independence in harmony with the environment.

Edited by Jeanée Ledoux and Brad Ring
Cover design by Meredith Maker
Cover photograph © Roderick Chen/SuperStock, Inc.
Text design by Mark Tomasi
Text production by Susan Bernier and Jennifer Jepson Smith
Indexed by Jeanée Ledoux

Printed in the United States by Malloy
10 9 8 7 6

Library of Congress Cataloging-in-Publication Data

Russell, Scott R., 1961-
  North American clonebrews: homebrew recipes for your favorite American & Canadian
  beers / Scott R. Russell.
    p.   cm.
  Includes bibliographical references and index.
  ISBN-13: 978-1-58017-246-2
  1. Beer-United States.   2. Beer-Canada.   3. Brewing-Amateur's manuals.   I. Title.
TP577 .R87 2000
641.8'73-dc21   00-026599

Dedication

I dedicate this book humbly, respectfully, and with love to the three men who first taught me about beer. Growing up, I thought beer was always yellow in color, came in cans, and was meant to be served ice cold. These men laughed at me when I came home from Europe — for the first time having seen and tasted amber beer, dark beer, cloudy beer, beer made from wheat, beer with spices and fruit, beer with a variety of strengths and flavors, and beer served at differing temperatures — and was no longer satisfied with what was in the fridge at home. Their "resistance" to my search for better beer, and then to my own homebrewing efforts, was one of the roots of this book. So, to my Uncle Bob Newton; my Grandfather Francis Newton; and my father, Pete Russell, I say thanks, and cheers!

Acknowledgments

There are many, many people to acknowledge and thank for their help in the writing of this book. There are those with whom I have brewed or talked about brewing and from whom I have learned much of what I know: Greg Noonan, Julian Zelazny, Mikel Redman, Paul White, Liz Trott, and especially my brother, Kirk Russell. I would also like to thank my original Storey Books editor, Brad Ring, for setting me up on this project, and Craig Bystrinski, my editor at *Brew Your Own* magazine, who helped me develop my first try at clone brewing. I should thank the Beer Judge Certification Program and the judges with whom I have spent many enjoyable hours over the past few years tasting, critiquing, arguing, socializing, and "geeking" — they are too numerous to list, but they know who they are.

I would like to thank the brewers who sent me samples of their products, provided technical data and product information, and in some cases even supplied recipes: Alaskan, Millstream, Great Lakes, Goose Island, Pike, Jasper Murdoch's, Tunbridge Quality Ales, Celis, Uinta, Acadian, Abita, Shiner, Bent River, Boulevard, Old Dominion, Pinehurst Village, Otto Bros., Stone Coast, Ybor City. For help in locating distant beers, thanks go to Don Younger at Belmont Station in Portland, Oregon; to Kenny at Vintage Cellars in Blacksburg, Virginia; and to Doug Alberhasky at John's Grocery in Iowa City, Iowa. Additional thanks to Brad Ring; Liz James; Dave Toth and Francis Newton; Kevin and Anna Rice; Ron Murdoch; Susan Ermer Locke; my wife, Eve Ermer; my sister, Leigh Russell; and my parents, Nadine and Pete Russell.

Contents

Introduction

This book is at the crossroads of 10 years of homebrewing, four years of judging homebrew, four years of managing a homebrew supply shop, and five years of writing about homebrewing. And, of course, this work is greatly aided by 20 years of drinking beer — good, bad, and indifferent.

I started homebrewing in 1990, and within two years, I was brewing regularly enough to need never buy beer again. I self-published a homebrewing manual. I brewed more, read a lot, and wrote another book, *The Basics of Homebrewing* (Optimus, 1994). When the Seven Barrel Brewery opened in nearby West Lebanon, New Hampshire, I was hired to run the homebrew supply shop. I was sales staff, stockboy, maintenance, purchasing agent, and brewing advisor. I learned more, especially from talking with the owner, Greg Noonan, and the head brewer, Mikel Redman. We wrote *The Seven Barrel Brewery Brewer's Handbook* together, perhaps the best all-around manual out there. At this time I also took the Beer Judge Certification Program exam and became a certified beer judge.

Next I hooked up with the national magazine *Brew Your Own* to write features and a monthly column, which I still do. One of my early features on "cloning" commercial beers was a popular article that got many letters and requests for more like it. Brad Ring, then an editor at Storey Books, saw the article and called me to propose this book. The rest is, well, history.

This book is a follow-up to Storey's 1998 title *CloneBrews: Homebrew Recipes for 150 Commercial Beers,* by Tess and Mark Szamatulski. But where their book was international in scope, including beers from six continents, this one deals exclusively with beers from the United States and Canada. Both my book and Tess and Mark's owe a debt to one of the pioneers in this industry, the late Dave Line, a British homebrewer and writer of the 1970s. Line's *Brewing Beers Like Those You Buy* (Argus Books Ltd, 1978) paved the way, and I must acknowledge him before going any further.

North American Clonebrews is first and foremost a manual, a workbook. You will find in it not arcane secret formulas, but straightforward, clear directions for making some of the best beers available in the United States and Canada. If your favorite beer is not here, I hope the methods and hints I give will help you figure out the recipe on your own. I can't promise that if you follow my recipes and instructions you will brew the perfect copy of your target beer. But if you use this book as the beginning point of your research, you will know more about beer, and you will probably brew better than when you started.

PART 1

The Basics of Clone Brewing

Before we look at the recipes for North American beers to be cloned, it is worthwhile to discuss reasons for cloning, processes involved, ingredients, brewing terminology, and equipment. I will also outline my basic procedure, step by step, and give you some practical tips to make things go more smoothly. If you are already a veteran brewer, or you have been cloning your favorite beers for a while now and are interested only in the recipes, then by all means skip ahead to parts 2 and 3.

What Is Cloning?

The typical homebrewer may approach recipe design and brewing itself in four ways: You take a preexisting recipe and brew it — no variation, no questions — and take the results as they come; you design a brew within certain fairly standard style guidelines; you take a preexisting recipe or style and change it, subtly or drastically, by adding or subtracting ingredients; or, you try to copy a specific example of a style or a unique commercial product. This latter procedure is what I and others call *cloning.*

The challenge of making beer forces us to consider issues of freedom, quality, creativity, economy, and art. By brewing our own beer at home we are making one or more sociopolitical statements. We are bored with commercially brewed beer; we are cheap and want to save money by making our own; we are trying to prove that we can do as well as the big guys; perhaps we just want to do something different, something original.

Whatever your reason for doing it, cloning is not a casual affair. It requires patience, research, and an eye for detail. To successfully clone your target beer, you need to learn as much as you can about that beer — its ingredients, style, brewer, process, history. But you must also learn as much as possible about general brewing procedures. Know what every ingredient does, what flavors and characteristics are contributed by each of them. Learn what different procedures can and can't do to the flavors and aromas you are seeking to reproduce, and find out what to expect from different types of packaging, aging, and temperatures.

Know Your Target Beer

For me, cloning a beer for the first time is a three-step process. First, I drink the target beer (obviously!), but with a critical eye and palate. I take notes on its appearance, its carbonation level, its color, clarity, head color and thickness, its aroma, flavor, body, and aftertaste. From these notes I make a rough thumbnail sketch, a preliminary guess at a recipe. Then I do some factual research and trial-and-error brewing.

Read the Label

Does the label say anything useful? Some brewers actually give you original gravity (OG), final gravity (FG), and alcohol by volume (abv) right there on the label. Others go so far as to give you a list of the ingredients, in the best cases including malt and hop varieties. The label may also list the brewery's Web site or product information phone line.

Ask for Help

Again, I know that the more information I can get my hands on before I start, the better my beer is going to turn out. For this book, my research included a few brewery tours and some phone calls and e-mails to the brewers themselves. You'd be surprised how forthcoming some of them are regarding their recipes and procedures. I guess that's because many of them started as homebrewers and still remember their humble beginnings. Hey, the way I see it, the whole craft brewing industry owes a huge debt to us, the consumers.

If you can't get information directly from your target brewers, use resources such as "beer tourist" guidebooks, like Michael Jackson's *Beer Companion* or the American Homebrewers Association 14-volume Classic Beer Style Series.

Brew and Brew Again

Once you have the necessary information, the real fun begins. You may have to brew a clone recipe three or four times to get it right, tweaking and fine-tuning after each batch ripens. Or maybe you'll get lucky, if you did enough research, and hit it right on or pretty darn close the first time. It's a good idea to share your brew with others who know and appreciate your target beer. Enter it in a local competition to see what trained judges think of it, and ask for their advice on how you can improve it. If the target beer is local, you may even be able to arrange to have the brewer taste it and give you some pointers.

Know Your Ingredients

Brew a lot and experiment with all the different types of extract, malt, adjunct grains, sugars, and so on. Use as many kinds of hops as you can find, getting accustomed to their different aromas and flavors; this will improve your ability to identify them in your target. Learn how the process of brewing affects the sweetness and bitterness, the body and color.

Select Your Yeast

The most important ingredient in duplicating a particular beer is usually the yeast. There is no way you are going to come close to that Belgian beer you like so much using a dry ale yeast. Nor will you re-create your favorite stout with a bock lager yeast.

In many ways, bottle-conditioned beers are the ultimate clonable beers, except that, in truth, more brewers nowadays bottle-condition with a yeast different from the one(s) with which they ferment. Many of the Belgian ales, for example, are fermented with carefully selected proprietary strains, then filtered and repitched with a special strain used only for bottling.

This protects a sort of informal "copyright" on yeasts. Chances are that the brewers who do bottle and ferment with the same yeast are using a common, commercially available strain, anyway, making their dregs not worth the trouble.

If you know that the brewer uses the same strain for fermentation and bottling, check to see whether it might be a variety that is available from your homebrew supplier — you'll have better luck getting a clean, viable culture that way. For those few beers that are bottle-conditioned with their main yeast and whose yeast strains are not commercially available, see Preparing Yeast on page 9 for the basics of reculturing. Of course, if you have connections within the brewery and can legally get a clean culture from them, go for it!

If you resort to buying a yeast culture for your brew, it is my opinion that you will always do better with a liquid yeast culture than with a dry yeast. Certain strains of dry yeast are wonderful, and certain liquid strains just don't cut it. But on the whole, the newer generations of liquid cultures are reliable, clean, authentic, efficient, and worth whatever they cost you. I have a particular fondness for the Wyeast strains, for both their variety and their packaging; hence, my recipes generally indicate a Wyeast product. If you are keen on another brand, by all means find the nearest equivalent to what I suggest and try it.

Select Your Hops

The recipes in this book use a variety of hops. We are fortunate today in that there is a huge selection of hops available. However, it would be very easy to get carried away and use too many different hops. Recipes for beers of a generally English style will include, if not English hops, then hops derived from English varieties. The same goes for German, Czech, and any other beer styles. Obvious American adaptations of European beer styles use typical American hops. By the same token, higher-alpha hops are nearly always used for bittering, while lower-alpha hops are used for flavor and aroma. If the hops recommended for a particular recipe are not available to you, check various style books, consult books on hops and hop use, or ask your homebrew supplier which substitutions would be best.

Brewing Terms Used in This Book

There are terms specific to the making of alcoholic beverages, and I will explain the most important ones here. Beginners can find more thorough coverage of the basics of homebrewing in *The Complete Handbook of Home Brewing* by Dave Miller (Storey Books, 1992); to learn about the science behind brewing, see *Brew Chem 101: The Basics of Homebrewing Chemistry* by Lee W. Janson, Ph.D. (Storey Books, 1996).

Alcohol by volume (abv). To determine abv, subtract the final gravity from the original gravity and multiply by .1275. Example: If your beer's original gravity is 1048 and its final gravity is 1008, the abv is 5.1% (40 x .1275 = 5.1% abv).

Ale. This is one of the two basic families of beer (see Lager below). Generally, ale is brewed with a strain of yeast that prefers slightly warmer temperatures. Ale also tends to be fruitier and coarser in flavor than lager. (See Beer Style Guidelines, page 162.)

Alpha acid units (AAUs). AAUs measure hops' bitterness. When you buy hops, they should be labeled with a percentage aa. For instance, Chinook hops are usually around 12% aa, but this will vary from crop to crop. Determine AAUs by multiplying the aa level of a given hop by the number of ounces used. (You will need to work backward for the recipes.) Example: You need 6 AAUs of Chinook hops. The Chinook your supplier has in stock is at 12% aa, so you need to use ½ ounce (½ x 12% = 6 AAUs).

Candi. A crystallized beet sugar used mainly in high-alcohol Belgian beers.

Dregs. The precipitated sediment, mainly yeast, at the bottom of a beer.

Fermentation. The process wherein wort (see page 7) is converted by yeast into beer. Yeast, a microscopic fungus, metabolizes sugars and other carbohydrates into alcohol and carbon dioxide (and other more or less desirable by-products).

Final gravity (FG) or terminal gravity (TG). Final gravity is the second hydrometer reading, done after fermentation is complete, as you bottle. The reading should be much lower than the original gravity since the density of beer decreases as the sugar is consumed by yeast.

International bittering units (IBUs). IBUs measure the bitterness of beer, relatively speaking. To determine IBUs, multiply AAUs by the hop utilization factor. (See the Hop Utilization Chart on page 6.)

Lager. One of the two basic families of beer (see Ale above), lager is brewed with strains of yeast that prefer colder temperatures and longer aging. (See Beer Style Guidelines, page 162.)

Lovibond, degrees (°L). A scale used to rate the color of grains and extracts.

Malt. 1) A grain that has been partially sprouted and dried, causing the conversion of starches to sugars and the release of enzymes and proteins. 2) An extract made by mashing malted grain and extracting its sugars. It is found in syrup and powdered form (DME). Malt extracts can be light, amber, or dark; they can be made from barley, wheat, rye, or other malted grains; and they can be hopped or unhopped.

Mash/partial mash. The time- and temperature-controlled soaking of malted grains in water to liberate enzymes, convert starches to sugars, and dissolve those sugars in order to remove them from the grains. Partial mashing is the compromise technique involving mashing grains to derive some of the fermentables in the wort (see next page) and supplementing them with ready-made extracts.

Original gravity (OG) or starting gravity (SG). This measurement, taken on a hydrometer before you pitch the yeast, is an indication of the sugar concentration in your wort. It's necessary to determine whether your mash has been efficient, and it's used to determine final alcohol content.

Pitch. Brewers use this term to mean adding yeast to wort.

Prime. This term is used by brewers to mean adding fermentables at the bottling stage to promote carbonation.

Rack. The process of siphoning beer from one vessel to another.

Reculture. The process of reviving suspended or dormant yeast to create a larger, pitchable quantity.

Runoff or runnings. The liquid that is drawn off from the mashed grains after conversion is complete.

Slurry. Yeast in a liquid suspension.

Sparge (or lauter). Gentle rinsing of mashed grains with water, usually at approximately 168°F to 170°F (76–77°C), to capture the maximum available fermentable material.

Hop Utilization Chart

A hop's utilization factor, or bitterness contributed to the recipe, is based on the volume brewed, the OG of the wort, and the length of the boil. Use this chart to determine the hop utilization factor of one AAU of a hop boiled in a 5-gallon (18.9 L) wort with a 1050 OG.

These factors are based on a general utilization rate of approximately 30%. A higher or lower OG will result in a slightly different utilization rate. Pellet hops will contribute more bitterness; whole, loose hops will contribute less bitterness, but more aroma.

Length of Boil (minutes)	Hop Utilization Factor (IBUs)
0	.7
5	.7
15	1.25
20	1.5
30	2.4
45	4.0
60	4.25
90	4.5

Tun. A vessel in which to mash, sparge, and sometimes ferment. Tuns were formerly barrels.

Wort. The liquid mixture before you add yeast to start fermentation. Sweet wort is the liquid mixture of fermentables before you add hops (or spices).

Basic Brewing Equipment

There is a bewildering array of brewing equipment available from shops, catalogs, and online sources. The investment can vary almost as much as the setups themselves, so here is what I recommend for the beginner. This equipment is essentially what I have used from my first batch to the present, and the total cost of these items should not set back the beginning brewer more than $100.

Airlock and stopper. These should fit the hole drilled in the lid of the fermenter. I prefer the three-piece, cylindrical type of airlock for the primary fermenter. For the secondary fermentation vessel, you'll probably need a #7 stopper and an S-shaped airlock.

Bottle capper. Use either the inexpensive, two-handled kind or the more reliable bench-type, one-handed model.

Fermenter, primary. Use a 6- or 7-gallon (22.7 or 26.5 L) food-grade plastic bucket with a tight-fitting lid (preferably with an inside O-ring seal). I like the lid to be drilled with a hole to fit a #2 rubber stopper.

Fermenter, secondary. Use a 5- or 6-gallon (18.9 or 22.7 L) glass carboy.

Heat source. A gas stove is better than an electric one, but the large units on any kitchen range will work for "small" batches. You will eventually want something bigger and better, but not until you advance in your techniques.

Hydrometer. This instrument measures the gravity of liquids. Buy one with a triple-scale, or at least with a specific gravity scale, and a sample cylinder.

Kettle. This should be stainless steel or enamelware, not aluminum. Buy a 4- or 5-gallon (15.1 or 18.9 L) kettle to start, but move up to an 8- or 10-gallon (30.3 or 37.9 L) monster when you're ready.

Siphoning equipment. You'll need this to transfer liquid and to bottle. Try 3 to 4 feet (91.5–122 cm) of ⅜-inch (1 cm) flexible, food-grade plastic tubing; a 24-inch (61 cm) stiff plastic, cane-shaped tube; and a plastic hose clamp. (You can make your life easier by also buying a spring-loaded bottle filler tip, but it isn't necessary for beginners.)

Spoons. Use long-handled, stainless-steel spoons for stirring liquids.

Thermometer. Get a long, glass, heavy-duty thermometer with a pot clip.

Thermometer strips. Buy one of these self-adhesive strips (as for aquariums, but specifically for beer fermenting temperatures) for each fermenter you own.

Brewing Step by Step

These are the brewing methods that I have found to work best with the equipment I own. I have a high success rate, mainly because I'm careful. You may have better equipment and better ideas, and that's fine. Following these guidelines carefully is still a good idea.

Brewing from Grains

Below is the basic step-by-step procedure for partial mash recipes. The main recipe for each beer is a partial mash recipe — some of the fermentables and much of the character of the beer will be derived from actually mashing a small portion of the grain, but this will be supplemented by some type of malt extract for the majority of the fermentables. For some of the "bigger" beers, however, even the partial mash will be as big as a full mash for lighter brews. If your equipment cannot handle the amount of grain to be mashed, you can usually substitute further, replacing 3 pounds (1.4 kg) of grain with 2 pounds (907 g) of dry malt extract. In any case, you will also find conversions for each recipe so that you can brew it principally from extract or as an all-grain recipe.

Use Fresh Ingredients

Don't crush the grains too far in advance; they get stale in a matter of days.

Step 1: Heat water as specified in the recipe.

Step 2: Crush grain, as required, and mix the grain into the mash liquor. Stir gently until all the grain is moistened.

Step 3: Check the temperature of the mixture and add a little more water (hot or cold) as necessary to adjust to steeping temperature. Cover the mash vessel and steep the grains for the recommended time.

Step 4: Heat more water for sparging according to the recipe.

Step 5: When the mash is done, quickly transfer the grains to your sparging tun for sparging. Think through this part of the process carefully — every brewer will find an appropriate setup, but it needs to be done efficiently and cleanly.

Step 6: When sparging is complete, add any extracts, sugars, and so on as indicated in the recipe. Put the kettle on the heat and boil the mixture. Add the hops and any other ingredients according to the recipe.

Step 7: After boiling for the recommended time, remove the kettle from the heat and chill it by setting it in a sinkful of ice or in a snowbank, siphoning the hot wort into a counterflow wort chiller, or setting an immersion chiller into the wort.

Step 8: When you have taken the edge off the wort's heat, pour the wort into your primary fermenter and add chilled, preboiled water to bring the volume up to 5¼ gallons (20 L). Set it to cool the rest of the way to your yeast-pitching temperature, if necessary.

Step 9: With a sanitized stirrer or spoon, stir the wort well or gently rock the fermenter back and forth, this will aerate it somewhat, providing oxygen for the yeast.

Step 10: Take and record a hydrometer reading.

Step 11: Pitch the yeast into the wort. Seal the fermenter, affix an airlock, and put the fermentation vessel in a place away from light, heat, and air currents.

Step 12: Wait. When initial fermentation is complete (usually one to two weeks, depending on the recipe), transfer the liquid to your secondary fermenter. Wait again.

Step 13: When conditioning is complete (usually three to eight weeks, depending on the recipe), rack the nearly finished beer to your bottling bucket, add priming sugar, and bottle.

Step 14: Wait yet again while the bottled beer ages (usually three to eight weeks, depending on the recipe).

Step 15: Reward yourself with a clonebrew!

Steeping Grains

Extract brews tend to lack slightly in depth and complexity; therefore, most homebrewers will use a small quantity of specialty grains to intensify the color, add character, and freshen up the grain aroma and flavor.

Step 1: Put the steeping grains in a muslin mesh bag, tie it shut, and place it in a kettle of water.

Step 2: Put the kettle on the heat, raise to the desired steeping temperature, and hold the temperature for the indicated time. Remove the grains.

Preparing Yeast

Below is the process for making a yeast starter. Follow the manufacturer's directions for preparing each particular brand, paying special attention to temperature recommendations. The temperature at which yeast is stored, cultured, and pitched is crucial. Extremely warm or cold temperatures will kill yeast, which, even in a dry or suspended state, is a living organism.

Step 1: Boil a small quantity of low-gravity wort. (I usually make about a quart at a time, using a quart [.95 L] of water and 3 or 4 tablespoons [44 or 59 ml] of dry malt extract.) A 15-minute boil is sufficient to sanitize it.

Step 2: Cool the wort. Pour it into a sanitized half-gallon (1.9 L) glass container (I use a milk bottle) and cover it with plastic wrap secured with a rubber band.

Step 3: When the wort has cooled to pitching temperature, pour in the yeast sample (either from the foil packet, in the case of Wyeast, or from the bottle dregs if you're reculturing a commercial, bottle-conditioned yeast).

Step 4: Affix an airlock, let the yeast work a day or two, then brew with it. If it looks like it will be a few days until you can brew, add another cup or so of chilled wort. This step can be repeated a couple of times, if necessary, but be careful not to expose the yeast to too much air or to shock the culture with either too cold or too hot wort.

General Considerations

At last we come to the recipes themselves — well, almost. There are just a few more things to consider before you start brewing one of them. The recipes assume you have the necessary and appropriate equipment to carry out the entire brewing process. If you don't, please review page 7, then put this book down and go directly to your homebrew supply shop and get whatever you need to start.

• All recipes are for 5 gallons (18.9 L), but I recommend a starting volume of 5¼ gallons (20 L) because some wort will inevitably be lost to spillage, evaporation, hydrometer measurement, and so on.

• The volume of water needed for mashing and sparging is based on a ratio between 1.1 and 1.3 quarts (1–1.2 L) of liquid per pound (454 g) of grain. Measure your water carefully since the thickness of the mash affects the final body of the beer.

• Always use chilled, preboiled water to top up the volume in the fermentation vessel.

• Sanitize anything and everything that will come in contact with the beer when it is cooler than 160°F (71°C).

• Unless otherwise indicated, always remove whole hops and spices at the end of the prescribed boiling or steeping time. Always remove steeped grains (in extract recipes) before proceeding to the boil.

• Note that the ingredients in the Alternate Methods section of each recipe may vary from those used in the main recipe. These are carefully calculated substitutions — combinations of colored grains or extracts, levels of fermentability, and other factors were considered to make partial-mash, all-extract, and all-grain versions look and taste the same.

• Brewers conventionally refer to only the last two digits of a standard hydrometer reading, or at least drop the decimal point (e.g., 1.054 = 1054); 1.000 or 00 is the density of water.

General Extract Values

Use this information if you wish to substitute ingredients for those I recommend. Recipe calculations are based on the following general extract values:

• malted grain = 30.7 gravity points/pound

• malt extract syrup = 36 gravity points/pound

• dry malt extract = 44 gravity points/pound

PART 2

Clone Recipes for U.S. Beers

Alaskan Amber

Alaskan Brewing, Juneau, Alaska

This alt-style amber ale has a bready, malty flavor balanced by German hop aroma.
It's a firm, smooth, rich brew, but not overwhelming, making it a pleasant session beer.

Original gravity: 1054   •   Final gravity: 1015   •   5% abv   •   20 IBU

Heat 1½ gallons (5.7 L) water to 164°F (73°C). Crush:

3 lb. (1.4 kg) Pilsner malt
1¼ lb. (567 g) Munich malt

Add to liquor and steep at 152°F (67°C) for 90 minutes. Sparge with 2½ gallons (9.5 L) water at 168°F (76°C). Add to runnings:

3½ lb. (1.6 kg) unhopped, light dry malt extract (DME)

Bring to a boil, then add:

4 AAUs Mt. Hood hops

Boil 45 minutes, then add:

4 AAUs Spalt hops

Boil 15 minutes, then remove from heat. Cool, then top up to 5¼ gallons (20 L) with chilled, preboiled water. Chill to 68°F (20°C), then pitch:

German ale yeast (Wyeast 1007 or equivalent)

Ferment at 68°F (20°C) for 2 weeks, then transfer to the secondary fermenter and condition cold (40°F [4°C]) for 3 to 4 weeks. Prime with:

⅞ cup (202 ml) pale dry malt extract

Bottle and age at 50°F (10°C) for 3 weeks.

Alternate Methods

All-extract: Steep 1 lb. (454 g) Pilsner malt and 1 lb. (454 g) Munich malt in 2½ gallons (9.5 L) water at 150°F (66°C) for 45 minutes. Increase DME to 5 lb. (2.3 kg) and follow directions from beginning of boil.

All-grain: Mash 8 lb. (3.6 kg) Pilsner malt and the Munich malt as in main recipe in 3 gallons (11 L) water at 152°F (67°C). Sparge with 4 gallons (15.1 L) water. Omit first DME and proceed as in main recipe, reducing wort volume to 5¼ gallons (20 L) or less.

Serve at 50°F (10°C) in a cylindrical alt glass.

Smoked Porter

Alaskan Brewing, Juneau, Alaska

A beer to warm an Alaska night, this porter is dark, rich, and semisweet with lots of malty flavor and aroma. As its name implies, though, the dominant flavor is smoke. Alaskan uses its own alder-smoked malt, but German beech-smoked malt will work if you don't have the capacity to smoke malt yourself.

Original gravity: 1065 • **Final gravity: 1015** • **6.1% abv** • **40 IBU**

Heat 1¾ gallons (6.6 L) water to 164°F (73°C). Crush:

3 lb. (1.4 kg) smoked pale malt
2 oz. (56.7 g) dark (90°L) crystal malt
8 oz. (227 g) black malt
2 oz. (56.7 g) chocolate malt

Add to liquor and steep at 152°F (67°C) for 90 minutes. Sparge with 2½ gallons (9.5 L) water at 168°F (76°C). Add to runnings:

5 lb. (2.3 kg) unhopped, amber dry malt extract (DME)

Bring to a boil, then add:

6 AAUs Goldings hops

Boil 30 minutes, then add:

3 AAUs Willamette hops

Boil 55 minutes, then add:

3 AAUs Goldings hops

Boil 5 minutes, then remove from heat. Cool, then top up to 5¼ gallons (20 L) with chilled, preboiled water. Cool to 68°F (20°C), then pitch:

American or English ale yeast (Wyeast 1056, 1098, or equivalent)

Ferment at 68°F (20°C) for 2 weeks, then transfer to secondary fermenter and condition cool (50–55°F [10–13°C]) for 3 to 4 weeks. Prime with:

1 cup (237 ml) pale dry malt extract

Bottle and age at 55–60°F (13–16°C) for 3 weeks.

Alternate Methods

All-extract: Steep 1½ lb. (680 g) smoked pale malt and the crystal, black, and chocolate malts as in main recipe in 2½ gallons (9.5 L) water at 150°F (66°C) for 45 minutes. Add 6 lb. (2.7 kg) dark DME, then follow directions from beginning of boil.

All-grain: Mash 4 lb. (1.8 kg) smoked pale malt, 6 lb. (2.7 kg) pale malt, and the crystal, black, and chocolate malts as above in 3½ gallons (13.2 L) water at 152°F (67°C). Sparge with 4½ gallons (17 L) water. Omit DME and proceed as in main recipe, reducing wort volume to 5¼ gallons (20 L) or less.

 Serve at 50°F (10°C) in a traditional pint glass.

Crazy Ed's Original Cave Creek Chili Beer

Black Mountain Brewing Co., Cave Creek, Arizona

Watch out — this looks like an ordinary, harmless golden lager, but the second you open the bottle, you know it isn't. Each bottle contains a 2-inch-long (5 cm) hot pepper (jalapeño, I'd guess), and you smell it and then taste it right away. Amazingly, though, there's also some beer in there!

Original gravity: 1046 • Final gravity: 1012 • 4.3% abv • 25 IBU

Heat 2 gallons (7.6 L) water to 164°F (73°C). Crush:
- **3 lb. (1.4 kg) lager malt**
- **1 lb. (454 g) carapils malt**
- **8 oz. (227 g) Vienna malt**
- **8 oz. (227 g) flaked maize**

Add to liquor and steep at 152°F (67°C) for 90 minutes. Sparge with 3 gallons (11 L) water at 168°F (76°C). Add to runnings:
- **2 lb. (907 g) unhopped, extra-light dry malt extract (DME)**

Bring to a boil, then add:
- **6 AAUs Hallertau hops**

Boil 60 minutes, then add:
- **4 AAUs Mt. Hood hops**

Remove from heat. Cool and top up to 5¼ gallons (20 L) with chilled, preboiled water. Cool to 68°F (20°C), then pitch:
- **German lager yeast (Wyeast 2007 or equivalent)**

Ferment at 45°F (7°C) for 2 weeks, then transfer to secondary fermenter and condition cold (40°F [4°C]) for 5 to 6 weeks. Prime with:
- **1 cup (237 ml) pale dry malt extract**

Add (one) to each bottle:
- **Small dried chili peppers (variety is up to you)**

Bottle and age at 40°F (4°C) for 6 weeks.

Alternate Methods

All-extract: Steep the carapils and Vienna malts and flaked maize as in main recipe in 2½ gallons (9.5 L) water at 150°F (66°C) for 45 minutes. Omit lager malt and increase DME to 4 lb. (1.8 kg). Follow directions from beginning of boil.

All-grain: Mash 6 lb. (2.7 kg) lager malt and the carapils and Vienna malts and flaked maize as in main recipe in 3 gallons (11 L) water at 152°F (67°C). Sparge with 3¾ gallons (14.2 L) water. Omit first DME and proceed as in main recipe, reducing wort volume to 5¼ gallons (20 L) or less.

 Serve at 40°F (4°C) in a traditional pint glass.

Anchor Porter

Anchor Brewing Co., San Francisco, California

A deep, dark, robust porter from one of the classic microbrewery pioneers, Anchor is opaque, black, and has a tight, creamy head with a noseful of dark malty aroma. Full bodied and rich with hints of coffee, treacle, fruit, and lots of hop bitterness, the flavors linger long after the glass is empty.

Original gravity: 1055 • Final gravity: 1018 • 4.7% abv • 30 IBU

Heat 1¾ gallons (6.6 L) water to 164°F (73°C). Crush:

- **3 lb. (1.4 kg) pale malt**
- **8 oz. (227 g) dark (120°L) crystal malt**
- **8 oz. (227 g) Munich malt**
- **8 oz. (227 g) black patent malt**

Add to liquor and steep at 152°F (67°C) for 90 minutes. Sparge with 2½ gallons (9.5 L) water at 168°F (76°C). Add to runnings:

- **3½ lb. (1.6 kg) unhopped, dark dry malt extract (DME)**

Bring to a boil, then add:

- **6 AAUs Northern Brewer hops**

Boil 75 minutes, then add:

- **4 AAUs Northern Brewer hops**

Boil 15 minutes, then remove from heat. Cool, then top up to 5¼ gallons (20 L) with chilled, preboiled water. Cool to 68°F (20°C), then pitch:

- **American ale yeast (Wyeast 1056 or equivalent)**

If desired, blend with:

- **California lager yeast (Wyeast 2112)**

Ferment at 68°F (20°C) for 2 weeks, then transfer to secondary fermenter and condition cold (40°F [4°C]) for 3 to 4 weeks. Prime with:

- **1 cup (237 ml) dark dry malt extract**

Bottle and age at 50°F (10°C) for 3 weeks.

Alternate Methods

All-extract: Steep the crystal, Munich, and black malts as in main recipe in 2½ gallons (9.5 L) water at 150°F (66°C) for 45 minutes. Omit pale malt and increase DME to 5½ lb. (2.5 kg). Follow directions from beginning of boil.

All-grain: Mash 8 lb. (3.6 kg) pale malt and the crystal, Munich, and black malts as in main recipe in 3 gallons (11 L) water at 152°F (67°C). Sparge with 3¾ gallons (14.2 L) water. Omit first DME and proceed as in main recipe, reducing wort volume to 5¼ gallons (20 L) or less.

 Serve at 50°F (10°C) in a traditional pint glass.

Barney Flats Oatmeal Stout

Anderson Valley Brewing Co., Boonville, California
The taste and aroma alternate between dark malt and hops; every sip of this black, smoky, roasty, and sweet stout seems to bring a different flavor perception.

Original gravity: 1055 • Final gravity: 1012 • 5.5% abv • 40 IBU

Heat 1¾ gallons (6.6 L) water to 164°F (73°C). Crush:

2 lb. (907 g) pale malt
12 oz. (340 g) dark (120°L) crystal malt
4 oz. (113 g) chocolate malt
1 lb. (454 g) flaked oats
8 oz. (227 g) roasted barley

Add to liquor and steep at 152°F (67°C) for 90 minutes. Sparge with 2½ gallons (9.5 L) water at 168°F (76°C). Add to runnings:

3½ lb. (1.6 kg) unhopped, dark dry malt extract (DME)

Bring to a boil, then add:

8 AAUs Goldings hops

Boil 75 minutes, then add:

4 AAUs Willamette hops

Boil 15 minutes, then remove from heat. Cool, then top up to 5¼ gallons (20 L) with chilled, preboiled water. Cool to 68°F (20°C), then pitch:

English ale yeast (Wyeast 1098 or equivalent)

Ferment at 68°F (20°C) for 2 weeks, then transfer to secondary fermenter and condition cool (50–55°F [10–13°C]) for 3 to 4 weeks. Prime with:

1 cup (237 ml) pale dry malt extract

Bottle and age at 55–60°F (13–16°C) for 3 weeks.

Alternate Methods

All-extract: Omit pale malt and steep the crystal and chocolate malts, flaked oats, and roasted barley as in main recipe in 2½ gallons (9.5 L) water at 150°F (66°C) for 45 minutes. Increase DME to 5 lb. (2.3 kg). Follow directions from beginning of boil.

All-grain: Mash 7 lb. (3.2 kg) pale malt and the crystal and chocolate malts, flaked oats, and roasted barley as in main recipe in 3 gallons (11 L) water at 152°F (67°C). Sparge with 3¾ gallons (14.2 L) water. Omit first DME and proceed as in main recipe, reducing wort volume to 5¼ gallons (20 L) or less.

 Serve at 50°F (10°C) in a traditional pint glass.

Bigfoot

Sierra Nevada Brewing Co., Chico, California

A barleywine-style ale from the brewers of a classic American pale ale, this deep reddish brown beer is big in malt, hop flavor, and aroma. It has an alcoholic warmth that will cheer you on the coldest night. With all that going on inside, Bigfoot is a very complex brew and will age well over several months. Be warned — this is not an inexpensive beer to make.

Original gravity: 1095 • **Final gravity: 1020** • **9.6% abv** • **80 IBU**

Heat 2½ gallons (9.5 L) water to 164°F (73°C). Crush:

- **6 lb. (2.7 kg) pale malt**
- **1¼ lb. (567 g) light (20°L) crystal malt**

Add to liquor and steep at 152°F (67°C) for 90 minutes. Sparge with 3 gallons (11 L) water at 168°F (76°C). Add to runnings:

- **7 lb. (3.2 kg) unhopped, light malt extract syrup**
- **8 oz. (227 g) unhopped, amber dry malt extract (DME)**

Boil 30 minutes, then add:

- **10 AAUs Nugget hops**
- **7 AAUs Cascade hops**

Boil 90 minutes, then remove from heat. Cool, then top up to 5¼ gallons (20 L) with chilled, preboiled water. Cool to 68°F (20°C), then pitch:

- **American ale yeast (recultured Bigfoot, Wyeast 1056, or equivalent)**

Ferment at 68°F (20°C) for 2 weeks. Transfer to secondary fermenter and add:

- **4 AAUs Cascade hops**
- **6 AAUs Centennial hops**
- **⅕ oz. (5.7 g) dry champagne yeast**

Condition cool (50–55°F [10–13°C]) for 6 to 8 weeks. Prime with:

- **¾ cup (177 ml) pale dry malt extract**

Bottle and age at 45–50°F (7–10°C) for 8 months.

Alternate Methods

All-extract: Steep 1 lb. (454 g) pale malt and the crystal malt as in main recipe in 2½ gallons (9.5 L) water at 150°F (66°C) for 45 minutes. Increase malt extract syrup to 12 lb. (5.4 kg) and omit DME. Follow directions from beginning of boil.

All-grain: Mash 15 lb. (6.8 kg) pale malt and the crystal malt as in main recipe in 5 gallons (18.9 L) water at 152°F (67°C). Sparge with 4 gallons (15.1 L) water. Omit malt extract syrup and DME and proceed as in main recipe, reducing wort volume to 5¼ gallons (20 L) or less.

Share with a friend at 50°F (10°C) in two brandy snifters.

Brickhouse Extra Pale Ale

SLO Brewing Co., San Luis Obispo, California
(contract-brewed in New Ulm, Minnesota)

A very pale, golden ale with lots of hop aroma, this beer is light in body and mild in flavor, making it seem hoppier than it really is. There are also notes of crackers, bread, toast, and grain.

Original gravity: 1048 • **Final gravity: 1010** • **4.8% abv** • **35 IBU**

Heat 1¾ gallons (6.6 L) water to 164°F (73°C). Crush:

3 lb. (1.4 kg) pale malt
1 lb. (454 g) light (20°L) crystal malt
4 oz. (113 g) toasted pale malt (toast at 350°F [177°C]
for 15 minutes)

Add to liquor and steep at 152°F (67°C) for 90 minutes. Sparge with 2½ gallons (9.5 L) water at 168°F (76°C). Add to runnings:

3¹/₃ lb. (1.5 kg) unhopped, extra-light malt extract syrup

Bring to a boil, then add:

4 AAUs Cluster hops
4 AAUs Goldings hops

Boil 60 minutes, then remove from heat. Cool, then top up to 5¼ gallons (20 L) with chilled, preboiled water. Cool to 68°F (20°C), then pitch:

American ale yeast (Wyeast 1056 or equivalent)

Ferment at 68°F (20°C) for 2 weeks, then transfer to secondary fermenter and add:

4 AAUs Cascade hops

Condition cool (50–55°F [10–13°C]) for 3 to 4 weeks. Prime with:

1 cup (237 ml) pale dry malt extract (DME)

Bottle and age at 55–60°F (13–16°C) for 3 weeks.

Alternate Methods

All-extract: Steep the crystal and toasted malts as in main recipe in 2¹/₂ gallons (9.5 L) water at 150°F (66°C) for 45 minutes. Omit pale malt and increase malt extract syrup to 6 lb. (2.7 kg). Follow directions from beginning of boil.

All-grain: Mash 7 lb. (3.2 kg) pale malt and the crystal and toasted malts as in main recipe in 3 gallons (11 L) water at 152°F (67°C). Sparge with 3³/₄ gallons (14.2 L) water. Omit malt extract syrup and proceed as in main recipe, reducing wort volume to 5¹/₄ gallons (20 L) or less.

Serve at 50°F (10°C) in a traditional pint glass.

Downtown Brown Ale

Lost Coast Brewery, Eureka, California

*Downtown is a classic example of an American brown ale: bigger, drier,
and hoppier than standard English brown ales, yet nutty and smooth.
The combination of burnt sugar and herbal hop bouquet is tantalizing.*

Original gravity: 1044 • Final gravity: 1008 • 4.6% abv • 25 IBU

Heat 1½ gallons (5.7 L) water to 164°F (73°C). Crush:

2 lb. (907 g) mild ale malt
1 lb. (454 g) brown malt
8 oz. (227 g) chocolate malt
8 oz. (227 g) medium (50°L) crystal malt
8 oz. (227 g) black malt

Add to liquor and steep at 152°F (67°C) for 90 minutes. Sparge with
2¼ gallons (8.5 L) water at 168°F (76°C). Add to runnings:

2 lb. (907 g) unhopped, amber dry malt extract (DME)

Boil 30 minutes, then add:

4 AAUs Willamette hops

Boil 30 minutes, then add:

4 AAUs Cascade hops

Boil 30 minutes, then remove from heat. Cool, then top up to 5¼ gallons
(20 L) with chilled, preboiled water. Cool to 65°F (18°C), then pitch:

**American or London ale yeast (Wyeast 1056, 1028, or
equivalent)**

Ferment at 65°F (18°C) for 2 weeks, then transfer to secondary fermenter
and condition cool (50–55°F [10–13°C]) for 3 to 4 weeks. Prime with:

½ cup (118 ml) pale dry malt extract
½ cup (118 ml) brown sugar

Bottle and age at 50°F (10°C) for 3 weeks.

Alternate Methods

All-extract: Steep 8 oz.
(227 g) brown malt and
the chocolate, crystal,
and black malts as in main
recipe in 2½ gallons (9.5 L)
water at 150°F (66°C) for
45 minutes. Omit mild ale
malt and increase DME
to 4 lb. (1.8 kg). Follow
directions from beginning
of boil.

All-grain: Mash 4 lb.
(1.8 kg) mild ale malt,
2 lb. (907 g) brown malt,
and the chocolate, crystal,
and black malts as in main
recipe in 2½ gallons (9.5 L)
water at 152°F (67°C).
Sparge with 3 gallons
(11 L) water. Omit first
DME and proceed as in
main recipe, reducing wort
volume to 5¼ gallons
(20 L) or less.

 Serve at 50°F (10°C) in a traditional pint glass.

Hübsch Märzen

Sudwerk Privatbrauerei Hübsch, Davis, California

Here's a rare example of an American-made but true-to-German-style Märzenbier (similar to an Oktoberfest). It is rich and malty but also fairly bitter, making it well balanced and very drinkable.

Original gravity: 1060 • **Final gravity: 1015** • **5.5% abv** • **25–30 IBU**

Heat 1¾ gallons (6.6 L) water to 163°F (73°C). Crush:

2 lb. (907 g) Pilsner malt
1 lb. (454 g) Munich malt
8 oz. (227 g) caramunich malt
8 oz. (227 g) carapils malt
4 oz. (113 g) malted wheat

Add to liquor and steep at 152°F (67°C) for 75 minutes. Sparge with 2½ gallons (9.5 L) water at 168°F (76°C). Add to runnings:

2 lb. (907 g) unhopped, pale dry malt extract (DME)
2 lb. (907 g) unhopped, amber dry malt extract

Bring to a boil, then add:

6 AAUs Tettnanger hops

Boil 60 minutes, then turn off heat and add:

3 AAUs Saaz hops

Steep 30 minutes, then remove as much of the hops as you can. Cool, then top up to 5¼ gallons (20 L) with chilled, preboiled water. Cool to 60°F (16°C), then pitch:

Bavarian lager yeast (Wyeast 2308, 2206, or equivalent)

Ferment at 50°F (10°C) for 1 week, then move to a cooler location (40°F [4°C]) for 2 weeks. Transfer to secondary fermenter and condition cold (38–40°F [3–4°C]) for 6 to 8 weeks. Prime with:

1 cup (237 ml) pale dry malt extract

Bottle and age at 40–45°F (5–7°C) for 6 weeks.

Alternate Methods

All-extract: Steep 8 oz. (227 g) each of Munich, caramunich, and carapils malts in 2½ gallons (9.5 L) water at 150°F (66°C) for 45 minutes. Omit the Pilsner malt and malted wheat and increase malt extracts to 3 lb. (1.4 kg) each. Follow directions from beginning of boil.

All-grain: Mash 5 lb. (2.3 kg) Pilsner malt and 1 lb. (454 g) each of Munich, caramunich, and carapils malts and malted wheat as in main recipe in 3½ gallons (13.2 L) water at 150°F (66°C). Sparge with 4 gallons (15.1 L) water. Omit pale and amber DME and proceed as in main recipe, reducing wort volume to 5¼ gallons (20 L) or less.

 Serve at 40°F (4°C) in a tall, fluted Pilsner glass or an Oktoberfest stein.

Liberty Ale

Anchor Brewing Co., San Francisco, California

A beautiful, deep golden ale, this one fits in somewhere between an extra special bitter and an India pale ale. This brew has the classic floral, pine, and lemon aroma of Cascade hops. It is dry hopped and naturally carbonated.

Original gravity: 1057 • **Final gravity: 1010** • **6% abv** • **45–50 IBU**

Heat 1¼ gallons (4.7 L) water to 164°F (73°C). Crush:
- **2 lb. (907 g) pale malt**
- **8 oz. (227 g) toasted pale malt**
- **8 oz. (227 g) light (20°L) crystal malt**

Add to liquor and steep at 152°F (67°C) for 90 minutes. Sparge with 2 gallons (7.6 L) water at 168°F (76°C). Add to runnings:
- **5 lb. (2.3 kg) unhopped, pale dry malt extract (DME)**

Bring to a boil, then add:
- **7 AAUs Cascade hops**

Boil 45 minutes, then add:
- **5 AAUs Cascade hops**

Boil 30 minutes, then remove from heat. Cool, then top up to 5¼ gallons (20 L) with chilled, preboiled water. Cool to 68°F (20°C), then pitch:
- **American ale yeast (Wyeast 1056 or equivalent)**

Ferment at 68°F (20°C) for 2 weeks, then transfer to secondary fermenter and add:
- **7 AAUs Cascade hops**

Condition cool (50–55°F [10–13°C]) for 3 to 4 weeks. Prime with:
- **1 cup (237 ml) pale dry malt extract**

Bottle and age at 55–60°F (13–16°C) for 3 weeks.

Alternate Methods

All-extract: Steep the toasted pale malt and the crystal malt as in main recipe in 2½ gallons (9.5 L) water at 150°F (66°C) for 45 minutes. Omit pale malt and increase DME to 6½ lb. (2.9 kg). Follow directions from beginning of boil.

All-grain: Mash 9 lb. (4.1 kg) pale malt and the toasted and crystal malts in 3¼ gallons (12.3 L) water at 152°F (67°C). Sparge with 3¾ gallons (14.2 L) water. Omit first DME and proceed as in main recipe, reducing wort volume to 5¼ gallons (20 L) or less.

 Serve at 50°F (10°C) in a traditional pint glass.

Pete's Signature Pilsner

Pete's Brewing Co., Palo Alto, California;
Winston-Salem, North Carolina; Seattle, Washington
*This surprisingly true-to-style, Bohemian-inspired golden lager is rich, bready, and has
a delicious Saaz aroma and flavor. The aftertaste is a slow fade
of malt and hops, leaving a clean and dry finish.*

Original gravity: 1048 • Final gravity: 1012 • 4.6% abv • 45 IBU

Heat 1½ gallons (5.7 L) water to 164°F (73°C). Crush:

3 lb. (1.4 kg) lager malt
1 lb. (454 g) carapils malt
4 oz. (113 g) Munich malt

Add to liquor and steep at 152°F (67°C) for 90 minutes. Sparge with
2¼ gallons (8.5 L) water at 168°F (76°C). Add to runnings:

3⅓ lb. (1.5 kg) unhopped, extra-light malt extract syrup

Bring to a boil, then add:

4 AAUs Saaz hops

Boil 30 minutes, then add:

4 AAUs Saaz hops

Boil 30 minutes, then add:

4 AAUs Hallertau hops

Remove from heat. Cool, then top up to 5¼ gallons (20 L) with chilled,
preboiled water. Cool to 62°F (17°C), then pitch:

**Bohemian or Czech lager yeast (Wyeast 2124, 2278, or
equivalent)**

Ferment at 50°F (10°C) for 2 weeks, then transfer to secondary fermenter
and condition cold (40°F [4°C]) for 6 to 8 weeks. Prime with:

⅞ cup (202 ml) corn sugar

Bottle and age at 45–50°F (7–10°C) for 3 weeks.

Alternate Methods

All-extract: Steep the carapils and Munich malts as in main recipe in 2½ gallons (9.5 L) water at 150°F (66°C) for 45 minutes. Omit lager malt and increase malt extract syrup to 5½ lb. (2.5 kg). Follow directions from beginning of boil.

All-grain: Mash 7 lb. (3.2 kg) lager malt and the carapils and Munich malts as in main recipe in 2½ gallons (9.5 L) water at 152°F (67°C). Sparge with 3 gallons (11 L) water. Omit malt extract syrup and proceed as in main recipe, reducing wort volume to 5¼ gallons (20 L) or less.

 Serve at 40°F (4°C) in a traditional Pilsner glass.

Pranqster

North Coast Brewing Co., Fort Bragg, California

This Belgian-style golden ale is fruity, citric, yeasty, and warming — very Belgian! It is bottle conditioned, of course, and has the characteristic softness and smoothness you'd expect. It comes adorned with one of the most interesting labels around.

Original gravity: 1075 • Final gravity: 1020 • 6.9% abv • 20 IBU

Heat 2 gallons (7.6 L) water to 164°F (73°C). Crush:

3 lb. (1.4 kg) Belgian pale malt
12 oz. (340 g) light (20°L) crystal malt
1 lb. (454 g) caravienne malt

Add to liquor and steep at 152°F (67°C) for 90 minutes. Sparge with 3 gallons (11 L) water at 168°F (76°C). Add to runnings:

6 lb. (2.7 kg) unhopped, light malt extract syrup
1 lb. (454 g) clear candi sugar

Bring to a boil, then add:

5 AAUs Willamette hops

Boil 90 minutes, then remove from heat. Cool, then top up to 5¼ gallons (20 L) with chilled, preboiled water. Cool to 68°F (20°C), then pitch:

Belgian Trappist ale yeast (recultured Pranqster, Wyeast 1214, or equivalent)

Ferment at 65°F (18°C) for 2 weeks, then transfer to secondary fermenter and condition cool (50°F [10°C]) for 3 to 4 weeks. Prime with:

1 cup (237 ml) pale dry malt extract (DME)

Bottle and age at 50°F (10°C) for 3 weeks.

Alternate Methods

All-extract: Steep 1 lb. (454 g) Belgian pale malt and the crystal and caravienne malts as in main recipe in 2½ gallons (9.5 L) water at 150°F (66°C) for 45 minutes. Add 8 lb. (3.6 kg) unhopped, light DME and 1 lb. (454 g) candi sugar. Follow directions from beginning of boil.

All-grain: Mash 10 lb. (4.5 kg) Belgian pale malt and the crystal and caravienne malts as in main recipe in 3¾ gallons (14.2 L) water at 152°F (67°C). Sparge with 4½ gallons (17 L) water. Omit malt extract syrup, but add the candi sugar and proceed as in main recipe, reducing wort volume to 5¼ gallons (20 L) or less.

 Serve at 50°F (10°C) in a Trappist-style chalice or goblet.

Pyramid Traditional ESB

Pyramid Breweries, Berkeley, California; Seattle and Kalama, Washington

This traditional-style, bottle-conditioned ale is reddish blond with a definite
English malt and hop character. It is fruity and grainy, reminiscent of strawberries,
pretzels, toasted bread, and caramel corn. The aftertaste is English hops.

Original gravity: 1055 • Final gravity: 1015 • 5.1% abv • 40 IBU

Heat 1½ gallons (5.7 L) water to 164°F (73°C). Crush:

- **2 lb. (907 g) pale malt**
- **8 oz. (227 g) toasted pale malt (toast at 350°F [177°C] for 30 minutes)**
- **8 oz. (227 g) medium (50°L) crystal malt**
- **8 oz. (227 g) torrefied wheat**

Add to liquor and steep at 152°F (67°C) for 90 minutes. Sparge with 2¼ gallons (8.5 L) water at 168°F (76°C). Add to runnings:

- **4 lb. (1.8 kg) unhopped, pale dry malt extract (DME)**

Bring to a boil, then add:

- **4 AAUs Goldings hops**

Boil 30 minutes, then add:

- **4 AAUs Goldings hops**

Boil 45 minutes, then add:

- **4 AAUs Goldings hops**

Boil 15 minutes, then remove from heat. Cool, then top up to 5¼ gallons (20 L) with chilled, preboiled water. Cool to 68°F (20°C), then pitch:

- **London ale yeast (Wyeast 1968 or equivalent)**

Ferment at 68°F (20°C) for 2 weeks, then transfer to secondary fermenter and add:

- **4 AAUs Goldings hops**

Condition cool (50–55°F [10–13°C]) for 3 to 4 weeks. Prime with:

- **1 cup (237 ml) pale dry malt extract**

Bottle and age at 50–55°F [10–13°C] for 3 weeks.

 Serve at 50°F (10°C) in a traditional pint glass.

Alternate Methods

All-extract: Steep the toasted pale and crystal malts and the torrefied wheat as in main recipe in 2½ gallons (9.5 L) water at 150°F (66°C) for 45 minutes. Omit pale malt and increase DME to 5½ lb. (2.5 kg). Follow directions from beginning of boil.

All-grain: Mash 8 lb. (3.6 kg) pale malt and the toasted pale malt, crystal malt, and torrefied wheat as in main recipe in 3¼ gallons (12.3 L) water at 152°F (67°C). Sparge with 4 gallons (15.1 L) water. Omit first DME and proceed as in main recipe, reducing wort volume to 5¼ gallons (20 L) or less.

Red Sky Ale

St. Stan's Brewing Co., Modesto, California

This ale comes from a pioneering microbrewery in north-central California. A malty, reddish, alt-style ale, Red Sky has a hint of wheat in the flavor and aroma. The malt sweetness is nicely balanced by an unexpected hop bitterness and floral aroma.

Original gravity: 1045 • Final gravity: 1010 • 4.5% abv • 35–40 IBU

Heat 1½ gallons (5.7 L) water to 164°F (73°C). Crush:

3 lb. (1.4 kg) pale malt
1 lb. (454 g) malted wheat
12 oz. (340 g) medium (50°L) crystal malt

Add to liquor and steep at 152°F (67°C) for 90 minutes. Sparge with 2¼ gallons (8.5 L) water at 168°F (76°C). Add to runnings:

2 lb. (907 g) unhopped, wheat dry malt extract (DME)

Bring to a boil, then add:

6 AAUs Chinook hops

Boil 45 minutes, then add:

4 AAUs Cascade hops
4 AAUs Willamette hops

Boil 15 minutes, then remove from heat. Cool, then top up to 5¼ gallons (20 L) with chilled, preboiled water. Cool to 68°F (20°C), then pitch:

American ale yeast (Wyeast 1056 or equivalent)

Ferment at 68°F (20°C) for 2 weeks, then transfer to secondary fermenter and condition cool (50–55°F [10–13°C]) for 3 to 4 weeks. Prime with:

1 cup (237 ml) pale dry malt extract

Bottle and age at 55–60°F (13–16°C) for 3 weeks.

Alternate Methods

All-extract: Steep the wheat and crystal malts as in main recipe in 2½ gallons (9.5 L) water at 150°F (66°C) for 45 minutes. Omit pale malt and increase DME to 4 lb. (1.8 kg). Follow directions from beginning of boil.

All-grain: Mash 5 lb. (2.3 kg) pale malt and 2 lb. (907 g) wheat and crystal malt as in main recipe in 2¾ gallons (10.2 L) water at 152°F (67°C). Sparge with 3½ gallons (13.2 L) water. Omit first DME and proceed as in main recipe, reducing wort volume to 5¼ gallons (20 L) or less.

 Serve at 50°F (10°C) in a traditional pint glass.

Sierra Nevada Porter

Sierra Nevada Brewing Co., Chico, California

A classic, Americanized version of an English style, this porter is rich and full flavored, reddish black, malty, and sweet and bitter at the same time.

Original gravity: 1054 • Final gravity: 1010 • 5.6% abv • 30–35 IBU

Heat 1½ gallons (5.7 L) water to 164°F (73°C). Crush:

2 lb. (907 g) pale malt
8 oz. (227 g) dark (90°L) crystal malt
8 oz. (227 g) black malt
4 oz. (113 g) chocolate malt

Add to liquor and steep at 152°F (67°C) for 90 minutes. Sparge with 2¼ gallons (8.5 L) water at 168°F (76°C). Add to runnings:

4 lb. (1.8 kg) unhopped, amber dry malt extract (DME)

Bring to a boil, then add:

6 AAUs Fuggles hops

Boil 90 minutes, then add:

6 AAUs Goldings hops

Remove from heat and steep last addition of hops 30 minutes. Cool, then top up to 5¼ gallons (20 L) with chilled, preboiled water. Cool to 68°F (20°C), then pitch:

American ale yeast (recultured Sierra Nevada yeast or Wyeast 1056 or equivalent)

Ferment at 68°F (20°C) for 2 weeks, then transfer to secondary fermenter and condition cool (50–55°F [10–13°C]) for 3 to 4 weeks. Prime with:

1 cup (237 ml) amber dry malt extract

Bottle and age at 50–55°F (10–13°C) for 3 weeks.

Alternate Methods

All-extract: Steep the crystal, black, and chocolate malts as in main recipe in 2½ gallons (9.5 L) water at 150°F (66°C) for 45 minutes. Omit pale malt and increase DME to 5½ lb. (2.5 kg). Follow directions from beginning of boil.

All-grain: Mash 7 lb. (3.2 kg) pale malt, 1 lb. (454 g) Munich malt, and the crystal, black, and chocolate malts as in main recipe in 3¼ gallons (12.3 L) water at 152°F (67°C). Sparge with 4 gallons (15.1 L) water. Omit first DME and proceed as in main recipe, reducing wort volume to 5¼ gallons (20 L) or less.

 Serve at 50°F (10°C) in a traditional pint glass.

Black Jack Porter

Left Hand Brewing Co., Longmont, Colorado

A fairly traditional London-style black porter, at least in terms of malt profile, Black Jack has more of an American-style hop aroma.

Original gravity: 1048 • **Final gravity: 1010** • **4.5% abv** • **30 IBU**

Heat 2¼ gallons (8.5 L) water to 164°F (73°C). Crush:

3½ lb. (1.6 kg) pale malt
8 oz. (227 g) Munich malt
8 oz. (227 g) black malt
8 oz. (227 g) chocolate malt
4 oz. (113 g) dark (90°L) crystal malt

Add to liquor and steep at 152°F (67°C) for 90 minutes. Sparge with 3 gallons (11 L) water at 168°F (76°C). Add to runnings:

2 lb. (907 g) unhopped, amber dry malt extract (DME)

Bring to a boil, then add:

6 AAUs Goldings hops

Boil 45 minutes, then add:

4 AAUs Cascade hops

Boil 15 minutes, then remove from heat. Cool, then top up to 5¼ gallons (20 L) with chilled, preboiled water. Cool to 68°F (20°C), then pitch:

London ale yeast (Wyeast 1028 or equivalent)

Ferment at 65°F (18°C) for 2 weeks, then transfer to secondary fermenter and condition cool (50–55°F [10–13°C]) for 3 to 4 weeks. Prime with:

1 cup (237 ml) pale dry malt extract

Bottle and age at 55–60°F (13–16°C) for 3 weeks.

Alternate Methods

All-extract: Steep 8 oz. (227 g) pale malt and the Munich, black, chocolate, and crystal malts as in main recipe in 2½ gallons (9.5 L) water at 150°F (66°C) for 45 minutes. Increase DME to 4 lb. (1.8 kg). Follow directions from beginning of boil.

All-grain: Mash 6½ lb. (2.9 kg) pale malt and the Munich, black, chocolate, and crystal malts as in main recipe in 3 gallons (11 L) water at 152°F (67°C). Sparge with 3¾ gallons (14.2 L) water. Omit first DME and proceed as in main recipe, reducing wort volume to 5¼ gallons (20 L) or less.

 Serve at 50°F (10°C) in a traditional pint glass.

Boulder Stout

Rockies Brewing Co., Boulder, Colorado

This nice, bitter, black stout has lots for everyone — fruitiness, raisiny sweetness, hop bitterness, roasty and dark malt notes, alcoholic warmth. It's all in there.

Original gravity: 1050 • Final gravity: 1010 • 5.1% abv • 30 IBU

Heat 2 gallons (7.6 L) water to 164°F (73°C). Crush:

3 lb. (1.4 kg) pale malt
1 lb. (454 g) dark (120°L) crystal malt
1 lb. (454 g) Munich malt
8 oz. (227 g) roasted barley

Add to liquor and steep at 152°F (67°C) for 90 minutes. Sparge with 3 gallons (11 L) water at 168°F (76°C). Add to runnings:

2 lb. (907 g) unhopped, amber dry malt extract (DME)

Bring to a boil, then add:

8 AAUs Northern Brewer hops

Boil 60 minutes, then remove from heat. Cool, then top up to 5¼ gallons (20 L) with chilled, preboiled water. Cool to 68°F (20°C), then pitch:

Irish ale yeast (Wyeast 1084 or equivalent)

Ferment at 65°F (18°C) for 2 weeks, then transfer to secondary fermenter and condition cool (50°F [10°C]) for 3 to 4 weeks. Prime with:

1 cup (237 ml) pale dry malt extract

Bottle and age at 50°F (10°C) for 3 weeks.

Alternate Methods

All-extract: Steep the crystal and Munich malts and roasted barley as in main recipe in 2½ gallons (9.5 L) water at 150°F (66°C) for 45 minutes. Omit pale malt and increase DME to 4 lb. (1.8 kg). Follow directions from beginning of boil.

All-grain: Mash 6 lb. (2.7 kg) pale malt, the crystal and Munich malts, and roasted barley as in main recipe in 3 gallons (11 L) water at 152°F (67°C). Sparge with 3¾ gallons (14.2 L) water. Omit first DME and proceed as in main recipe, reducing wort volume to 5¼ gallons (20 L) or less.

Serve at 50°F (10°C) in a traditional pint or tulip glass.

Fat Tire Ale

New Belgium Brewing Co., Fort Collins, Colorado

A legendary amber ale in a Belgian style, Fat Tire comes from one of the most respected breweries in the Mountain States. This rich, nutty ale is bottle conditioned and dry hopped, giving it a fresh aroma and a smooth texture.

Original gravity: 1058 • Final gravity: 1012 • 5.9% abv • 28 IBU

Heat 2½ gallons (9.5 L) water to 164°F (73°C). Crush:

5 lb. (2.3 kg) Belgian pale malt
1 lb. (454 g) Belgian Special B malt
8 oz. (227 g) dark (120°L) crystal malt
8 oz. (227 g) Munich malt

Add to liquor and steep at 152°F (67°C) for 90 minutes. Sparge with 3¼ gallons (12.3 L) water at 168°F (76°C). Add to runnings:

2 lb. (907 g) unhopped, amber dry malt extract (DME)

Bring to a boil, then add:

5 AAUs Brewer's Gold hops

Boil 45 minutes, then add:

4 AAUs Saaz hops

Boil 45 minutes, then remove from heat. Cool, then top up to 5¼ gallons (20 L) with chilled, preboiled water. Cool to 65°F (18°C), then pitch:

Recultured Fat Tire yeast or Belgian ale yeast (Wyeast 1214 or equivalent)

Ferment at 65°F (18°C) for 2 weeks, then transfer to secondary fermenter and condition cool (50–55°F [10–13°C]) for 3 to 4 weeks. Prime with:

1 cup (237 ml) pale dry malt extract

Bottle and age at 55–60°F (13–16°C) for 3 weeks.

Alternate Methods

All-extract: Steep 2 lb. (907 g) Belgian pale malt and the Belgian Special B, crystal, and Munich malts as in main recipe in 2½ gallons (9.5 L) water at 150°F (66°C) for 45 minutes. Increase DME to 4 lb. (1.8 kg). Follow directions from beginning of boil.

All-grain: Mash 8 lb. (3.6 kg) pale malt and the Belgian Special B, crystal, and Munich malts as in main recipe in 3 gallons (11 L) water at 152°F (67°C). Sparge with 3¾ gallons (14.2 L) water. Omit first DME and proceed as in main recipe, reducing wort volume to 5¼ gallons (20 L) or less.

  Serve at 50°F (10°C) in a Trappist-style goblet.

Hibernation Ale

Great Divide Brewing Co., Denver, Colorado

A deep reddish brown, Hibernation is in the Old English ale style. It has a huge aroma of malt, hops, and alcohol and an equally huge flavor. Medium bodied, this beer has echoes of burnt sugar, roasted barley, and lingering hop bitterness.

Original gravity: 1080 • Final gravity: 1016 • 8.1% abv • 55–60 IBU

Heat 3 gallons (11 L) water to 164°F (73°C). Crush:

5 lb. (2.3 kg) pale malt
1 lb. (454 g) medium (50°L) crystal malt
8 oz. (227 g) brown malt
8 oz. (227 g) roasted barley
12 oz. (340 g) malted wheat

Add to liquor and steep at 152°F (67°C) for 90 minutes. Sparge with 3¾ gallons (14.2 L) water at 168°F (76°C). Add to runnings:

4 lb. (1.8 kg) unhopped, amber dry malt extract (DME)

Bring to a boil, then add:

8 AAUs Magnum hops

Boil 75 minutes, then add:

6 AAUs Goldings hops

Boil 15 minutes, then remove from heat. Cool, then top up to 5¼ gallons (20 L) with chilled, preboiled water. Cool to 68°F (20°C), then pitch:

Scottish ale yeast (Wyeast 1728 or equivalent)

Ferment at 65°F (18°C) for 2 weeks, then transfer to secondary fermenter and condition cool (50–55°F [10–13°C]) for 6 to 8 weeks. Prime with:

1 cup (237 ml) pale dry malt extract

Bottle and age at 50°F (10°C) for 8 weeks or longer.

Alternate Methods

All-extract: Steep 2 lb. (907 g) pale malt and the crystal and brown malts, roasted barley, and malted wheat as in main recipe in 2½ gallons (9.5 L) water at 150°F (66°C) for 45 minutes. Increase DME to 6 lb. (2.7 kg). Follow directions from beginning of boil.

All-grain: Mash 11 lb. (5 kg) pale malt and the crystal and brown malts, roasted barley, and malted wheat as in main recipe in 2½ gallons (9.5 L) water at 152°F (67°C). Sparge with 3 gallons (11 L) water. Omit first DME and proceed as in main recipe, reducing wort volume to 5¼ gallons (20 L) or less.

 Share it with a friend at 50°F (10°C) in two brandy snifters.

Mountain Kölsch Ale

H. C. Berger Brewing Co., Fort Collins, Colorado

*A bright golden ale, this brew boasts a mild, true German-style hop aroma.
Buttery but dry and medium bodied, this light ale is a good example
of a light beer that is still flavorful and interesting.*

Original gravity: 1042 • **Final gravity: 1008** • **4.3% abv** • **15 IBU**

Heat 1½ gallons (5.7 L) water to 164°F (73°C). Crush:

3½ lb. (1.6 kg) lager malt
12 oz. (340 g) carapils malt

Add to liquor and steep at 152°F (67°C) for 90 minutes. Sparge with
2¼ gallons (8.5 L) water at 168°F (76°C). Add to runnings:

2 lb. (907 g) unhopped, extra-light dry malt extract (DME)

Bring to a boil, then add:

4 AAUs Spalt hops

Boil 45 minutes, then add:

2 AAUs Spalt hops

Boil 5 minutes, then remove from heat. Cool, then top up to 5¼ gallons
(20 L) with chilled, preboiled water. Cool to 68°F (20°C), then pitch:

German ale yeast (Wyeast 1007, 2565, or equivalent)

Ferment at 65°F (18°C) for 2 weeks, then transfer to secondary fermenter
and condition cool (50°F [10°C]) for 3 to 4 weeks. Prime with:

¾ cup (177 ml) corn sugar

Bottle and age at 50°F (10°C) for 3 weeks.

Alternate Methods

All-extract: Steep 8 oz.
(227 g) lager malt and the
carapils malt as in main
recipe in 2½ gallons (9.5 L)
water at 150°F (66°C) for
45 minutes. Increase DME
to 4 lb. (1.8 kg). Follow
directions from beginning
of boil.

All-grain: Mash 6½ lb.
(3 kg) lager malt and the
carapils malt as in main
recipe in 3 gallons (11 L)
water at 152°F (67°C).
Sparge with 3¾ gallons
(14.2 L) water. Omit DME
and proceed as in main
recipe, reducing wort volume to 5¼ gallons (20 L)
or less.

 Serve at 50°F (10°C) in a traditional cylindrical Kölsch glass.

Railyard Ale

Wynkoop Brewing Co., Denver, Colorado

A light amber, bottle-conditioned pale ale, Railyard is sweet, yeasty, and hoppy in the nose. Fruity from the yeast strain, bitter from the hops, and fragrant from dry-hopping, this is nevertheless a mild, light ale.

Original gravity: 1045 • Final gravity: 1010 • 4.5% abv • 25–30 IBU

Heat 1½ gallons (5.7 L) water to 164°F (73°C). Crush:

3 lb. (1.4 kg) pale malt
1 lb. (454 g) malted wheat
12 oz. (340 g) light (20°L) crystal malt

Add to liquor and steep at 152°F (67°C) for 90 minutes. Sparge with 2¼ gallons (8.5 L) water at 168°F (76°C). Add to runnings:

2 lb. (907 g) unhopped, pale dry malt extract (DME)

Bring to a boil, then add:

4 AAUs Goldings hops

Boil 30 minutes, then add:

4 AAUs Cascade hops

Boil 30 minutes, then remove from heat. Cool, then top up to 5¼ gallons (20 L) with chilled, preboiled water. Cool to 68°F (20°C), then pitch:

Recultured Wynkoop yeast or American ale yeast (Wyeast 1056 or equivalent)

Ferment at 68°F (20°C) for 2 weeks, then transfer to secondary fermenter and add:

4 AAUs Cascade hops

Condition cool (50–55°F [10–13°C]) for 3 to 4 weeks. Prime with:

1 cup (237 ml) pale dry malt extract

Bottle and age at 55–60°F (13–16°C) for 3 weeks.

Alternate Methods

All-extract: Steep the wheat and crystal malts as in main recipe in 2½ gallons (9.5 L) water at 150°F (66°C) for 45 minutes. Omit pale malt and increase DME to 4 lb. (1.8 kg). Follow directions from beginning of boil.

All-grain: Mash 6 lb. (2.7 kg) pale malt and the wheat and crystal malts as in main recipe in 2¾ gallons (10.2 L) water at 152°F (67°C). Sparge with 3¼ gallons (12.3 L) water. Omit first DME and proceed as in main recipe, reducing wort volume to 5¼ gallons (20 L) or less.

 Serve at 50°F (10°C) in a traditional pint glass.

Road Dog Ale

Broadway Brewing Co., Denver, Colorado
(for Flying Dog Brewpub, Aspen, Colorado)

A malty, caramelly, Scottish-style ale, Road Dog has a complex fruity-sweet aroma and a mildly sweet flavor profile. Medium bodied and warming, this beer is fairly rich for its OG.

Original gravity: 1048 • Final gravity: 1008 • 5.1% abv • 18–20 IBU

Heat 1¾ gallons (6.6 L) water to 164°F (73°C). Crush:
- **3 lb. (1.4 kg) pale malt**
- **1 lb. (454 g) medium (50°L) crystal malt**
- **2 oz. (56.7 g) roasted barley**

Add to liquor and steep at 152°F (67°C) for 90 minutes. Sparge with 2½ gallons (9.5 L) water at 168°F (76°C). Add to runnings:
- **3½ lb. (1.6 kg) unhopped, pale malt extract syrup**

Bring to a boil, then add:
- **5 AAUs Target hops**

Boil 60 minutes, then remove from heat. Cool, then top up to 5¼ gallons (20 L) with chilled, preboiled water. Cool to 68°F (20°C), then pitch:
- **Scottish or Irish ale yeast (Wyeast 1728, 1084, or equivalent)**

Ferment at 65°F (18°C) for 2 weeks, then transfer to secondary fermenter and condition cold (40–45°F [5–7°C]) for 5 to 6 weeks. Prime with:
- **½ cup (118 ml) pale dry malt extract (DME)**
- **½ cup (118 ml) brown sugar**

Bottle and age at 55–60°F (13–16°C) for 4 weeks.

 **Alternate Methods**

All-extract: Steep the crystal malt and roasted barley as in main recipe in 2½ gallons (9.5 L) water at 150°F (66°C) for 45 minutes. Omit pale malt and increase malt extract syrup to 6 lb. (2.7 kg). Follow directions from beginning of boil.

All-grain: Mash 7¼ lb. (3.3 kg) pale malt and the crystal malt and roasted barley in 3 gallons (11 L) water at 152°F (67°C). Sparge with 3½ gallons (13.2 L) water. Omit malt extract syrup and proceed as in main recipe, reducing wort volume to 5¼ gallons (20 L) or less.

 Serve at 50°F (10°C) in a Scottish thistle glass.

Tabernash Weiss

Tabernash Brewing Co., Longmont, Colorado

Here's an authentic German-style hefeweizen, complete with a good dose of hefe in the bottom. This wheat beer is cloudy, fruity, and slightly sour and has notes of bananas and spice. It's like a brew you'd find at the Weihenstephen Institute.

Original gravity: 1045 • Final gravity: 1010 • 4.5% abv • 20 IBU

Heat 1½ gallons (4.7 L) water to 164°F (73°C). Crush:

2 lb. (907 g) pale malt
1 lb. (454 g) malted wheat
12 oz. (340 g) carapils malt

Add to liquor and steep at 152°F (67°C) for 90 minutes. Sparge with 2 gallons (7.6 L) water at 168°F (76°C). Add to runnings:

3½ lb. (1.6 kg) unhopped, wheat malt extract syrup

Bring to a boil, then add:

4 AAUs Hallertau hops

Boil 40 minutes, then add:

4 AAUs Spalt hops

Boil 5 minutes, then remove from heat. Cool, then top up to 5¼ gallons (20 L) with chilled, preboiled water. Cool to 68°F (20°C), then pitch:

Recultured Tabernash yeast or German wheat yeast (Wyeast 3056 or equivalent)

Ferment at 68°F (20°C) for 2 weeks, then transfer to secondary fermenter and condition cool (50–55°F [10–13°C]) for 3 to 4 weeks. Prime with:

⅞ cup (202 ml) corn sugar

Bottle and age at 50°F (10°C) for 3 weeks.

Alternate Methods

All-extract: Steep 1 lb. (454 g) pale malt, 1 lb. (454 g) malted wheat, and 12 oz. (340 g) carapils in 2½ gallons (9.5 L) water at 150°F (66°C) for 45 minutes. Increase malt extract to 4½ lb. (2 kg). Follow directions from beginning of boil.

All-grain: Mash 4 lb. (1.8 kg) pale malt, 3 lb. (1.4 kg) malted wheat, and the carapils as in main recipe in 3 gallons (11 L) water at 152 °F (67 °C). Sparge with 3¾ gallons (14.2 L) water. Omit malt extract and proceed as in main recipe, reducing wort volume to 5¼ gallons (20 L) or less.

 Serve at 50°F (10°C) in a traditional fluted weizen glass.

Frog 'n' Hound Pub Ale

Olde Wyndham Brewery, Willamantic, Connecticut

Frog 'n' Hound is a creamy, amber ale, mild in flavor and aroma, that is reminiscent of an ordinary English bitter. It has a semisweet, nutty aftertaste.

Original gravity: 1044 • **Final gravity: 1010** • **4.3% abv** • **35 IBU**

Heat 1¼ gallons (4.7 L) water to 164°F (73°C). Crush:

2 lb. (907 g) pale malt
8 oz. (227 g) medium (40°L) crystal malt

Add to liquor and steep at 152°F (67°C) for 90 minutes. Sparge with 2 gallons (7.6 L) water at 168°F (76°C). Add to runnings:

3½ lb. (1.6 kg) unhopped, amber dry malt extract (DME)

Bring to a boil, then add:

6 AAUs Cascade hops

Boil 30 minutes, then add:

4 AAUs Willamette hops

Boil 30 minutes, then remove from heat. Cool, then top up to 5¼ gallons (20 L) with chilled, preboiled water. Cool to 68°F (20°C), then pitch:

English ale yeast (Wyeast 1098 or equivalent)

Ferment at 68°F (20°C) for 2 weeks, then transfer to secondary fermenter and condition cool (50–55°F [10–13°C]) for 3 to 4 weeks. Prime with:

⅞ cup (202 ml) pale dry malt extract

Bottle and age at 50–55°F (10–13°C) for 3 weeks.

Alternate Methods

All-extract: Steep 8 oz. (227 g) pale malt and the crystal malt as in main recipe in 2½ gallons (9.5 L) water at 150°F (66°C) for 45 minutes. Increase DME to 4½ lb. (2 kg). Follow directions from beginning of boil.

All-grain: Mash 7 lb. (3.2 kg) pale malt and the crystal malt as in main recipe in 2½ gallons (9.5 L) water at 152°F (67°C). Sparge with 3 gallons (11 L) water. Omit DME and proceed as in main recipe, reducing wort volume to 5¼ gallons (20 L) or less.

 Serve at 50°F (10°C) in a traditional pint glass.

Hammer & Nail Brown Ale

Hammer & Nail Brewers, Watertown, Connecticut

A tart and hoppy American-style brown ale, this one is light in body, copper colored, and aromatic. It's a highly carbonated and fairly bitter take on a relatively new style of beer.

Original gravity: 1045 • Final gravity: 1010 • 4.5% abv • 25–30 IBU

Heat 1 gallon (3.8 L) water to 164°F (73°C). Crush:

2 lb. (907 g) mild ale malt
8 oz. (227 g) medium (50°L) crystal malt
4 oz. (113 g) chocolate malt

Add to liquor and steep at 152°F (67°C) for 90 minutes. Sparge with 1½ gallons (5.7 L) water at 168°F (76°C). Add to runnings:

3½ lb. (1.6 kg) unhopped, pale dry malt extract (DME)

Bring to a boil, then add:

4 AAUs Willamette hops

Boil 30 minutes, then add:

4 AAUs Willamette hops

Boil 30 minutes, then remove from heat. Cool, then top up to 5¼ gallons (20 L) with chilled, preboiled water. Cool to 68°F (20°C), then pitch:

American ale yeast (Wyeast 1056 or equivalent)

Ferment at 68°F (20°C) for 2 weeks, then transfer to secondary fermenter and condition cool (50–55°F [10–13°C]) for 3 to 4 weeks. Prime with:

⅓ cup (76 ml) pale dry malt extract
½ cup (118 ml) light brown sugar

Bottle and age at 55–60°F (13–16°C) for 3 weeks.

Alternate Methods

All-extract: Steep the crystal and chocolate malts as in main recipe in 2½ gallons (9.5 L) water at 150°F (66°C) for 45 minutes. Omit mild ale malt and DME and add 6 lb. (2.7 kg) light malt extract syrup. Follow directions from beginning of boil.

All-grain: Mash 7 lb. (3.2 kg) mild ale malt and the crystal and chocolate malts as in main recipe in 3 gallons (11 L) water at 152°F (67°C). Sparge with 3¾ gallons (14.2 L) water. Omit first DME and proceed as in main recipe, reducing wort volume to 5¼ gallons (20 L) or less.

 Serve at 50°F (10°C) in a traditional pint glass.

Hammer & Nail Vienna-Style Lager

Hammer & Nail Brewers, Watertown, Connecticut

*A nice, clean, malty, reddish brown lager, H & N is a bit light for
the traditional Vienna style, but it's refreshing, tasty, and malty nevertheless.
It has a dry and clean aftertaste with hints of tea, peaches, and apples.*

Original gravity: 1045 • Final gravity: 1010 • 4.5% abv • 20 IBU

Heat 1¼ gallons (4.7 L) water to 164°F (73°C). Crush:

1 lb. (454 g) Pilsner malt
1 lb. (454 g) Vienna malt
8 oz. (227 g) carapils malt
8 oz. (227 g) Munich malt
8 oz. (227 g) light (20°L) crystal malt

Add to liquor and steep at 152°F (67°C) for 90 minutes. Sparge with
2 gallons (7.6 L) water at 168°F (76°C). Add to runnings:

3 lb. (1.4 kg) unhopped, light malt extract syrup
8 oz. (227 g) unhopped, extra-light dry malt extract (DME)

Bring to a boil, then add:

3 AAUs Hallertau hops

Boil 30 minutes, then add:

4 AAUs Saaz hops

Boil 30 minutes, then remove from heat. Cool, then top up to 5¼ gallons
(20 L) with chilled, preboiled water. Cool to 60°F (16°C), then pitch:

Munich lager yeast (Wyeast 2308 or equivalent)

Ferment at 50°F (10°C) for 2 weeks, then transfer to secondary fermenter
and condition cold (35–40°F [2–4°C]) for 4 to 6 weeks. Prime with:

1 cup (237 ml) pale dry malt extract

Bottle and age at 35–40°F (2–4°C) for 3 weeks.

 **Alternate Methods**

All-extract: Steep 4 oz.
(113 g) Vienna malt and
the carapils, Munich, and
crystal malts as in main
recipe in 2½ gallons (9.5 L)
water at 150°F (66°C) for
45 minutes. Omit Pilsner
malt and malt syrup and
increase DME to 4 lb.
(1.8 kg). Follow directions
from beginning of boil.

All-grain: Mash 5 lb.
(2.3 kg) Pilsner malt, 1¼ lb.
(567 g) Vienna malt, and
the carapils, Munich, and
crystal malts as in main
recipe in 2½ gallons (9.5 L)
water at 152°F (67°C).
Sparge with 3 gallons (11 L)
water. Omit malt extract
syrup and DME and pro-
ceed as in main recipe,
reducing wort volume to
5¼ gallons (20 L) or less.

 Serve at 50°F (10°C) in a tall Pilsner glass.

Old Yankee Ale

Cottrell Brewing, Pawcatuck, Connecticut

A traditional English-style pale ale with a complex, malty profile and a mild hop finish, this beer glows with rich copper hues and has a pleasant burnt sugar/caramel aftertaste.

Original gravity: 1048 • Final gravity: 1012 • 4.6% abv • 35 IBU

Heat 1¼ gallons (4.7 L) water to 164°F (73°C). Crush:

1½ lb. (680 g) pale malt
12 oz. (340 g) medium (50°L) crystal malt

Add to liquor and steep at 152°F (67°C) for 90 minutes. Sparge with 2 gallons (7.6 L) water at 168°F (76°C). Add to runnings:

4 lb. (1.8 kg) unhopped, amber dry malt extract (DME)

Bring to a boil, then add:

6 AAUs Fuggles hops

Boil 30 minutes, then add:

4 AAUs Goldings hops

Boil 30 minutes, then remove from heat. Cool, then top up to 5¼ gallons (20 L) with chilled, preboiled water. Cool to 68°F (20°C), then pitch:

English ale yeast (Wyeast 1098 or equivalent)

Ferment at 65°F (18°C) for 2 weeks, then transfer to secondary fermenter and condition cool (50–55°F [10–13°C]) for 3 to 4 weeks. Prime with:

1 cup (237 ml) pale dry malt extract

Bottle and age at 55–60°F (13–16°C) for 3 weeks.

Alternate Methods

All-extract: Steep 8 oz. (227 g) pale malt and 8 oz. (227 g) medium crystal malt in 2½ gallons (9.5 L) water at 150°F (66°C) for 45 minutes. Increase DME to 5 lb. (2.3 kg). Follow directions from beginning of boil.

All-grain: Mash 7½ lb. (3.4 kg) pale malt and the crystal malt as in main recipe in 3 gallons (11 L) water at 152°F (67°C). Sparge with 3¾ gallons (14.2 L) water. Omit first DME and proceed as in main recipe, reducing wort volume to 5¼ gallons (20 L) or less.

 Serve at 50°F (10°C) in a traditional pint glass.

Immortale

Dogfish Head Brewing Co., Lewes, Delaware

A rich, strong ale — I still don't understand how they get that much malt into that little bottle! Immortale has notes of smoke, sweet malt, toasted and roasted malt, caramel, raisins, vanilla, alcohol, and maple. It's almost a "kitchen sink" sort of beer.

Original gravity: 1105 • Final gravity: 1019 • 11% abv • 60 IBU

Heat 3¾ gallons (14.2 L) water to 164°F (73°C). Crush:

7 lb. (3.2 kg) pale malt
3 lb. (1.4 kg) biscuit malt
1 lb. (454 g) medium (50°L) crystal malt
8 oz. (227 g) malted wheat
4 oz. (113 g) roasted barley
4 oz. (113 g) peat-smoked malt

Add to liquor and steep at 152°F (67°C) for 90 minutes. Sparge with 4½ gallons (17 L) water at 168°F (76°C). Add to runnings:

4 lb. (1.8 kg) unhopped, amber dry malt extract (DME)

Bring to a boil, then add:

10 AAUs Northern Brewer hops

Boil 60 minutes, then add:

6 AAUs Centennial hops

Boil 30 minutes, then remove from heat. Cool, then top up to 5¼ gallons (20 L) with chilled, preboiled water. Cool to 68°F (20°C), then pitch:

Scottish ale yeast (Wyeast 1728 or equivalent)

Ferment at 68°F (20°C) for 4 weeks, then transfer to secondary fermenter and condition cool (50–55°F [10–13°C]) for 6 to 8 weeks. Prime with:

1 cup (237 ml) maple syrup

Bottle and age at 50°F (10°C) for at least 6 to 8 months (it will keep much longer than that).

Alternate Methods

All-extract: Steep 3 lb. (1.4 kg) pale malt, 1 lb. (454 g) biscuit malt, and the crystal malt, malted wheat, roasted barley, and peat-smoked malt as in main recipe in 3 gallons water at 150°F (66°C) for 45 minutes. Increase DME to 8 lb. (3.6 kg). Follow directions from beginning of boil.

All-grain: Mash 12 lb. (5.4 kg) pale malt, 4 lb. (1.8 kg) biscuit malt, the crystal malt, malted wheat, roasted barley, and peat-smoked malt as in main recipe in 5½ gallons (20.8 L) water at 152°F (67°C). Sparge with 6 gallons (22.7 L) water. Omit DME and proceed as in main recipe, reducing wort volume to 5¼ gallons (20 L) or less.

 Share it with a friend at 50°F (10°C) in two brandy snifters.

Calusa Wheat Beer

Ybor City Brewing Co., Tampa, Florida

Here's a light, delicious, and refreshing wheat beer from an unexpected place — a renovated cigar factory in the heart of Florida's Cuban community. Calusa has wheat flavor, malt sweetness, and a very bright and fresh hop aroma, and it's not at all heavy or cloying.

Original gravity: 1040 • **Final gravity: 1008** • **4.1% abv** • **15 IBU**

Heat 1¼ gallons (4.7 L) water to 164°F (73°C). Crush:

1 lb. (454 g) malted wheat
2 lb. (907 g) lager malt
12 oz. (340 g) carapils malt

Add to liquor and steep at 152°F (67°C) for 90 minutes. Sparge with 2 gallons (7.6 L) water at 168°F (76°C). Add to runnings:

2 lb. (907 g) unhopped, wheat dry malt extract (DME)

Bring to a boil, then add:

2 AAUs Hallertau hops

Boil 45 minutes, then add:

2 AAUs Hallertau hops

Boil 15 minutes, then remove from heat. Add:

3 AAUs Hallertau hops

Steep 15 minutes, then cool and top up to 5¼ gallons (20 L) with chilled, preboiled water. Cool to 68°F (20°C), then pitch:

American ale yeast (Wyeast 1056 or equivalent)

Ferment at 68°F (20°C) for 2 weeks, then transfer to secondary fermenter and condition cool (50–55°F [10–13°C]) for 3 to 4 weeks. Prime with:

1 cup (237 ml) corn sugar

Bottle and age at 50°F (10°C) for 3 weeks.

Alternate Methods

All-extract: Steep 8 oz. (227 g) lager malt, 8 oz. (227 g) malted wheat, and the carapils malt as in main recipe in 2½ gallons (9.5 L) water at 150°F (66°C) for 45 minutes. Increase DME to 3½ lb. (1.6 kg). Follow directions from beginning of boil.

All-grain: Mash 3 lb. (1.4 kg) malted wheat, 3 lb. (1.4 kg) lager malt, and the carapils malt as in main recipe in 2¼ gallons (8.5 L) water at 152°F (67°C). Sparge with 3 gallons (11 L) water. Omit DME and proceed as in main recipe, reducing wort volume to 5¼ gallons (20 L) or less.

Serve at 40°F (4°C) in a traditional weizen glass.

Bohemian Pilsner

Bent River Brewing Co., Moline, Illinois

*A well-balanced, semisweet Pilsner, Bohemian has lots of floral hop aroma and a
lingering bitter finish. Medium gold with a huge white head,
it's also medium bodied and mellow.*

Original gravity: 1044 • Final gravity: 1010 • 4.3% abv • 40 IBU

Heat 1½ gallons (5.7 L) water to 164°F (73°C). Crush:

3 lb. (1.4 kg) lager malt
8 oz. (227 g) carapils malt

Add to liquor and steep at 152°F (67°C) for 90 minutes. Sparge with
2¼ gallons (8.5 L) water at 168°F (76°C). Add to runnings:

3⅓ lb. (1.5 kg) unhopped, extra-light malt extract syrup

Bring to a boil, then add:

3 AAUs Saaz hops

Boil 30 minutes, then add:

4 AAUs Saaz hops

Boil 30 minutes, then add:

4 AAUs Saaz hops

Boil 30 minutes, then add:

4 AAUs Saaz hops

Remove from heat and let the hops steep 15 minutes. Cool, then top up
to 5¼ gallons (20 L) with chilled, preboiled water. Cool to 62°F (17°C),
then pitch:

Bohemian or Czech lager yeast (Wyeast 2278 or equivalent)

Ferment at 55°F (13°C) for 2 weeks, then transfer to secondary fermenter
and condition cold (40°F [4°C]) for 4 to 6 weeks. Prime with:

⅞ cup (210 ml) corn sugar

Bottle and age at 45–50°F (7–10°C) for 6 weeks.

Alternate Methods

All-extract: Steep the carapils malt as in main recipe and 1 lb. (454 g) lager malt in 2½ gallons (9.5 L) water at 150°F (66°C) for 45 minutes. Increase malt extract syrup to 5 lb. (2.3 kg). Follow directions from beginning of boil.

All-grain: Mash 7 lb. (3.2 kg) lager malt and the carapils as in main recipe in 2½ gallons (9.5 L) water at 152°F (67°C). Sparge with 3 gallons (11 L) water. Omit malt extract syrup and proceed as in main recipe, reducing wort volume to 5¼ gallons (20 L) or less.

 Serve at 40°F (4°C) in a traditional Pilsner glass.

Hex Nut Brown Ale

Goose Island Beer Co., Chicago, Illinois

A sweet, nutty, caramelly brown ale, Hex Nut is somewhere between copper and reddish amber in color and light to medium in body. It's smooth, easy to get to know, and pleasant company over a long session.

Original gravity: 1044 • Final gravity: 1008 • 4.6% abv • 15–18 IBU

Heat 2 gallons (7.6 L) water to 164°F (73°C). Crush:

2½ lb. (1.1 kg) pale malt
1 lb. (454 g) medium (50°L) crystal malt
8 oz. (227 g) chocolate malt
8 oz. (227 g) brown malt

Add to liquor and steep at 152°F (67°C) for 90 minutes. Sparge with 2½ gallons (9.5 L) water at 168°F (76°C). Add to runnings:

2 lb. (907 g) unhopped, amber dry malt extract (DME)

Bring to a boil, then add:

6 AAUs Willamette hops

Boil 45 minutes, then remove from heat. Cool, then top up to 5¼ gallons (20 L) with chilled, preboiled water. Cool to 68°F (20°C), then pitch:

American ale yeast (Wyeast 1056 or equivalent) or Irish ale yeast (Wyeast 1084)

Ferment at 65°F (18°C) for 2 weeks, then transfer to secondary fermenter and condition cool (50–55°F [10–13°C]) for 3 to 4 weeks. Prime with:

1 cup (237 ml) amber dry malt extract

Bottle and age at 50°F (10°C) for 3 weeks.

Alternate Methods

All-extract: Steep 12 oz. (340 g) crystal malt and the chocolate and brown malts as in main recipe in 2½ gallons (9.5 L) water at 150°F (66°C) for 45 minutes. Omit pale malt and increase DME to 4 lb. (1.8 kg). Follow directions from beginning of boil.

All-grain: Mash 5½ lb. (2.5 kg) pale malt and the crystal, chocolate, and brown malts as in main recipe in 3 gallons (11 L) water at 152°F (67°C). Sparge with 3¾ gallons (14.2 L) water. Omit first DME and proceed as in main recipe, reducing wort volume to 5¼ gallons (20 L) or less.

 Serve at 50°F (10°C) in a traditional pint or tulip glass.

John's Generations Ale

Stone City Brewing Co., Solon, Iowa

This is a Belgian-style witbier brewed by Stone City for the folks at John's Grocery in Iowa City, who, by the way, have a marvelous selection of great beers and glassware, available by mail and on-line! This beer is cloudy, tangy, and spicy — very much in keeping with the witbier style.

Original gravity: 1048 • **Final gravity: 1013** • **4.5% abv** • **20 IBU**

Heat 2¼ gallons (8.5 L) water to 164°F (73°C). Crush:

2 lb. (907 g) Belgian Pilsner malt
2 lb. (907 g) malted wheat
8 oz. (227 g) flaked wheat
12 oz. (340 g) carapils malt

Add to liquor and steep at 152°F (67°C) for 90 minutes. Sparge with 3 gallons (11 L) water at 168°F (76°C). Add to runnings:

2 lb. (907 g) unhopped, wheat dry malt extract (DME)

Boil 30 minutes, then add:

4 AAUs Saaz hops

Boil 25 minutes, then add:

⅛ oz. (3.5 g) crushed (not ground) coriander seed
¼ oz. (7 g) dried curaçao orange peel

Boil 5 minutes, then remove from heat. Steep 15 minutes, then remove spices. Cool, then top up to 5¼ gallons (20 L) with chilled, preboiled water. Cool to 65°F (18°C), then pitch:

Belgian white ale yeast (Wyeast 3944 or any recultured witbier yeast)

Ferment at 62°F (17°C) for 2 weeks, then transfer to secondary fermenter and condition cool (50–55°F [10–13°C]) for 3 to 4 weeks. Prime with:

1 cup (237 ml) wheat dry malt extract

Bottle and age at 55–60°F (13–16°C) for 3 weeks.

Alternate Methods

All-extract: Steep 1 lb. (454 g) malted wheat and the flaked wheat and carapils malt as in main recipe in 2½ gallons (9.5 L) water at 150°F (66°C) for 45 minutes. Omit Pilsner malt and increase DME to 4 lb. (1.8 kg). Follow directions from beginning of boil.

All-grain: Mash 4 lb. (1.8 kg) Belgian Pilsner malt, 3 lb. (1.4 kg) malted wheat, and the flaked wheat and carapils malt as in main recipe in 3 gallons (11 L) water at 152°F (67°C). Sparge with 3¾ gallons (14.2 L) water. Omit first DME and proceed as in main recipe, reducing wort volume to 5¼ gallons (20 L) or less.

Serve at 50°F (10°C) in a witbier chalice-style glass or lambic tumbler.

Schild Brau Amber

Millstream Brewing Co., Amana, Iowa

This amber is a rich, Vienna-style lager with lots of buttery, caramel, toasty flavors and a complex yet balanced hop and malt nose.

Original gravity: 1057 • Final gravity: 1014 • 5.7% abv • 20–25 IBU

Heat 2¼ gallons (8.5 L) water to 164°F (73°C). Crush:

4 lb. (1.8 kg) lager malt
1 lb. (454 g) carapils malt
8 oz. (227 g) medium (80°L) crystal malt
2 oz. (56.7 g) roasted barley

Add to liquor and steep at 152°F (67°C) for 90 minutes. Sparge with 3 gallons (11 L) water at 168°F (76°C). Add to runnings:

3⅓ lb. (1.5 kg) unhopped, light malt extract syrup

Bring to a boil, then add:

4 AAUs Cluster hops

Boil 30 minutes, then add:

4 AAUs Hallertau hops

Boil 30 minutes, then remove from heat. Cool, then top up to 5¼ gallons (20 L) with chilled, preboiled water. Cool to 60°F (16°C), then pitch:

Bavarian lager yeast (Wyeast 2206 or equivalent)

Ferment at 48°F (9°C) for 2 weeks, then transfer to secondary fermenter and condition cold (40°F [4°C]) for 5 to 6 weeks. Prime with:

1 cup (237 ml) pale dry malt extract (DME)

Bottle and age at 45°F (7°C) for 6 weeks.

Alternate Methods

All-extract: Steep the carapils and crystal malts and roasted barley as in main recipe in 2½ gallons (9.5 L) water at 150°F (66°C) for 45 minutes. Omit lager malt and increase malt extract syrup to 6⅔ lb. (3 kg). Follow directions from beginning of boil.

All-grain: Mash 8 lb. (3.6 kg) lager malt, the carapils and crystal malts, and the roasted barley as in main recipe in 3 gallons (11 L) water at 152°F (67°C). Sparge with 3¾ gallons (14.2 L) water. Omit malt extract syrup and proceed as in main recipe, reducing wort volume to 5¼ gallons (20 L) or less.

Serve at 50°F (10°C) in a tall, footed Pilsner glass.

Stein Bock

Stone City Brewing Co., Solon, Iowa

This is not a steinbier, but instead is a blond maibock, bottle conditioned, full bodied, and light amber. The blend of yeast, caramel malt, and mild German-style hops in the aroma is echoed by the balance in the flavor.

Original gravity: 1055 • **Final gravity: 1014** • **5.2% abv** • **45 IBU**

Heat 2½ gallons (9.5 L) water to 164°F (73°C). Crush:

5 lb. (2.3 kg) lager malt
1 lb. (454 g) Vienna malt
8 oz. (227 g) carapils malt

Add to liquor and steep at 152°F (67°C) for 90 minutes. Sparge with 3¼ gallons (12.3 L) water at 168°F (76°C). Add to runnings:

2 lb. (907 g) unhopped, pale dry malt extract (DME)

Bring to a boil, then add:

6 AAUs Hallertau hops

Boil 45 minutes, then add:

4 AAUs Perle hops

Boil 30 minutes, then add:

4 AAUs Tettnang hops

Boil 15 minutes, then remove from heat. Cool, then top up to 5¼ gallons (20 L) with chilled, preboiled water. Cool to 62°F (17°C), then pitch:

Recultured Stone City yeast or Munich lager yeast (Wyeast 2308 or equivalent)

Ferment at 40°F (4°C) for 4 weeks, then transfer to secondary fermenter and condition cold (40–45°F [4–7°C]) for 6 weeks. Prime with:

1 cup (237 ml) pale dry malt extract

Bottle and age at 50°F (10°C) for 6 weeks.

Alternate Methods

All-extract: Steep 2 lb. (907 g) lager malt and the Vienna and carapils malts as in main recipe in 2½ gallons (9.5 L) water at 150°F (66°C) for 45 minutes. Increase DME to 4 lb. (1.8 kg). Follow directions from beginning of boil.

All-grain: Mash 8 lb. (3.6 kg) lager malt and the Vienna and carapils malts as in main recipe in 3¼ gallons (12.3 L) water at 152°F (67°C). Sparge with 3¾ gallons (14.2 L) water. Omit first DME and proceed as in main recipe, reducing wort volume to 5¼ gallons (20 L) or less.

 Serve at 45°F (7°C) in a ceramic stein.

Xtra Pale Ale

3 Floyds Brewing Co., Dubuque, Iowa

Here's a crisp, refreshing golden ale with lots of hops and spicy flavors reminding one of rye, caraway, sassafras, and lemongrass. The hop bitterness lingers, and the hop aroma is bright and lively up front.

Original gravity: 1045 • Final gravity: 1008 • 4.7% abv • 40 IBU

Heat 1¾ gallons (6.6 L) water to 164°F (73°C). Crush:

3 lb. (1.4 kg) pale malt
1 lb. (454 g) light (20°L) crystal malt
12 oz. (340 g) malted wheat

Add to liquor and steep at 152°F (67°C) for 90 minutes. Sparge with 2½ gallons (9.5 L) water at 168°F (76°C). Add to runnings:

2 lb. (907 g) unhopped, extra-light dry malt extract (DME)

Bring to a boil, then add:

6 AAUs Goldings hops
4 AAUs Cascade hops

Boil 60 minutes, then add:

6 AAUs Cascade hops

Remove from heat and steep 15 minutes. Cool, then top up to 5¼ gallons (20 L) with chilled, preboiled water. Cool to 68°F (20°C), then pitch:

American ale yeast (Wyeast 1056 or equivalent)

Ferment at 65°F (18°C) for 2 weeks, then transfer to secondary fermenter and condition cool (50–55°F [10–13°C]) for 3 to 4 weeks. Prime with:

1 cup (237 ml) pale dry malt extract

Bottle and age at 55–60°F (13–16°C) for 3 weeks.

 **Alternate Methods**

All-extract: Steep the crystal malt and malted wheat as in main recipe in 2½ gallons (9.5 L) water at 150°F (66°C) for 45 minutes. Omit pale malt and increase DME to 4 lb. (1.8 kg). Follow directions from beginning of boil.

All-grain: Mash 6 lb. (2.7 kg) pale malt and the crystal malt and malted wheat as in main recipe in 3 gallons (11 L) water at 152°F (67°C). Sparge with 3¾ gallons (14.2 L) water. Omit first DME and proceed as in main recipe, reducing wort volume to 5¼ gallons (20 L) or less.

 Serve at 50°F (10°C) in a traditional pint glass.

Abita Amber

Abita Brewing Co., Abita Springs, Louisiana

*This is a richly flavored, amber- to copper-colored, Vienna-style lager.
Abita Amber has an earthy, tart flavor suggesting apples and cinnamon,
with just a hint of sulfur from the lager yeast.*

Original gravity: 1048 • **Final gravity: 1012** • **4.6% abv** • **20 IBU**

Heat 1¾ gallons (6.6 L) water to 164°F (73°C). Crush:

2 lb. (907 g) lager malt
1 lb. (454 g) Vienna malt
1 lb. (454 g) Munich malt
4 oz. (113 g) medium (50°L) crystal malt

Add to liquor and steep at 152°F (67°C) for 90 minutes. Sparge with
2½ gallons (9.5 L) water at 168°F (76°C). Add to runnings:

3⅓ lb. (1.5 kg) unhopped, light malt extract syrup

Bring to a boil, then add:

3 AAUs Tettnang hops

Boil 30 minutes, then add:

3 AAUs Tettnang hops

Boil 30 minutes, then remove from heat. Cool, then top up to 5¼ gallons
(20 L) with chilled, preboiled water. Cool to 60°F (16°C), then pitch:

Munich lager yeast (Wyeast 2308 or equivalent)

Ferment at 55°F (13°C) for 2 weeks, then transfer to secondary fermenter
and condition cold (35°F [2°C]) for 5 to 6 weeks. Prime with:

1 cup (237 ml) pale dry malt extract

Bottle and age at 40°F (4°C) for 8 weeks.

Alternate Methods

All-extract: Steep 1 lb.
(454 g) lager malt, 8 oz.
(227 g) Vienna malt, 8 oz.
(227 g) Munich malt, and
the crystal malt as in main
recipe in 2½ gallons (9.5 L)
water at 150°F (66°C) for
45 minutes. Increase malt
extract syrup to 5¼ lb.
(2.4 kg). Follow directions
from beginning of boil.

All-grain: Mash 5 lb.
(2.3 kg) lager malt and 2 lb.
(907 g) Vienna malt with
the Munich and crystal
malts as in main recipe in
3 gallons (11 L) water at
152°F (67°C). Sparge with
3¾ gallons (14.2 L) water.
Omit malt extract syrup
and proceed as in main
recipe, reducing wort volume to 5¼ gallons (20 L)
or less.

Serve at 50°F (10°C) in a tall, fluted Pilsner glass.

Acadian Pilsener

Acadian Brewing Co., New Orleans, Louisiana

Try this hoppy, Bohemian-style Pilsner from the heart of Cajun country (the labels are even in French and English). The aroma and aftertaste are reminiscent of crackers, pretzels, and biscuits, but there is a sharp hint of Saaz hops as well.

Original gravity: 1050 • Final gravity: 1012 • 4.8% abv • 40 IBU

Heat 1¾ gallons (6.6 L) water to 164°F (73°C). Crush:
- **4 lb. (1.8 kg) lager malt**
- **8 oz. (227 g) Vienna malt**
- **1 lb. (454 g) carapils malt**

Add to liquor and steep at 152°F (67°C) for 90 minutes. Sparge with 2½ gallons (9.5 L) water at 168°F (76°C). Add to runnings:
- **2 lb. (907 g) unhopped, extra-light dry malt extract (DME)**

Bring to a boil, then add:
- **6 AAUs Saaz hops**

Boil 60 minutes, then add:
- **4 AAUs Saaz hops**

Boil 15 minutes, then add:
- **4 AAUs Saaz hops**

Boil 15 minutes, then remove from heat. Cool, then top up to 5¼ gallons (20 L) with chilled, preboiled water. Cool to 60°F (16°C), then pitch:
- **Bohemian or Czech lager yeast (Wyeast 2278, 2124, or equivalent)**

Ferment at 55°F (13°C) for 2 weeks, then transfer to secondary fermenter and condition cold (35°F [2°C]) for 5 to 6 weeks. Prime with:
- **¾ cup (177 ml) corn sugar**

Bottle and age at 45°F (7°C) for 6 weeks.

Alternate Methods

All-extract: Steep the Vienna and carapils malts as in main recipe in 2½ gallons (9.5 L) water at 150°F (66°C) for 45 minutes. Omit lager malt and increase DME to 5 lb. (2.3 kg). Follow directions from beginning of boil.

All-grain: Mash 7 lb. (3.2 kg) pale malt and the Vienna and carapils malts as in main recipe in 3 gallons (11 L) water at 152°F (67°C). Sparge with 3¾ gallons (14.2 L) water. Omit DME and proceed as in main recipe, reducing wort volume to 5¼ gallons (20 L) or less.

 Serve at 45°F (7°C) in a traditional Pilsner glass.

Allegash Grand Cru

Allegash Brewing Co., Portland, Maine

Grand Cru is a bottle conditioned, spiced wheat beer from a Maine brewery specializing in Belgian-style beers. This auburn-colored brew is soft and malty with a pleasant spice and fruit aroma. It's slightly alcoholic and warming with a hint of smoke — very complex and satisfying.

Original gravity: 1060 • **Final gravity: 1015** • **5.7% abv** • **20 IBU**

Heat 1½ gallons (5.7 L) water to 164°F (73°C). Crush:

- **2 lb. (907 g) Belgian pale malt**
- **1 lb. (454 g) caravienne malt**
- **1 lb. (454 g) malted wheat**
- **1 tbsp. (15 ml) peat-smoked malt**

Add to liquor and steep at 152°F (67°C) for 90 minutes. Sparge with 2¼ gallons (8.5 L) water at 168°F (76°C). Add to runnings:

- **3½ lb. (1.6 kg) unhopped, wheat dry malt extract (DME)**
- **1 lb. (454 g) clear candi sugar**

Boil 30 minutes, then add:

- **8 AAUs Brewer's Gold hops**

Boil 30 minutes, then remove from heat. Add:

- **1 oz. (28 g) dried sweet orange peel**
- **½ oz. (14 g) star anise**

Steep 15 minutes, then remove orange peel and cool. Top up to 5¼ gallons (20 L) with chilled, preboiled water. Cool to 68°F (20°C), then pitch:

- **Belgian witbier yeast (Wyeast 3944 or recultured Allegash, Hoegaarden, or Blanche de Bruges)**

Ferment at 60°F (16°C) for 3 weeks, then transfer to secondary fermenter and condition cool (50–55°F [10–13°C]) for 3 to 4 weeks. Prime with:

- **⅞ cup (210 ml) corn sugar**

Bottle and age at 50°F (10°C) for 3 weeks.

 Serve at 50°F (10°C) in a tulip glass or snifter.

 **Alternate Methods**

All-extract: Steep 1 lb. (454 g) Belgian pale malt, 8 oz. (227 g) each of caravienne malt and malted wheat, and a pinch of peat-smoked malt in 2½ gallons (9.5 L) water at 150°F (66°C) for 45 minutes. Add 6 lb. (2.7 kg) unhopped, malted wheat extract syrup and the clear candi sugar as in main recipe. Follow directions from beginning of boil.

All-grain: Mash 5 lb. (2.3 kg) Belgian pale malt, 3 lb. (1.4 kg) malted wheat, and the caravienne and peat-smoked malts as in main recipe in 3¼ gallons (12.3 L) water at 152°F (67°C). Sparge with 3¾ gallons (14.2 L) water. Omit DME, but add the clear candi sugar and proceed as in main recipe, reducing wort volume to 5¼ gallons (20 L) or less.

Black Fly Stout

Gritty McDuff's Brewing Co., Portland, Maine

Black Fly is a very American adaptation of a dry Irish stout. It has American hops, which give it a distinct taste of grapefruit and other citrus flavors, balanced by a burnt sugar and chocolate aroma and roasty flavor.

Original gravity: 1048 • Final gravity: 1012 • 4.6% abv • 32 IBU

Heat 2 gallons (7.6 L) water to 164°F (73°C). Crush:

3 lb. (1.4 kg) pale malt
12 oz. (340 g) dark (90°L) crystal malt
8 oz. (227 g) black malt
8 oz. (227 g) roasted barley

Add to liquor and steep at 152°F (67°C) for 90 minutes. Sparge with 2½ gallons (9.5 L) water at 168°F (76°C). Add to runnings:

2½ lb. (1.1 kg) unhopped, dark dry malt extract (DME)

Bring to a boil, then add:

4 AAUs Chinook hops

Boil 60 minutes, then add:

4 AAUs Goldings hops

Boil 15 minutes, then add:

4 AAUs Cascade hops

Boil 15 minutes, then remove from heat. Cool, then top up to 5¼ gallons (20 L) with chilled, preboiled water. Cool to 68°F (20°C), then pitch:

Irish ale yeast (Wyeast 1084 or equivalent)

Ferment at 68°F (20°C) for 2 weeks, then transfer to secondary fermenter and condition cool (50–55°F [10–13°C]) for 3 to 4 weeks. Prime with:

1 cup (237 ml) pale dry malt extract

Bottle and age at 50°F (10°C) for 3 weeks.

Alternate Methods

All-extract: Steep the crystal and black malts and the roasted barley as in main recipe in 2½ gallons (9.5 L) water at 150°F (66°C) for 45 minutes. Omit pale malt and increase DME to 4½ lb. (2.1 kg). Follow directions from beginning of boil.

All-grain: Mash 6½ lb. (3 kg) pale malt, the crystal and black malts, and the roasted barley as in main recipe in 3 gallons (11 L) water at 152°F (67°C). Sparge with 3¾ gallons (14.2 L) water. Omit first DME and proceed as in main recipe, reducing wort volume to 5¼ gallons (20 L) or less.

Serve at 50°F (10°C) in a traditional pint glass.

Fuggles IPA

Shipyard Brewing Co., Portland, Maine

An English-style IPA, Fuggles is buttery, creamy, earthy, and aromatic.
Much of its character comes from the distinctive Ringwood yeast,
but even more distinguishing is the use of only Fuggles hops.

Original gravity: 1055 • Final gravity: 1015 • 5.1% abv • 50 IBU

Heat 1½ gallons (5.7 L) water to 164°F (73°C). Crush:
2½ lb. (1.1 kg) pale malt
1 lb. (454 g) light (35°L) crystal malt

Add to liquor and steep at 152°F (67°C) for 90 minutes. Sparge with 2½ gallons (9.5 L) water at 168°F (76°C). Add to runnings:
5 lb. (2.3 kg) unhopped, light malt extract syrup

Bring to a boil, then add:
6 AAUs Fuggles hops

Boil 45 minutes, then add:
4 AAUs Fuggles hops

Boil 45 minutes, then remove from heat and add:
8 AAUs Fuggles hops

Steep 15 minutes, then remove hops. Cool, then top up to 5¼ gallons (20 L) with chilled, preboiled water. Cool to 68°F (20°C), then pitch:
Ringwood ale yeast (available from EasYeast) or
other English ale yeast

Ferment at 68°F (20°C) for 2 weeks, then transfer to secondary fermenter and add:
4 AAUs Fuggles hops

Condition cool (50–55°F [10–13°C]) for 3 to 4 weeks. Prime with:
1 cup (237 ml) pale dry malt extract (DME)

Bottle and age at 55–60°F (13–16°C) for 3 weeks.

Alternate Methods

All-extract: Steep 12 oz. (340 g) toasted pale malt (toast at 350°F [177°C] for 15 minutes) and the crystal malt as in main recipe in 2½ gallons (9.5 L) water at 150°F (66°C) for 45 minutes. Omit pale malt and increase malt extract syrup to 6½ lb. (3 kg). Follow directions from beginning of boil.

All-grain: Mash 8½ lb. (3.9 kg) pale malt and the crystal malt as in main recipe in 3 gallons (11 L) water at 152°F (67°C). Sparge with 3¾ gallons (14.2 L) water. Omit malt extract syrup and proceed as in main recipe, reducing wort volume to 5¼ gallons (20 L) or less.

 Serve at 50°F (10°C) in a traditional pint glass.

Hampshire Special Ale

Geary's Brewing, Portland, Maine

This traditional, English-style strong ale, or "winter warmer," is brewed seasonally or when the weather's dreary. It is rich, malty, fruity, aromatic, and alcoholic. Deep copper with a firm white head, Hampshire Special finishes dry and pleasantly bitter.

Original gravity: 1070 • Final gravity: 1018 • 6.6% abv • 35 IBU

Heat 1½ gallons (5.7 L) water to 164°F (73°C). Crush:

2½ lb. (1.1 kg) pale malt
1¼ lb. (567 g) medium (50°L) crystal malt
4 oz. (113 g) chocolate malt

Add to liquor and steep at 152°F (67°C) for 90 minutes. Sparge with 2¼ gallons (8.5 L) water at 168°F (76°C). Add to runnings:

5½ lb. (2½ kg) unhopped, pale dry malt extract (DME)

Bring to a boil, then add:

4 AAUs Cascade hops
3 AAUs Mt. Hood hops

Boil 90 minutes, then add:

5 AAUs Goldings hops

Remove from heat. Cool, then top up to 5¼ gallons (20 L) with chilled, preboiled water. Cool to 68°F (20°C), then pitch:

Ringwood ale yeast (available from EasYeast) or English ale yeast such as Wyeast 1098

Ferment at 68°F (20°C) for 2 weeks, then transfer to secondary fermenter and condition cool (50–55°F [10–13°C]) for 3 to 4 weeks. Prime with:

1 cup (237 ml) pale dry malt extract

Bottle and age at 55–60°F (13–16°C) for 3 weeks.

Alternate Methods

All-extract: Steep 12 oz. (340 g) pale malt and the crystal and chocolate malts as in main recipe in 2½ gallons (9.5 L) water at 150°F (66°C) for 45 minutes. Add 7 lb. (3.2 kg) unhopped, light malt extract syrup and 1 lb. (454 g) amber DME. Follow directions from beginning of boil.

All-grain: Mash 8 lb. (3.6 kg) pale malt and the crystal and chocolate malts as in main recipe in 4 gallons (15.1 L) water at 152°F (67°C). Sparge with 4 gallons (15.1 L) water. Omit first DME and proceed as in main recipe, reducing wort volume to 5¼ gallons (20 L) or less.

Serve at 50°F (10°C) in a traditional pint glass.

Riverdriver Hazelnut Porter

Sea Dog Brewing Co., Bangor, Maine

This rich, dark porter is sweet, bitter, and then sweet again, with an additional complexity from hazelnut flavoring. It's deep reddish brown and medium to full bodied, and there are many different flavors one can pursue when brewing it.

Original gravity: 1045 • **Final gravity: 1010** • **4.5% abv** • **25 IBU**

Heat 1¼ gallons (4.7 L) water to 164°F (73°C). Crush:

- **1 lb. (454 g) pale malt**
- **4 oz. (113 g) toasted pale malt (toast at 350°F [177°C] for 15 minutes)**
- **4 oz. (113 g) black malt**
- **4 oz. (113 g) chocolate malt**
- **8 oz. (227 g) dark (90°L) crystal malt**

Add to liquor and steep at 152°F (67°C) for 90 minutes. Sparge with 2 gallons (7.6 L) water at 168°F (76°C). Add to runnings:

- **4½ lb. (2 kg) unhopped, amber malt extract syrup**

Bring to a boil, then add:

- **6 AAUs B. C. Goldings hops**

Boil 60 minutes, then remove from heat. Cool, then top up to 5¼ gallons (20 L) with chilled, preboiled water. Cool to 68°F (20°C), then pitch:

- **London ale yeast (Wyeast 1968 or equivalent)**

Ferment at 68°F (20°C) for 2 weeks, then transfer to secondary fermenter and condition cool (50–55°F [10–13°C]) for 3 to 4 weeks.

At bottling, prime with:

- **1 cup (237 ml) pale dry malt extract (DME)**
- **2 oz. (57 g) Noirot Hazelnut liqueur concentrate**

Bottle and age at 55–60°F (13–16°C) for 3 weeks.

Alternate Methods

All-extract: Steep the toasted pale, black, chocolate, and crystal malts as in main recipe in 2½ gallons (9.5 L) water at 150°F (66°C) for 45 minutes. Omit pale malt and increase malt extract syrup to 5½ lb. (2.5 kg). Follow directions from beginning of boil.

All-grain: Mash 6¼ lb. (2.8 kg) pale malt and the toasted pale, black, chocolate, and crystal malts as in main recipe in 2½ gallons (9.5 L) water at 152°F (67°C). Sparge with 3 gallons (11 L) water. Omit malt extract syrup and proceed as in main recipe, reducing wort volume to 5¼ gallons (20 L) or less.

 Serve at 50°F (10°C) in a traditional pint glass.

Sunsplash Golden Ale

Stone Coast Brewing Co., Portland, Maine; Bethel, Maine

Here's a surprisingly complex, golden ale from a brewery that operates both at the seacoast and in western Maine's ski country. It has malty, bready, and crackery notes and several layers of hop flavor and aroma. This is a beer to chew on; it finishes nutty and dry.

Original gravity: 1048 • Final gravity: 1010 • 4.8% abv • 22 IBU

Heat 2 gallons (7.6 L) water to 164°F (73°C). Crush:

- **3 lb. (1.4 kg) pale malt**
- **1 lb. (454 g) light (20°L) crystal malt**
- **1 lb. (454 g) carapils malt**
- **4 oz. (113 g) malted wheat**

Add to liquor and steep at 152°F (67°C) for 90 minutes. Sparge with 3 gallons (11 L) water at 168°F (76°C). Add to runnings:

- **2 lb. (907 g) unhopped, extra-light dry malt extract (DME)**

Bring to a boil, then add:

- **4 AAUs Mt. Hood hops**

Boil 15 minutes, then add:

- **3 AAUs Willamette hops**

Boil 30 minutes, then remove from heat and add:

- **4 AAUs Mt. Hood hops**

Steep 30 minutes, then remove from heat. Cool, then top up to 5¼ gallons (20 L) with chilled, preboiled water. Cool to 68°F (20°C), then pitch:

- **American ale yeast (Wyeast 1056 or equivalent)**

Ferment at 68°F (20°C) for 2 weeks, then transfer to secondary fermenter and condition cool (50–55°F [10–13°C]) for 3 to 4 weeks. Prime with:

- **1 cup (237 ml) pale dry malt extract**

Bottle and age at 50°F (10°C) for 3 weeks.

Alternate Methods

All-extract: Steep the crystal and carapils malts and malted wheat as in main recipe in 2½ gallons (9.5 L) water at 150°F (66°C) for 45 minutes. Omit pale malt and increase DME to 4 lb. (1.8 kg). Follow directions from beginning of boil.

All-grain: Mash 6 lb. (2.7 kg) pale malt, the crystal and carapils malts, and the malted wheat as in main recipe in 3 gallons (11 L) water at 152°F (67°C). Sparge with 3¾ gallons (14.2 L) water. Omit first DME and proceed as in main recipe, reducing wort volume to 5¼ gallons (20 L) or less.

 Serve at 50°F (10°C) in a traditional pint glass.

Whale Tail Brown Ale

Whale Tail Brewing Co., Old Orchard Beach, Maine

A newish brewpub in the summer tourist town of Old Orchard Beach,
Whale Tail produces this southern England–style brown ale. It's mild and relatively
sweet and smooth with hints of burnt sugar, figs, and raisins.

Original gravity: 1043 • **Final gravity: 1010** • **4.2% abv** • **20 IBU**

Heat 1¾ gallons (6.6 L) water to 164°F (73°C). Crush:

2 lb. (907 g) pale malt
1 lb. (454 g) brown malt
8 oz. (227 g) dark (90°L) crystal malt
8 oz. (227 g) black malt
8 oz. (227 g) chocolate malt

Add to liquor and steep at 152°F (67°C) for 90 minutes. Sparge with 2½ gallons (9.5 L) water at 168°F (76°C). Add to runnings:

2 lb. (907 g) unhopped, pale dry malt extract (DME)
1 cup (237 ml) brown sugar

Boil 30 minutes, then add:

4 AAUs Fuggles hops

Boil 45 minutes, then add:

4 AAUs Cascade hops

Boil 15 minutes, then remove from heat. Cool, then top up to 5¼ gallons (20 L) with chilled, preboiled water. Cool to 68°F (20°C), then pitch:

London ale yeast (Wyeast 1028 or equivalent)

Ferment at 65°F (18°C) for 2 weeks, then transfer to secondary fermenter and condition cool (50–55°F [10–13°C]) for 3 to 4 weeks. Prime with:

¾ cup (177 ml) pale dry malt extract

Bottle and age at 55–60°F (13–16°C) for 3 weeks.

Alternate Methods

All-extract: Steep the crystal, black, and chocolate malts as in main recipe in 2½ gallons (9.5 L) water at 150°F (66°C) for 45 minutes. Omit pale and brown malts and increase DME to 4 lb. (1.8 kg). Follow directions from beginning of boil.

All-grain: Mash 4 lb. (1.8 kg) pale malt, 2 lb. (907 g) brown malt, and the crystal, black, and chocolate malts as in main recipe in 3 gallons (11 L) water at 152°F (67°C). Sparge with 3¾ gallons (14.2 L) water. Omit first DME, but add brown sugar and proceed as in main recipe, reducing wort volume to 5¼ gallons (20 L) or less.

Serve at 50°F (10°C) in a traditional pint glass.

Clipper City Pale Ale

Clipper City Brewing Co., Baltimore, Maryland

Clipper City is a pleasant, mildly sweet, relatively hoppy pale ale with a distinctly English aroma profile. This beer is dark gold and has a tangy, clean bitterness.

Original gravity: 1050 • **Final gravity: 1012** • **4.8% abv** • **40 IBU**

Heat 1¼ gallons (4.7 L) water to 164°F (73°C). Crush:
- **3 lb. (1.4 kg) pale malt**
- **1 lb. (454 g) medium (50°L) crystal malt**

Add to liquor and steep at 152°F (67°C) for 90 minutes. Sparge with 2 gallons (7.6 L) water at 168°F (76°C). Add to runnings:
- **3 lb. (1.4 kg) unhopped, pale dry malt extract (DME)**

Bring to a boil, then add:
- **6 AAUs Goldings hops**

Boil 45 minutes, then add:
- **6 AAUs Goldings hops**

Boil 15 minutes, then remove from heat. Cool, then top up to 5¼ gallons (20 L) with chilled, preboiled water. Cool to 68°F (20°C), then pitch:
- **English ale yeast (Wyeast 1098 or equivalent)**

Ferment at 68°F (20°C) for 2 weeks, then transfer to secondary fermenter and add:
- **4 AAUs Fuggles hops**

Condition cool (50–55°F [10–13°C]) for 3 to 4 weeks. Prime with:
- **1 cup (237 ml) pale dry malt extract**

Bottle and age at 55–60°F (13–16°C) for 3 weeks.

Alternate Methods

All-extract: Steep the crystal malt as in main recipe in 2½ gallons (9.5 L) water at 150°F (66°C) for 45 minutes. Omit pale malt and increase DME to 5 lb. (2.3 kg). Follow directions from beginning of boil.

All-grain: Mash 7½ lb. (3.4 kg) pale malt and the crystal malt as in main recipe in 2½ gallons (9.5 L) water at 152°F (67°C). Sparge with 3 gallons (11 L) water. Omit first DME and proceed as in main recipe, reducing wort volume to 5¼ gallons (20 L) or less.

 Serve at 50°F (10°C) in a traditional pint glass.

DeGroen's Märzen

Baltimore Brewing Co., Baltimore, Maryland

Here's a nice malty, bready, mellow Märzenbier from a brewery known for authentic German-style lagers and specialty beers (including a legendary steinbier). This one has a rich, deep golden color and lots of caramel and biscuit flavor notes cut by a pleasant noble hop bitterness.

Original gravity: 1054 • Final gravity: 1012 • 5.4% abv • 38–40 IBU

Heat 2½ gallons (9.5 L) water to 164°F (73°C). Crush:
- **4½ lb. (2 kg) lager malt**
- **1 lb. (454 g) Munich malt**
- **12 oz. (340 g) carapils malt**

Add to liquor and steep at 152°F (67°C) for 90 minutes. Sparge with 3¼ gallons (12.3 L) water at 168°F (76°C). Add to runnings:
- **2 lb. (907 g) unhopped, pale dry malt extract (DME)**

Bring to a boil, then add:
- **4 AAUs Perle hops**

Boil 45 minutes, then add:
- **4 AAUs Hallertau hops**
- **4 AAUs Tettnang hops**

Boil 45 minutes, then add:
- **4 AAUs Hallertau hops**

Boil 5 minutes, then remove from heat. Cool, then top up to 5¼ gallons (20 L) with chilled, preboiled water. Cool to 62°F (17°C), then pitch:
- **Munich lager yeast (Wyeast 2308 or equivalent)**

Ferment at 40°F (4°C) for 2 weeks, then transfer to secondary fermenter and condition cool (45°F [7°C]) for 4 to 6 weeks. Prime with:
- **1 cup (237 ml) pale dry malt extract**

Bottle and age at 45–50°F (7–10°C) for 6 weeks.

Alternate Methods

All-extract: Steep 1½ lb. (680 g) lager malt and the Munich and carapils malts as in main recipe in 2½ gallons (9.5 L) water at 150°F (66°C) for 45 minutes. Increase DME to 4 lb. (1.8 kg). Follow directions from beginning of boil.

All-grain: Mash 7½ lb. (3.4 kg) lager malt and the Munich and carapils malts as in main recipe in 3 gallons (11 L) water at 152°F (67°C). Sparge with 3¾ gallons (14.2 L) water. Omit first DME and proceed as in main recipe, reducing wort volume to 5¼ gallons (20 L) or less.

 Serve at 50°F (10°C) in a glass or ceramic stein.

Hempen Ale

Frederick Brewing Co., Frederick, Maryland

Hempen Ale is a light brown ale that's amber, mildly hoppy, crisp, and refreshing. On top of that, it has the nutty flavor of hemp seeds, but there's nothing illegal about it!

Original gravity: 1045 • **Final gravity: 1012** • **4.2% abv** • **20 IBU**

Heat 1¼ gallons (4.7 L) water to 164°F (73°C). Crush:

2 lb. (907 g) mild ale malt
1 lb. (454 g) brown malt
8 oz. (227 g) medium (50°L) crystal malt
1 lb. (454 g) hemp seeds, toasted on a cookie sheet at 350°F (177°C) for 30 minutes

Add to liquor and steep at 152°F (67°C) for 90 minutes. Sparge with 2 gallons (7.6 L) water at 168°F (76°C). Add to runnings:

3 lb. (1.4 kg) unhopped, amber malt extract syrup
8 oz. (227 g) brown sugar

Bring to a boil, then add:

4 AAUs Cascade hops

Boil 30 minutes, then add:

8 oz. (227 g) hemp seeds

Boil 60 minutes, then remove from heat. Cool, then top up to 5¼ gallons (20 L) with chilled, preboiled water. Cool to 68°F (20°C), then pitch:

English ale yeast (Wyeast 1098 or equivalent)

Ferment at 68°F (20°C) for 2 weeks, then transfer to secondary fermenter and condition cool (50–55°F [10–13°C]) for 3 to 4 weeks. Prime with:

1 cup (237 ml) pale dry malt extract

Bottle and age at 55–60°F (13–16°C) for 3 weeks.

Alternate Methods

All-extract: Steep the brown and crystal malts and the hemp seeds as in main recipe in 2½ gallons (9.5 L) water at 150°F (66°C) for 45 minutes. Omit mild malt and increase malt extract syrup to 4½ lb. (2 kg). Follow directions from beginning of boil.

All-grain: Mash 5 lb. (2.3 kg) mild ale malt, the brown and crystal malts, and hemp seeds in 2½ gallons (9.5 L) water at 152°F (67°C). Sparge with 3 gallons (11 L) water. Omit malt extract syrup and proceed as in main recipe, reducing wort volume to 5¼ gallons (20 L) or less.

Serve at 50°F (10°C) in a traditional pint glass.

Subliminator Doppelbock

Blue Ridge Brewing Co., Frederick, Maryland

*A glowing red doppelbock, Subliminator greets you with notes of toast and coffee,
then alcohol, then sweet malt and bitter hops — something for everyone.
This beer finishes bigger than it starts.*

Original gravity: 1073 • Final gravity: 1020 • 6.8% abv • 45 IBU

Heat 2¼ gallons (8.5 L) water to 164°F (73°C). Crush:

4 lb. (1.8 kg) lager malt
1 lb. (454 g) carapils malt
1 lb. (454 g) Munich malt

Add to liquor and steep at 152°F (67°C) for 90 minutes. Sparge with
3 gallons (11 L) water at 168°F (76°C). Add to runnings:

2 lb. (907 g) unhopped, pale dry malt extract (DME)

Bring to a boil, then add:

4 AAUs Tettnang hops

Boil 30 minutes, then add:

3 AAUs Hallertau hops
3 AAUs Mt. Hood hops

Boil 45 minutes, then add:

3 AAUs Mt. Hood hops

Boil 15 minutes, then remove from heat. Cool, then top up to 5¼ gallons
(20 L) with chilled, preboiled water. Cool to 60°F (16°C), then pitch:

Munich lager yeast (Wyeast 2308 or equivalent)

Ferment at 50°F (10°C) for 2 weeks, then transfer to secondary fermenter
and condition cold (40°F [4°C]) for 5 to 6 weeks. Prime with:

1 cup (237 ml) pale dry malt extract

Bottle and age at 45°F (7°C) for 8 weeks.

Alternate Methods

All-extract: Steep the carapils and Munich malts as in main recipe in 2½ gallons (9.5 L) water at 150°F (66°C) for 45 minutes. Omit lager malt and increase DME to 5 lb. (2.3 kg). Follow directions from beginning of boil.

All-grain: Mash 7 lb. (3.2 kg) lager malt and the carapils and Munich malts as in main recipe in 3 gallons (11 L) water at 152°F (67°C). Sparge with 3¾ gallons (14.2 L) water. Omit first DME and proceed as in main recipe, reducing wort volume to 5¼ gallons (20 L) or less.

Serve at 50°F (10°C) in a glass or ceramic stein.

Wild Goose IPA

Wild Goose Brewery, Frederick, Maryland

*Deep golden to amber, with caramel and fruity notes, particularly apple,
this IPA is a mild example of the style. The hops are there, for sure,
but are more balanced than in most American-made IPAs.*

Original gravity: 1050 • Final gravity: 1015 • 4.5% abv • 45 IBU

Heat 1¾ gallons (6.6 L) water to 164°F (73°C). Crush:
- **3 lb. (1.4 kg) pale malt**
- **8 oz. (227 g) medium (20°L) crystal malt**
- **8 oz. (227 g) malted wheat**

Add to liquor and steep at 152°F (67°C) for 90 minutes. Sparge with
2½ gallons (9.5 L) water at 168°F (76°C). Add to runnings:
- **3 lb. (1.4 kg) unhopped, pale dry malt extract (DME)**

Bring to a boil, then add:
- **8 AAUs Target hops**

Boil 45 minutes, then add:
- **4 AAUs Fuggles hops**

Boil 15 minutes, then remove from heat. Add:
- **6 AAUs Cascade hops**

Steep last hops for 15 minutes, then top up to 5¼ gallons (20 L) with
chilled, preboiled water. Cool to 68°F (20°C), then pitch:
- **English or American ale yeast (Wyeast 1098, 1056, or
equivalent)**

Ferment at 68°F (20°C) for 2 weeks, then transfer to secondary fermenter
and condition cool (50–55°F [10–13°C]) for 3 to 4 weeks. Prime with:
- **1 cup (237 ml) pale dry malt extract**

Bottle and age at 55–60°F (13–16°C) for 4 weeks.

Alternate Methods

All-extract: Steep 8 oz.
(227 g) toasted pale malt
(toast at 350°F [177°C] for
30 minutes) and the crystal
malt and malted wheat as
in main recipe in 2½ gal-
lons (9.5 L) water at 150°F
(66°C) for 45 minutes. Add
6 lb. (2.7 kg) unhopped,
light malt extract syrup.
Follow directions from
beginning of boil.

All-grain: Mash 7½ lb.
(3.4 kg) pale malt and the
crystal malt and malted
wheat as in main recipe in
3 gallons (11 L) water at
152°F (67°C). Sparge with
3¾ gallons (14.2 L) water.
Omit first DME and pro-
ceed as in main recipe,
reducing wort volume to
5¼ gallons (20 L) or less.

Serve at 50°F (10°C) in a traditional pint glass.

Wild Goose Oatmeal Stout

Wild Goose Brewery, Frederick, Maryland

*Smooth and roasty, bold and smoky, sweet and dark, this is a satisfying stout.
American hops give this one an aroma and flavor profile slightly different
from those of your average English stout, and the combination
of burnt sugar and oats makes an interesting contrast.*

Original gravity: 1065 • **Final gravity: 1015** • **6.4% abv** • **35 IBU**

Heat 2½ gallons (9.5 L) water to 164°F (73°C). Crush:

3¼ lb. (1.5 kg) pale malt
1 lb. (454 g) flaked oats
8 oz. (227 g) roasted barley
8 oz. (227 g) Munich malt
4 oz. (113 g) black malt
4 oz. (113 g) chocolate malt
8 oz. (227 g) dark (90°L) crystal malt

Add to liquor and steep at 152°F (67°C) for 90 minutes. Sparge with
3 gallons (11 L) water at 168°F (76°C). Add to runnings:

3½ lb. (1.6 kg) unhopped, amber dry malt extract (DME)

Bring to a boil, then add:

3 AAUs Cascade hops
3 AAUs Willamette hops
3 AAUs Tettnang hops

Boil 45 minutes, then add:

2 AAUs Cascade hops
2 AAUs Willamette hops

Boil 15 minutes, then remove from heat. Cool, then top up to 5¼ gallons
(20 L) with chilled, preboiled water. Cool to 68°F (20°C), then pitch:

English ale yeast (Wyeast 1098 or equivalent)

Ferment at 65°F (18°C) for 2 weeks, then transfer to secondary fermenter
and condition cool (50–55°F [10–13°C]) for 3 to 4 weeks. Prime with:

1 cup (237 ml) pale dry malt extract

Bottle and age at 50°F (10°C) for 3 weeks.

 Serve at 50°F (10°C) in a traditional pint glass.

 **Alternate Methods**

All-extract: Omit pale malt
and steep the flaked oats,
roasted barley, and the
Munich, black, chocolate,
and crystal malts as in
main recipe in 2½ gallons
(9.5 L) water at 150°F
(66°C) for 45 minutes.
Increase DME to 6 lb. (2.7
kg). Follow directions from
beginning of boil.

All-grain: Mash 8¼ lb.
(3.7 kg) pale malt and the
flaked oats, roasted barley,
and the Munich, black,
chocolate, and crystal
malts as in main recipe in
3½ gallons (13.2 L) water
at 152°F (67°C). Sparge
with 4 gallons (15.1 L)
water. Omit first DME and
proceed as in main recipe,
reducing wort volume to
5¼ gallons (20 L) or less.

Buzzards Bay Stock Ale

Buzzards Bay Brewing Co., Westport, Massachusetts

This beer is hearty and warming with a rich nutty taste and a lingering hop flavor and bitterness. A portion of the profits from this stock ale go to help farmland preservation.

Original gravity: 1060 • Final gravity: 1015 • 5.7% abv • 40 IBU

Heat 2 gallons (7.6 L) water to 164°F (73°C). Crush:

3 lb. (1.4 kg) pale malt
1 lb. (454 g) dark (120°L) crystal malt
8 oz. (227 g) black malt
4 oz. (113 g) malted wheat

Add to liquor and steep at 152°F (67°C) for 90 minutes. Sparge with 3 gallons (11 L) water at 168°F (76°C). Add to runnings:

2 lb. (907 g) unhopped, amber dry malt extract (DME)

Bring to a boil, then add:

6 AAUs Fuggles hops

Boil 45 minutes, then add:

4 AAUs Cascade hops

Boil 45 minutes, then remove from heat. Cool, then top up to 5¼ gallons (20 L) with chilled, preboiled water. Cool to 68°F (20°C), then pitch:

London ale yeast (Wyeast 1028, 1968, or equivalent)

Ferment at 65°F (18°C) for 2 weeks, then transfer to secondary fermenter and condition cool (50–55°F [10–13°C]) for 3 to 4 weeks. Prime with:

1 cup (237 ml) pale dry malt extract

Bottle and age at 50°F (10°C) for 6 weeks.

Alternate Methods

All-extract: Steep the crystal and black malts and malted wheat as in main recipe in 2½ gallons (9.5 L) water at 150°F (66°C) for 45 minutes. Omit pale malt and increase DME to 4 lb. (1.8 kg). Follow directions from beginning of boil.

All-grain: Mash 6 lb. (2.7 kg) pale malt and the crystal and black malts and malted wheat as in main recipe in 3 gallons (11 L) water at 152°F (67°C). Sparge with 3¾ gallons (14.2 L) water. Omit first DME and proceed as in main recipe, reducing wort volume to 5¼ gallons (20 L) or less.

Serve at 50°F (10°C) in a traditional pint glass.

Harpoon Spring Maibock

Harpoon Brewery, Boston, Massachusetts

This is a nice, rich lager, lighter than your average bock but darker than most maibocks. Smooth and tasty, aromatic and malty, this is a beer that awakens the senses.

Original gravity: 1060 • Final gravity: 1015 • 5.8% abv • 36 IBU

Heat 1¼ gallons (4.7 L) water to 164°F (73°C). Crush:

2 lb. (907 g) lager malt
1 lb. (454 g) Munich malt
4 oz. (113 g) medium (40–50°L) crystal malt

Add to liquor and steep at 152°F (67°C) for 90 minutes. Sparge with 2 gallons (7.6 L) water at 168°F (76°C). Add to runnings:

6 lb. (2.7 kg) unhopped, light malt extract syrup

Bring to a boil, then add:

6 AAUs Spalt hops

Boil 45 minutes, then add:

4 AAUs Tettnang hops

Boil 30 minutes, then remove from heat. Cool, then top up to 5¼ gallons (20 L) with chilled, preboiled water. Cool to 68°F (20°C), then pitch:

Munich lager yeast (Wyeast 2308 or equivalent)

Ferment at 68°F (20°C) for 3 days, then move to a cooler place and ferment at 45–50°F (7–10°C) for 2 weeks. Transfer to secondary fermenter and condition cold (38–40°F [3–4°C]) for 6 weeks. Prime with:

¾ cup (177 ml) corn sugar

Bottle and age at 40–45°F (4–7°C) for 6 weeks.

Alternate Methods

All-extract: Steep 8 oz. (227 g) Munich malt, 12 oz. (340 g) lager malt, and the crystal malt as in main recipe in 2½ gallons (9.5 L) water at 150°F (66°C) for 45 minutes. Remove grains and add 6 lb. (2.7 kg) light, unhopped dry malt extract. Follow directions from beginning of boil.

All-grain: Mash 4 lb. (1.8 kg) Munich malt, 6 lb. (2.7 kg) lager malt, and the crystal malt as in main recipe in 3¼ gallons (12.3 L) water at 152°F (67°C). Sparge with 3¾ gallons (14.2 L) water. Omit malt extract syrup and proceed as in main recipe, reducing wort volume to 5¼ gallons (20 L) or less.

Serve at 45°F (7°C) in a tall Pilsner glass.

Harpoon UFO Hefeweizen

Harpoon Brewery., Boston, Massachusetts

*UFO stands for unfiltered offering, and this German-style wheat beer is just that —
cloudy with suspended proteins and yeast, and chock-full of wheat and
spicy flavors. This is an authentic version of a true classic, with all the fruit, cloves,
bread, and hops in the nose that you'd expect in a beer from Bavaria.*

Original gravity: 1050 • Final gravity: 1012 • 4.8% abv • 15 IBU

Heat 2 gallons (7.6 L) water to 164°F (73°C). Crush:

2 lb. (907 g) lager malt
2 lb. (907 g) malted wheat
8 oz. (227 g) carapils malt

Add to liquor and steep at 152°F (67°C) for 90 minutes. Sparge with
3 gallons (11 L) water at 168°F (76°C). Add to runnings:

3⅓ lb. (1.5 kg) unhopped, malted wheat extract syrup

Bring to a boil, then add:

4 AAUs Hallertau hops

Boil 60 minutes, then remove from heat. Add:

2 AAUs Hallertau hops

Steep 30 minutes, then cool and top up to 5¼ gallons (20 L) with chilled,
preboiled water. Cool to 68°F (20°C), then pitch:

**Recultured Harpoon UFO weizen yeast (or German weizen
yeast, Wyeast 3333, or equivalent)**

Ferment at 65°F (18°C) for 2 weeks, then transfer to secondary fermenter
and condition cool (50°F [10°C]) for 3 to 4 weeks. Prime with:

⅞ cup (210 ml) corn sugar

Bottle and age at 50°F (10°C) for 3 weeks.

Alternate Methods

All-extract: Steep 1 lb.
(454 g) lager malt, 1 lb.
(454 g) malted wheat, and
the carapils malt as in main
recipe in 2½ gallons (9.5 L)
water at 150°F (66°C) for
45 minutes. Increase malt
extract syrup to 5 lb.
(2.3 kg). Follow directions
from beginning of boil.

All-grain: Mash 4 lb.
(1.8 kg) lager malt, 4 lb.
(1.8 kg) malted wheat, and
the carapils malt as in main
recipe in 3 gallons (11 L)
water at 152°F (67°C).
Sparge with 3 gallons (11 L)
water. Omit malt extract
syrup and proceed as in
main recipe, reducing
wort volume to 5¼ gallons
(20 L) or less.

Serve at 50°F (10°C) in a traditional weizen glass.

Hyland's American Pale Ale

Hyland Orchard and Brewery, Sturbridge, Massachusetts

From my original hometown, this classically styled American pale ale is all about balance. The malt and hops complement each other beautifully to create a clean, chewy ale that positively glows a golden amber.

Original gravity: 1048 • **Final gravity: 1012** • **4.6% abv** • **35 IBU**

Heat 2 gallons (7.6 L) water to 164°F (73°C). Crush:

4½ lb. (2 kg) pale malt
12 oz. (340 g) medium (50°L) crystal malt

Add to liquor and steep at 152°F (67°C) for 90 minutes. Sparge with 3 gallons (11 L) water at 168°F (76°C). Add to runnings:

2 lb. (907 g) unhopped, pale dry malt extract (DME)

Bring to a boil, then add:

6 AAUs Nugget hops

Boil 30 minutes, then add:

4 AAUs Cascade hops

Boil 15 minutes, then add:

4 AAUs Cascade hops

Boil 15 minutes, then remove from heat. Cool, then top up to 5¼ gallons (20 L) with chilled, preboiled water. Cool to 68°F (20°C), then pitch:

American ale yeast (Wyeast 1056 or equivalent)

Ferment at 68°F (20°C) for 2 weeks, then transfer to secondary fermenter and add:

4 AAUs Willamette hops

Condition cool (50–55°F [10–13°C]) for 3 to 4 weeks. Prime with:

1 cup (237 ml) pale dry malt extract

Bottle and age at 50°F (10°C) for 3 weeks.

Alternate Methods

All-extract: Steep 1½ lb. (680 g) pale malt and the crystal malt as in main recipe in 2½ gallons (9.5 L) water at 150°F (66°C) for 45 minutes. Increase DME to 4 lb. (1.8 kg). Follow directions from beginning of boil.

All-grain: Mash 7½ lb. (3.4 kg) pale malt and the crystal malt as in main recipe in 3 gallons (11 L) water at 152°F (67°C). Sparge with 3¾ gallons (14.2 L) water. Omit first DME and proceed as in main recipe, reducing wort volume to 5¼ gallons (20 L) or less.

 Serve at 50°F (10°C) in a traditional pint glass.

Ipswich Extra Special Bitter

Ipswich Brewing Co., Ipswich, Massachusetts; Baltimore, Maryland

A rich, reddish amber beer, Ipswich has a big floral hop bouquet balancing a caramel malt and bready-grainy flavor. They call it a session beer for malt lovers, but it's not a bad beer for hop lovers, either.

Original gravity: 1046   •   Final gravity: 1010   •   4.6% abv   •   22 IBU

Heat 1 gallon (3.8 L) water to 164°F (73°C). Crush:

1 lb. (454 g) pale malt
1 lb. (454 g) malted wheat
8 oz. (227 g) medium (50°L) crystal malt

Add to liquor and steep at 152°F (67°C) for 90 minutes. Sparge with 1½ gallons (5.7 L) water at 168°F (76°C). Add to runnings:

2 lb. (907 g) unhopped, amber dry malt extract (DME)
2 lb. (907 g) unhopped, light malt extract syrup

Bring to a boil, then add:

4 AAUs Cascade hops

Boil 60 minutes, then add:

8 AAUs Chinook hops

Remove from heat. Cool, then top up to 5¼ gallons (20 L) with chilled, preboiled water. Cool to 68°F (20°C), then pitch:

American or British ale yeast (Wyeast 1056, 1098, or equivalent)

Ferment at 68°F (20°C) for 2 weeks, then transfer to secondary fermenter and condition cool (50–55°F [10–13°C]) for 3 to 4 weeks. Prime with:

1 cup (237 ml) pale dry malt extract

Bottle and age at 55–60°F (13–16°C) for 3 weeks.

Alternate Methods

All-extract: Steep 8 oz. (227 g) malted wheat and the crystal malt as in main recipe in 2½ gallons (9.5 L) water at 150°F (66°C) for 45 minutes. Omit pale malt, but add 1 lb. (454 g) amber DME, 2 lb. (907 g) light DME, and the light malt extract syrup as in main recipe. Follow directions from beginning of boil.

All-grain: Mash 5 lb. (2.3 kg) pale malt, 2¼ lb. (1 kg) malted wheat, and 12 oz. (340 g) medium crystal malt in 3 gallons (11 L) water at 152°F (67°C). Sparge with 3¾ gallons (14.2 L) water. Omit first DME and malt extract syrup and proceed as in main recipe, reducing wort volume to 5¼ gallons (20 L) or less.

Serve at 50°F (10°C) in a traditional pint glass.

Martha's Vineyard Extra Stout

Forrest Williams Brewing Co., Martha's Vineyard, Massachusetts
(contract-brewed by Catamount, Windsor, Vermont)
A reddish brown, dry stout with nice roasted barley notes and a very dry finish,
Martha's Vineyard has an aroma of sweet malt and roasted barley.
The aftertaste is of dark malt and hop bitterness.

Original gravity: 1052 • Final gravity: 1010 • 5.4% abv • 35 IBU

Heat 2¼ gallons (8.5 L) water to 164°F (73°C). Crush:

4 lb. (1.8 kg) pale malt
1 lb. (454 g) dark (120°L) crystal malt
8 oz. (227 g) roasted barley
8 oz. (227 g) malted wheat

Add to liquor and steep at 152°F (67°C) for 90 minutes. Sparge with 3 gallons (11 L) water at 168°F (76°C). Add to runnings:

2 lb. (907 g) unhopped, amber dry malt extract (DME)

Bring to a boil, then add:

6 AAUs Northern Brewer hops

Boil 75 minutes, then add:

4 AAUs Willamette hops

Boil 15 minutes, then remove from heat. Cool, then top up to 5¼ gallons (20 L) with chilled, preboiled water. Cool to 68°F (20°C), then pitch:

Irish ale yeast (Wyeast 1084 or equivalent)

Ferment at 65°F (18°C) for 2 weeks, then transfer to secondary fermenter and condition cool (50–55°F [10–13°C]) for 3 to 4 weeks. Prime with:

1 cup (237 ml) pale dry malt extract

Bottle and age at 55–60°F (13–16°C) for 3 weeks.

Alternate Methods

All-extract: Steep 1 lb. (454 g) pale malt and the crystal malt, roasted barley, and malted wheat as in main recipe in 2½ gallons (9.5 L) water at 150°F (66°C) for 45 minutes. Increase DME to 4 lb. (1.8 kg). Follow directions from beginning of boil.

All-grain: Mash 7 lb. (3.2 kg) pale malt and the crystal malt, roasted barley, and malted wheat as in main recipe in 3 gallons (11 L) water at 152°F (67°C). Sparge with 3¾ gallons (14.2 L) water. Omit first DME and proceed as in main recipe, reducing wort volume to 5¼ gallons (20 L) or less.

Serve at 50°F (10°C) in a traditional pint glass.

Private Stock Imperial Stout

Berkshire Brewing Co., South Deerfield, Massachusetts

Big and rich, dark and warming, this seasonal beer brings lots of malt flavor and hop bitterness along with burnt sugar, caramel, and roasted barley notes. By a roaring fire in the middle of winter, you'll appreciate this full-bodied beer that is sweet but not cloying.

Original gravity: 1072 • Final gravity: 1025 • 6% abv • 45 IBU

Heat 2½ gallons (9.5 L) water to 164°F (73°C). Crush:

5 lb. (2.3 kg) pale malt
1 lb. (454 g) dark (120°L) crystal malt
8 oz. (227 g) chocolate malt
8 oz. (227 g) roasted barley

Add to liquor and steep at 152°F (67°C) for 90 minutes. Sparge with 3¼ gallons (12.3 L) water at 168°F (76°C). Add to runnings:

3 lb. (1.4 kg) unhopped, dark dry malt extract (DME)
1 lb. (454 g) unsulfured molasses

Bring to a boil, then add:

6 AAUs Styrian Goldings hops

Boil 30 minutes, then add:

4 AAUs Cascade hops

Boil 55 minutes, then add:

4 AAUs Styrian Goldings hops

Boil 5 minutes, then remove from heat. Cool, then top up to 5¼ gallons (20 L) with chilled, preboiled water. Cool to 68°F (20°C), then pitch:

English or Irish ale yeast (Wyeast 1098, 1084, or equivalent)

Ferment at 68°F (20°C) for 2 weeks, then transfer to secondary fermenter and condition cool (50–55°F [10–13°C]) for 6 to 8 weeks. Prime with:

¾ cup (177 ml) corn sugar

Bottle and age at 55–60°F (13–16°C) for 8 weeks.

Alternate Methods

All-extract: Steep 2 lb. (907 g) pale malt and the crystal and chocolate malts and roasted barley as in main recipe in 2½ gallons (9.5 L) water at 150°F (66°C) for 45 minutes. Increase DME to 5 lb. (2.3 kg) and add the molasses. Follow directions from beginning of boil.

All-grain: Mash 9 lb. (4.1 kg) pale malt and the crystal and chocolate malts and roasted barley as in main recipe in 3¾ gallons (14.2 L) water at 152°F (67°C). Sparge with 4½ gallons (17 L) water. Omit DME, but add the molasses and proceed as in main recipe, reducing wort volume to 5¼ gallons (20 L) or less.

 Serve at 50°F (10°C) in a traditional pint glass.

Quinn's Irish-Style Ale

Wachusett Brewing Co., Winchester, Massachusetts

Quinn's is a nice bottle-conditioned red ale, hoppy and sweet at the same time. It's well balanced and has a beautifully smooth texture.

Original gravity: 1048 • Final gravity: 1010 • 4.8% abv • 40 IBU

Heat 2 gallons (7.6 L) water to 164°F (73°C). Crush:

4 lb. (1.8 kg) pale malt
8 oz. (227 g) medium (50°L) crystal malt
4 oz. (113 g) black malt
4 oz. (113 g) brown malt
4 oz. (113 g) roasted barley

Add to liquor and steep at 152°F (67°C) for 90 minutes. Sparge with 3 gallons (11 L) water at 168°F (76°C). Add to runnings:

2 lb. (907 g) unhopped, pale dry malt extract (DME)

Bring to a boil, then add:

4 AAUs Target hops

Boil 60 minutes, then add:

8 AAUs Northern Brewer hops

Boil 15 minutes, then add:

4 AAUs Goldings hops

Boil 15 minutes, then remove from heat. Cool, then top up to 5¼ gallons (20 L) with chilled, preboiled water. Cool to 68°F (20°C), then pitch:

Recultured Wachusett yeast or Irish ale yeast (Wyeast 1084 or equivalent)

Ferment at 65°F (18°C) for 2 weeks, then transfer to secondary fermenter and condition cool (50–55°F [10–13°C]) for 3 to 4 weeks. Prime with:

1 cup (237 ml) pale dry malt extract (DME)

Bottle and age at 55–60°F (13–16°C) for 3 weeks.

Alternate Methods

All-extract: Steep 1 lb. (454 g) pale malt and the crystal, black, and brown malts and roasted barley as in main recipe in 2½ gallons (9.5 L) water at 150°F (66°C) for 45 minutes. Increase DME to 4 lb. (1.8 kg). Follow directions from beginning of boil.

All-grain: Mash 7 lb. (3.2 kg) pale malt and the crystal, black, and brown malts as in main recipe in 3 gallons (11 L) water at 152°F (67°C). Sparge with 3¾ gallons (14.2 L) water. Omit first DME and proceed as in main recipe, reducing wort volume to 5¼ gallons (20 L) or less.

Serve at 50°F (10°C) in a traditional pint glass.

Samuel Adams Scotch Ale

Boston Beer Co., Boston, Massachusetts

Try this malty, smoky Scotch ale that's hearty and smooth. It has enough hops to keep it from being sweet, but enough malt to support the peat-smoked, whiskey malt flavor and aroma.

Original gravity: 1052 • Final gravity: 1012 • 5.1% abv • 24 IBU

Heat 2¼ gallons (8.5 L) water to 164°F (73°C). Crush:

3 lb. (1.4 kg) pale malt
1 lb. (454 g) peat-smoked malt
4 oz. lb. (113 g) roasted barley
8 oz. (227 g) dark (120°L) crystal malt
8 oz. (227 g) medium (60°L) crystal malt
8 oz. (227 g) Munich malt

Add to liquor and steep at 152°F (67°C) for 90 minutes. Sparge with 3 gallons (11 L) water at 168°F (76°C). Add to runnings:

2 lb. (907 g) unhopped, amber dry malt extract (DME)

Boil 60 minutes, then add:

5 AAUs Galena hops

Boil 60 minutes, then remove from heat. Cool, then top up to 5¼ gallons (20 L) with chilled, preboiled water. Cool to 65°F (18°C), then pitch:

Scottish ale yeast (Wyeast 1728 or equivalent)

Ferment at 62°F (17°C) for 2 weeks, then transfer to secondary fermenter and condition cool (50°F [10°C]) for 3 to 4 weeks. Prime with:

1 cup (237 ml) pale dry malt extract

Bottle and age at 50°F (10°C) for 3 weeks.

Alternate Methods

All-extract: Steep the peat-smoked malt, roasted barley, and crystal and Munich malts as in main recipe in 2½ gallons (9.5 L) water at 150°F (66°C) for 45 minutes. Omit pale malt and increase DME to 4 lb. (1.8 kg). Follow directions from beginning of boil.

All-grain: Mash 6 lb. (2.7 kg) pale malt and the peat-smoked malt, roasted barley, and crystal and Munich malts as in main recipe in 3 gallons (11 L) water at 152°F (67°C). Sparge with 3¾ gallons (14.2 L) water. Omit first DME and proceed as in main recipe, reducing wort volume to 5¼ gallons (20 L) or less.

 Serve at 50°F (10°C) in a Scottish thistle glass.

Samuel Adams Summer Ale

Boston Beer Co., Boston, Massachusetts

Based on a Belgian witbier (white beer) recipe, this hazy, refreshing, wheat-based ale has the unusual spicy flavors and aromas of grains of paradise and lemon. An intriguing beer.

Original gravity: 1055 • Final gravity: 1012 • 5.5% abv • 15 IBU

Alternate Methods

All-extract: Steep the carapils malt and flaked wheat as in main recipe in 2½ gallons (9.5 L) water at 150°F (66°C) for 45 minutes. Omit Pilsner malt and increase wheat and light malt extract syrups to 3½ lb. (1.6 kg) each. Follow directions from beginning of boil.

All-grain: Mash 4 lb. (1.8 kg) malted wheat, 5 lb. (2.3 kg) Pilsner malt, and the carapils malt and flaked wheat as in main recipe in 3½ gallons (13.2 L) water at 152°F (67°C). Sparge with 4 gallons (15.1 L) water. Omit malt extract syrups and proceed as in main recipe, reducing wort volume to 5¼ gallons (20 L) or less.

Heat 1¼ gallons (4.7 L) water to 164°F (73°C). Crush:

1 lb. (454 g) Pilsner malt
8 oz. (227 g) carapils malt

Add to liquor along with:

1 lb. (454 g) flaked wheat

Steep at 152°F (67°C) for 90 minutes. Sparge with 2 gallons (7.6 L) water at 168°F (76°C). Add to runnings:

3 lb. (1.4 kg) unhopped, malted wheat extract syrup
3 lb. (1.4 kg) unhopped, light malt extract syrup

Boil 15 minutes, then add:

4 AAUs Hallertau hops

Boil 40 minutes, then add:

½ oz. (14 g) lightly crushed grains of paradise
1 oz. (28 g) shredded lemon zest

Boil 5 minutes, then turn off heat and add:

2 AAUs Hallertau hops

Steep 5 minutes, then remove last addition of hops. Cool, then top up to 5¼ gallons (20 L) with chilled, preboiled water. Cool to 68°F (20°C), then pitch:

Belgian white beer yeast (Wyeast 3944 or equivalent)

Ferment at 68°F (20°C) for 2 weeks, then transfer to secondary fermenter and condition cool (50–55°F [10–13°C]) for 3 to 4 weeks. Prime with:

¾ cup (177 ml) corn sugar

Bottle and age at 55–60°F (13–16°C) for 3 weeks.

 Serve at 50°F (10°C) in a footed goblet.

Winter Solstice Ale

Paper City Brewing, Holyoke, Massachusetts

This is a strong seasonal ale with characteristics of English strong ales, Scotch ales, and Belgian strong ales all in one. It's warming, alcoholic, and sweet, yet with a solid malt profile and a noticeable hop presence as well. The use of a little Belgian candi sugar makes it powerful without becoming cloying. Aging in oak (or on oak chips) will add an interesting depth of flavor.

Original gravity: 1078 • Final gravity: 1020 • 7.4% abv • 60 IBU

Heat 2¾ gallons (10.2 L) water to 164°F (73°C). Crush:
- **5 lb. (2.3 kg) pale malt (Maris Otter 2-row)**
- **1 lb. (454 g) medium (50°L) crystal malt**

Add to liquor and steep at 152°F (67°C) for 90 minutes. Sparge with 3¾ gallons (14.2 L) water at 168°F (76°C). Add to runnings:
- **4 lb. (1.8 kg) unhopped, pale dry malt extract (DME)**
- **8 oz. (227 g) light candi sugar**
- **8 oz. (227 g) dark candi sugar**

Bring to a boil, then add:
- **10 AAUs Magnum hops**

Boil 30 minutes, then add:
- **6 AAUs Saaz hops**

Boil 60 minutes, then remove from heat. Cool, then top up to 5¼ gallons (20 L) with chilled, preboiled water. Cool to 68°F (20°C), then pitch:
- **English ale yeast (Wyeast 1098 or equivalent) and**
- **Belgian Strong Ale yeast (Wyeast 3787 or equivalent)**

Ferment at 68°F (20°C) for 3 weeks, then transfer to secondary fermenter and condition cool (50–55°F [10–13°C]) for 4 to 6 weeks. Prime with:
- **1 cup (237 ml) pale dry malt extract**

Bottle and age at 55–60°F (13–16°C) for 5 weeks.

Alternate Methods

All-extract: Steep 2 lb. (907 g) pale malt and the crystal malt as in main recipe in 2½ gallons (9.5 L) water at 150°F (66°C) for 45 minutes. Increase DME to 6 lb. (2.7 kg) and add both candi sugars. Follow directions from beginning of boil.

All-grain: Mash 11 lb. (5 kg) pale malt and the crystal malt as in main recipe in 3¾ gallons (14.2 L) water at 152°F (67°C). Sparge with 4½ gallons (17 L) water. Omit first DME and proceed as in main recipe, including adding both candi sugars. Reduce wort volume to 5¼ gallons (20 L) or less.

 Serve at 50°F (10°C) in a brandy snifter.

Bell's Oberon Ale

Kalamazoo Brewing Co., Kalamazoo, Michigan

A bottle-conditioned Belgian white beer, Bell's has its emphasis more on the yeast and malt flavors and less on the traditional spices. It's a light, thirst-quenching beer, perfect for midsummer weather.

Original gravity: 1042 • Final gravity: 1008 • 4.3% abv • 18–20 IBU

Heat 2 gallons (7.6 L) water to 164°F (73°C). Crush:

2 lb. (907 g) lager malt
2½ lb. (1.1 kg) malted wheat
12 oz. (340 g) carapils malt

Add to liquor and steep at 152°F (67°C) for 90 minutes. Sparge with 2½ gallons (9.5 L) water at 168°F (76°C). Add to runnings:

2 lb. (907 g) unhopped, wheat dry malt extract (DME)

Bring to a boil, then add:

4 AAUs Saaz hops

Boil 60 minutes, then add:

⅛ tsp. (.13 ml) crushed coriander seeds

Remove from heat. Cool, then top up to 5¼ gallons (20 L) with chilled, preboiled water. Cool to 68°F (20°C), then pitch:

Recultured Oberon yeast or Belgian witbier yeast (Wyeast 3944 or equivalent)

Ferment at 65°F (18°C) for 2 weeks, then transfer to secondary fermenter and condition cool (50–55°F [10–13°C]) for 3 to 4 weeks. Prime with:

1 cup (237 ml) wheat dry malt extract

Bottle and age at 50°F (10°C) for 3 weeks.

 **Alternate Methods**

All-extract: Steep 1 lb. (454 g) lager malt, 8 oz. (227 g) malted wheat, and the carapils malt as in main recipe in 2½ gallons (9.5 L) water at 150°F (66°C) for 45 minutes. Increase DME to 4 lb. (1.8 kg). Follow directions from beginning of boil.

All-grain: Mash 4½ lb. (2.1 kg) malted wheat, 3 lb. (1.4 kg) lager malt, and the carapils malt as in main recipe in 3 gallons (11 L) water at 152°F (67°C). Sparge with 3¾ gallons (14.2 L) water. Omit first DME and proceed as in main recipe, reducing wort volume to 5¼ gallons (20 L) or less.

 Serve at 50°F (10°C) in a witbier chalice-style glass or lambic tumbler.

Bell's Porter

Kalamazoo Brewing Co., Kalamazoo, Michigan

This rich brown porter is bottle conditioned, giving it a stoutlike firmness and creaminess. The hop flavor is modest, and the roasted malt notes don't undermine the smoothness of the sweet, fruity flavors.

Original gravity: 1050 • Final gravity: 1015 • 5.7% abv • 25 IBU

Heat 1½ gallons (5.7 L) water to 164°F (73°C). Crush:

1¾ lb. (794 g) pale malt
1 lb. (454 g) black malt
1 lb. (454 g) chocolate malt
8 oz. (227 g) dark (120°L) crystal malt

Add to liquor and steep at 152°F (67°C) for 90 minutes. Sparge with 2¼ gallons (8.5 L) water at 168°F (76°C). Add to runnings:

3 lb. (1.4 kg) unhopped, dark dry malt extract (DME)

Bring to a boil, then add:

4 AAUs Goldings hops

Boil 60 minutes, then add:

4 AAUs Fuggles hops

Boil 30 minutes, then remove from heat. Cool, then top up to 5¼ gallons (20 L) with chilled, preboiled water. Cool to 68°F (20°C), then pitch:

Irish ale yeast (Wyeast 1084 or equivalent)

Ferment at 68°F (20°C) for 2 weeks, then transfer to secondary fermenter and condition cool (50°F [10°C]) for 3 to 4 weeks. Prime with:

1 cup (237 ml) pale dry malt extract

Bottle and age at 50°F (10°C) for 3 weeks.

Alternate Methods

All-extract: Steep the black, chocolate, and crystal malts as in main recipe in 2½ gallons (9.5 L) water at 150°F (66°C) for 45 minutes. Omit pale malt and increase DME to 4¼ lb. (1.9 kg). Follow directions from beginning of boil.

All-grain: Mash 6 lb. (2.7 kg) pale malt and the black, chocolate, and crystal malts as in main recipe in 3 gallons (11 L) water at 152°F (67°C). Sparge with 3¾ gallons (14.2 L) water. Omit first DME and proceed as in main recipe, reducing wort volume to 5¼ gallons (20 L) or less.

 Serve at 50°F (10°C) in a traditional pint glass.

McSorley's Black & Tan

McSorley's Brewing, Detroit, Michigan

Traditionally a blend of two finished beers, this recipe can be brewed quite easily as one batch. It combines the rich, roasty flavor of a dry stout and the clean, hoppy aroma and flavor of a Pilsner. The finished product is sweeter than a stout, roasty like a schwarzbier, and smooth and clean.

Original gravity: 1044 • Final gravity: 1010 • 4.3% abv • 30 IBU

Heat 1½ gallons (5.7 L) water to 164°F (73°C). Crush:

1 lb. (454 g) pale malt
1 lb. (454 g) lager malt
8 oz. (227 g) carapils malt
8 oz. (227 g) Munich malt
8 oz. (227 g) medium (60°L) crystal malt
8 oz. (227 g) roasted barley

Add to liquor and steep at 152°F (67°C) for 90 minutes. Sparge with 2¼ gallons (8.5 L) water at 168°F (76°C). Add to runnings:

2½ lb. (1.1 kg) unhopped, pale dry malt extract (DME)

Bring to a boil, then add:

5 AAUs Northern Brewer hops

Boil 30 minutes, then add:

4 AAUs Hallertau hops

Boil 30 minutes, then remove from heat and add:

4 AAUs Northern Brewer hops

Steep for 15 minutes, then remove hops. Cool, then top up to 5¼ gallons (20 L) with chilled, preboiled water. Cool to 65°F (18°C), then pitch a blend of:

Irish Ale yeast (Wyeast 1084 or equivalent)
and
Pilsner lager yeast (Wyeast 2007 or equivalent)

Ferment at 60°F (16°C) for 2 weeks, then transfer to secondary fermenter and condition cool (50°F [10°C]) for 3 to 4 weeks. Prime with:

1 cup (237 ml) pale dry malt extract

Bottle and age at 50°F (10°C) for 3 weeks.

 Serve at 50°F (10°C) in a traditional pint glass.

 **Alternate Methods**

All-extract: Steep the carapils, Munich, and crystal malts and the roasted barley as in main recipe in 2½ gallons (9.5 L) water at 150°F (66°C) for 45 minutes.

Omit pale and lager malts and increase DME to 4 lb. (1.8 kg). Follow directions from beginning of boil.

All-grain: Mash 3 lb. (1.4 kg) pale malt, 2½ lb. (1.1 kg) lager malt, and the carapils, Munich, and crystal malts and the roasted barley as in main recipe in 2½ gallons (9.5 L) water at 152°F (67°C). Sparge with 3¼ gallons (12.3 L) water. Omit first DME and proceed as in main recipe, reducing wort volume to 5¼ gallons (20 L) or less.

Old Mission Lighthouse Ale

Traverse Brewing Co., Williamsburg, Michigan

Here's a brisk, light, pale ale with lots of herbal and floral hop aroma and a very refreshing carbonation level.

Original gravity: 1048 • Final gravity: 1012 • 4.3% abv • 45 IBU

Heat 2 gallons (7.6 L) water to 164°F (73°C). Crush:
- **3 lb. (1.4 kg) pale malt**
- **1 lb. (454 g) light (20°L) crystal malt**
- **12 oz. (340 g) malted wheat**

Add to liquor and steep at 152°F (67°C) for 90 minutes. Sparge with 3 gallons (11 L) water at 168°F (76°C). Add to runnings:
- **2 lb. (907 g) unhopped, pale dry malt extract (DME)**

Bring to a boil, then add:
- **6 AAUs Cluster hops**

Boil 45 minutes, then add:
- **4 AAUs Cascade hops**

Boil 15 minutes, then remove from heat. Add:
- **4 AAUs Cascade hops**

Steep 15 minutes. Cool, then top up to 5¼ gallons (20 L) with chilled, preboiled water. Cool to 68°F (20°C), then pitch:
- **American ale yeast (Wyeast 1056 or equivalent)**

Ferment at 68°F (20°C) for 2 weeks, then transfer to secondary fermenter and condition cool (50–55°F [10–13°C]) for 3 to 4 weeks. Prime with:
- **1 cup (237 ml) pale dry malt extract**

Bottle and age at 55–60°F (13–16°C) for 3 weeks.

Alternate Methods

All-extract: Steep the crystal malt and malted wheat as in main recipe in 2½ gallons (9.5 L) water at 150°F (66°C) for 45 minutes. Omit pale malt and increase DME to 4 lb. (1.8 kg). Follow directions from beginning of boil.

All-grain: Mash 6 lb. (2.7 kg) pale malt and the crystal malt and malted wheat as in main recipe in 2¾ gallons (10.2 L) water at 152°F (67°C). Sparge with 3¼ gallons (12.3 L) water. Omit first DME and proceed as in main recipe, reducing wort volume to 5¼ gallons (20 L) or less.

 Serve at 50°F (10°C) in a traditional pint glass.

Grain Belt Premium Beer

Minnesota Brewing Co., St. Paul, Minnesota

*This is a surprisingly malty and freshly hopped, standard American light-style lager.
It has obvious (but pleasant) adjunct flavor, and it's a little fuller bodied
than the usual examples of this style.*

Original gravity: 1044 • Final gravity: 1010 • 4.3% abv • 18–20 IBU

Heat 1¾ gallons water to 164°F (73°C). Crush:
- **2 lb. (907 g) lager malt**
- **2 lb. (907 g) brewer's flaked rice**
- **8 oz. (227 g) carapils malt**

Add to liquor and steep at 152°F (67°C) for 90 minutes. Sparge with
2½ gallons (9.5 L) water at 168°F (76°C). Add to runnings:
- **2 lb. (907 g) unhopped, extra-light dry malt extract (DME)**

Bring to a boil, then add:
- **4 AAUs Tettnang hops**

Boil 30 minutes, then add:
- **4 AAUs Perle hops**

Boil 15 minutes, then remove from heat. Cool, then top up to 5¼ gallons
(20 L) with chilled, preboiled water. Cool to 65°F (18°C), then pitch:
- **American lager yeast (Wyeast 2035 or equivalent)**

Ferment at 50°F (10°C) for 2 weeks, then transfer to secondary fermenter
and condition cool (40°F [4°C]) for 5 to 6 weeks. Prime with:
- **¾ cup (177 ml) corn sugar**

Bottle and age at 40°F (4°C) for 6 weeks.

 **Alternate Methods**

All-extract: Steep the carapils malt as in main recipe in 2½ gallons (9.5 L) water at 150°F (66°C) for 45 minutes. Omit lager malt and flaked rice and increase DME to 4 lb. (1.8 kg). Add 1 lb. (454 g) rice syrup solids. Follow directions from beginning of boil.

All-grain: Mash 5 lb. (2.3 kg) lager malt and the flaked rice and carapils malt as in main recipe in 2½ gallons (9.5 L) water at 152°F (67°C). Sparge with 3 gallons (11 L) water. Omit DME and proceed as in main recipe, reducing wort volume to 5¼ gallons (20 L) or less.

 Serve at 40°F (4°C) in a traditional Pilsner glass.

Great Northern Porter

Summit Brewing Co., St. Paul, Minnesota

*This is a deep reddish brown porter reminiscent of the porters of Scandinavia.
A robust chocolate and black malt aroma, with herbal hops and an
almost stoutlike creaminess, makes this one smooth porter.*

Original gravity: 1048 • Final gravity: 1012 • 4.6% abv • 25 IBU

Heat 2¼ gallons (8.5 L) water to 164°F (73°C). Crush:

3½ lb. (1.6 kg) pale malt
8 oz. (227 g) black malt
8 oz. (227 g) chocolate malt
12 oz. (340 g) dark (120°L) crystal malt

Add to liquor and steep at 152°F (67°C) for 90 minutes. Sparge with
3 gallons (11 L) water at 168°F (76°C). Add to runnings:

2 lb. (907 g) unhopped, amber dry malt extract (DME)

Bring to a boil, then add:

6 AAUs Styrian Goldings hops

Boil 55 minutes, then add:

3 AAUs Styrian Goldings hops

Boil 5 minutes, then remove from heat. Cool, then top up to 5¼ gallons
(20 L) with chilled, preboiled water. Cool to 65°F (18°C), then pitch:

Swedish ale yeast (Wyeast 1742 or equivalent)

Ferment at 65°F (18°C) for 2 weeks, then transfer to secondary fermenter
and condition cool (50°F [10°C]) for 3 to 4 weeks. Prime with:

1 cup (237 ml) pale dry malt extract

Bottle and age at 50°F (10°C) for 3 weeks.

Alternate Methods

All-extract: Steep 8 oz.
(227 g) pale malt and the
black, chocolate, and crystal malts as in main recipe
in 2½ gallons (9.5 L) water
at 150°F (66°C) for 45 minutes. Increase DME to 4 lb.
(1.8 kg). Follow directions
from beginning of boil.

All-grain: Mash 6½ lb.
(3 kg) pale malt and the
black, chocolate, and crystal malts as in main recipe
in 3 gallons (11 L) water at
152°F (67°C). Sparge with
3¾ gallons (14.2 L) water.
Omit first DME and pro-
ceed as in main recipe,
reducing wort volume to
5¼ gallons (20 L) or less.

Serve at 50°F (10°C) in a traditional pint glass.

Maifest

August Schell Brewing Co., New Ulm, Minnesota

Here's a blond double bock from one of the largest independent brewers in the Midwest, also well known for contract brewing for several nationally known craft breweries. This medium-bodied beer is smooth and fruity with pear or pineapple aromas and a hoppy, dry finish.

Original gravity: 1055 • Final gravity: 1015 • 5.1% abv • 25–30 IBU

Heat 2 gallons (7.6 L) water to 164°F (73°C). Crush:

3 lb. (1.4 kg) lager malt
1 lb. (454 g) carapils malt
1 lb. (454 g) malted wheat
8 oz. (227 g) Vienna malt

Add to liquor and steep at 152°F (67°C) for 90 minutes. Sparge with 3 gallons (11 L) water at 168°F (76°C). Add to runnings:

3⅓ lb. (1.4 kg) unhopped, light malt extract syrup

Bring to a boil, then add:

6 AAUs Tettnang hops

Boil 60 minutes, then remove from heat. Add:

3 AAUs Hallertau hops

Steep 15 minutes. Cool, then top up to 5¼ gallons (20 L) with chilled, preboiled water. Cool to 68°F (20°C), then pitch:

Munich lager yeast (Wyeast 2308 or equivalent)

Ferment at 55°F (13°C) for 2 weeks, then transfer to secondary fermenter and condition cold (40°F [4°C]) for 4 to 6 weeks. Prime with:

1 cup (237 ml) pale dry malt extract (DME)

Bottle and age at 40°F (4°C) for 8 weeks.

Alternate Methods

All-extract: Steep the carapils, wheat, and Vienna malts as in main recipe in 2½ gallons (9.5 L) water at 150°F (66°C) for 45 minutes. Omit lager malt and increase malt extract syrup to 6 lb. (2.7 kg). Follow directions from beginning of boil.

All-grain: Mash 7 lb. (3.2 kg) lager malt and the carapils, wheat, and Vienna malts as in main recipe in 3 gallons (11 L) water at 152°F (67°C). Sparge with 3¾ gallons (14.2 L) water. Omit malt extract syrup and proceed as in main recipe, reducing wort volume to 5¼ gallons (20 L) or less.

 Serve at 45°F (7°C) in a cylindrical bock glass or ceramic stein.

Bully Porter

Boulevard Brewing Co., Kansas City, Missouri

Bully is a rich, malty, bottle-conditioned porter with a touch of wheat. Black with red highlights, this porter emphasizes dark malts and remains smooth, not bitter.

Original gravity: 1055 • Final gravity: 1015 • 5.1% abv • 30 IBU

Heat 2 gallons (7.6 L) water to 164°F (73°C). Crush:

3 lb. (1.4 kg) pale malt
8 oz. (227 g) black malt
8 oz. (227 g) chocolate malt
1 lb. (454 g) malted wheat
8 oz. (227 g) dark (90°L) crystal malt

Add to liquor and steep at 152°F (67°C) for 90 minutes. Sparge with 3 gallons (11 L) water at 168°F (76°C). Add to runnings:

2¾ lb. (1.3 kg) unhopped, amber dry malt extract (DME)

Bring to a boil, then add:

4 AAUs Nugget hops
2 AAUs Willamette hops

Boil 30 minutes, then add:

4 AAUs Mt. Hood hops

Boil 30 minutes, then remove from heat. Cool, then top up to 5¼ gallons (20 L) with chilled, preboiled water. Cool to 68°F (20°C), then pitch:

American ale yeast (recultured Boulevard yeast, Wyeast 1056, or equivalent)

Ferment at 65°F (18°C) for 2 weeks, then transfer to secondary fermenter and condition cool (50–55°F [10–13°C]) for 3 to 4 weeks. Prime with:

¾ cup (177 ml) pale dry malt extract

Bottle and age at 55–60°F (13–16°C) for 3 weeks.

Alternate Methods

All-extract: Steep the black, chocolate, and crystal malts as in main recipe, plus 8 oz. (227 g) malted wheat, in 2½ gallons (9.5 L) water at 150°F (66°C) for 45 minutes. Omit pale malt and increase DME to 5¼ lb. (2.4 kg). Follow directions from beginning of boil.

All-grain: Mash 7 lb. (3.2 kg) pale malt, the black, chocolate, and crystal malts, and the malted wheat as in main recipe in 3 gallons (11 L) water at 152°F (67°C). Sparge with 3¾ gallons (14.2 L) water. Omit first DME and proceed as in main recipe, reducing wort volume to 5¼ gallons (20 L) or less.

 Serve at 50°F (10°C) in a traditional pint glass.

Black Dog Ale

Spanish Peaks Brewing, Bozeman, Montana
(contract-brewed by Schell, New Ulm, Minnesota)

This pale ale is more sweet than bitter, more malty than hoppy, soft and mild, and clean and easy to drink. It's deep gold with hints of caramel and popcorn and a touch of peppery spice in the nose.

Original gravity: 1045 • Final gravity: 1010 • 4.5% abv • 20 IBU

Heat 1½ gallons (5.7 L) water to 164°F (73°C). Crush:

2 lb. (907 g) pale malt
1 lb. (454 g) medium (50°L) crystal malt
12 oz. (340 g) malted wheat

Add to liquor and steep at 152°F (67°C) for 90 minutes. Sparge with 2¼ gallons (8.5 L) water at 168°F (76°C). Add to runnings:

3½ lb. (1.6 kg) unhopped, light malt extract syrup

Bring to a boil, then add:

4 AAUs Willamette hops

Boil 45 minutes, then add:

4 AAUs Mt. Hood hops

Boil 15 minutes, then remove from heat. Cool, then top up to 5¼ gallons (20 L) with chilled, preboiled water. Cool to 68°F (20°C), then pitch:

American ale yeast (Wyeast 1056 or equivalent)

Ferment at 68°F (20°C) for 2 weeks, then transfer to secondary fermenter and condition cool (50–55°F [10–13°C]) for 3 to 4 weeks. Prime with:

1 cup (237 ml) pale dry malt extract (DME)

Bottle and age at 50°F (10°C) for 3 weeks.

Alternate Methods

All-extract: Steep the crystal malt and malted wheat as in main recipe in 2½ gallons (9.5 L) water at 150°F (66°C) for 45 minutes. Omit pale malt and increase malt extract syrup to 6½ lb. (3 kg). Follow directions from beginning of boil.

All-grain: Mash 6 lb. (2.7 kg) pale malt and the crystal malt and malted wheat as in main recipe in 3 gallons (11 L) water at 152°F (67°C). Sparge with 3¾ gallons (14.2 L) water. Omit malt extract syrup and proceed as in main recipe, reducing wort volume to 5¼ gallons (20 L) or less.

 Serve at 50°F (10°C) in a traditional pint glass.

Phil's Pils

Barley Boys Brewing, Omaha, Nebraska
(contract-brewed in St. Paul, Minnesota)

Here's a German-style Pilsner that's sweet, malty, and lightly but freshly hopped. It's also well rounded and flavorful with a nutty, almost licorice aftertaste.

Original gravity: 1048 • Final gravity: 1012 • 4.6% abv • 20 IBU

Heat 1¾ gallons water to 164°F (73°C). Crush:
- **3¼ lb. (1.5 kg) lager malt**
- **1 lb. (454 g) carapils malt**
- **8 oz. (227 g) Vienna malt**

Add to liquor and steep at 152°F (67°C) for 90 minutes. Sparge with 2½ gallons (9.5 L) water at 168°F (76°C). Add to runnings:
- **2 lb. (907 g) unhopped, extra-light dry malt extract (DME)**

Bring to a boil, then add:
- **6 AAUs Hallertau hops**

Boil 45 minutes, then add:
- **4 AAUs Saaz hops**

Boil 15 minutes, then remove from heat. Cool, then top up to 5¼ gallons (20 L) with chilled, preboiled water. Cool to 62°F (17°C), then pitch:
- **Czech Pilsner lager yeast (Wyeast 2278 or equivalent)**

Ferment at 38°F (3°C) for 2 weeks, then transfer to secondary fermenter and condition cool (35–38°F [2–3°C]) for 5 to 6 weeks. Prime with:
- **¾ cup (177 ml) corn sugar**

Bottle and age at 40°F (4°C) for 6 weeks.

Alternate Methods

All-extract: Steep the carapils and Vienna malts as in main recipe, plus 4 oz. (113 g) lager malt, in 2½ gallons (9.5 L) water at 150°F (66°C) for 45 minutes. Increase DME to 4 lb. (1.8 kg). Follow directions from beginning of boil.

All-grain: Mash 6¼ lb. (2.8 kg) lager malt and the carapils and Vienna malts as in main recipe in 3 gallons (11 L) water at 152°F (67°C). Sparge with 3¾ gallons (14.2 L) water. Omit DME and proceed as in main recipe, reducing wort volume to 5¼ gallons (20 L) or less.

Serve at 40°F (4°C) in a traditional Pilsner glass.

Black 47 Stout

Old Nutfield Brewing Co., Derry, New Hampshire

This pleasant, dry Irish stout comes from a town founded by Irish immigrants at the time of the great potato famine. Black 47 has all the hallmarks of a classic stout — roasted barley in the nose and flavor, a slightly acidic, metallic sourness in the finish, and a creamy, thick, tan head that you can write your name in.

Original gravity: 1047 • Final gravity: 1010 • 4.7% abv • 28 IBU

Heat 2 gallons (7.6 L) water to 164°F (73°C). Crush:

3 lb. (1.4 kg) pale malt
1 lb. (454 g) roasted barley
8 oz. (227 g) black malt
8 oz. (227 g) dark (120°L) crystal malt

Add to liquor and steep at 152°F (67°C) for 90 minutes. Sparge with 3 gallons (11 L) water at 168°F (76°C). Add to runnings:

2 lb. (907 g) unhopped, amber dry malt extract (DME)

Bring to a boil, then add:

6 AAUs Northern Brewer hops

Boil 55 minutes, then add:

4 AAUs Fuggles hops

Boil 5 minutes, then remove from heat. Cool, then top up to 5¼ gallons (20 L) with chilled, preboiled water. Cool to 68°F (20°C), then pitch:

Irish ale yeast (Wyeast 1084 or equivalent)

Ferment at 65°F (18°C) for 2 weeks, then transfer to secondary fermenter and condition cool (50°F [10°C]) for 3 to 4 weeks. Prime with:

1 cup (237 ml) pale dry malt extract

Bottle and age at 50°F (10°C) for 3 weeks.

Alternate Methods

All-extract: Steep the roasted barley and black and crystal malts as in main recipe in 2½ gallons (9.5 L) water at 150°F (66°C) for 45 minutes. Omit pale malt and increase DME to 4 lb. (1.8 kg). Follow directions from beginning of boil.

All-grain: Mash 6 lb. (2.7 kg) pale malt and the roasted barley and the black and crystal malts as in main recipe in 3 gallons (11 L) water at 152°F (67°C). Sparge with 3¾ gallons (14.2 L) water. Omit first DME and proceed as in main recipe, reducing wort volume to 5¼ gallons (20 L) or less.

 Serve at 50°F (10°C) in a traditional stout glass.

Blackhook Porter

Redhook Brewery, Seattle, Washington; Portsmouth, New Hampshire
*A very dark, rich, aromatic London-style porter, Blackhook has great
chocolate and roasty maltiness balanced with hop bitterness
and aroma. This is a very complex porter.*

Original gravity: 1056 • Final gravity: 1015 • 5.3% abv • 35–40 IBU

Heat 1¼ gallons (4.7 L) water to 164°F (73°C). Crush:

2 lb. (907 g) pale malt
8 oz. (227 g) dark (90°L) crystal malt
8 oz. (227 g) black patent malt

Add to liquor and steep at 152°F (67°C) for 75 minutes. Sparge with
2 gallons (7.6 L) water at 168°F (76°C). Add to runnings:

4½ lb. (2 kg) unhopped, amber dry malt extract (DME)

Bring to a boil, then add:

8 AAUs Eroica hops

Boil 60 minutes, then add:

6 AAUs Tettnang hops

Remove from heat and steep 15 minutes. Cool, then top up to 5¼ gallons
(20 L) with chilled, preboiled water. Cool to 68°F (20°C), then pitch:

London ale yeast (Wyeast 1028, 1968, or equivalent)

Ferment at 65°F (18°C) for 2 weeks, then transfer to secondary fermenter
and condition cool (50–55°F [10–13°C]) for 3 to 4 weeks. Prime with:

1 cup (237 ml) amber dry malt extract

Bottle and age at 55–60°F (13–16°C) for 3 weeks.

Alternate Methods

All-extract: Steep the crystal and black malts as in main recipe in 2½ gallons (9.5 L) water at 150°F (66°C) for 45 minutes. Omit pale malt and increase DME to 7¼ lb. (3.3 kg). Follow directions from beginning of boil.

All-grain: Mash 8½ lb. (3.9 kg) pale malt and the crystal and black malts as in main recipe in 3 gallons (11 L) water at 152°F (67°C). Sparge with 3¾ gallons (14.2 L) water. Omit first DME and proceed as in main recipe, reducing wort volume to 5¼ gallons (20 L) or less.

Serve at 50°F (10°C) in a traditional pint glass.

Lucknow Munich-Style Lager

Castle Springs Brewing Co., Moultenborough, New Hampshire
A glowing, golden, Munich-style helles lager, this beer has all the big malty flavor plus the pleasant buttery notes of diacetyl commonly found in the better examples from Bavaria. It tastes like bread fresh from the oven. The brewery uses water from its own mountain spring, which it also bottles.

Original gravity: 1046 • **Final gravity: 1010** • **4.6% abv** • **25 IBU**

Heat 3 quarts (2.8 L) water to 140°F (60°C). Crush:

2 lb. (907 g) Pilsner malt
1 lb. (454 g) Munich malt
8 oz. (227 g) caramunich malt

Add to liquor and steep at 130°F (55°C) for 30 minutes. Heat another 3 quarts (2.8 L) water to 180°F (83°C), add it to mash, and steep at 150°F (66°C) for 45 minutes. Sparge with 2 gallons (7.6 L) water at 168°F (76°C). Add to runnings:

3¾ lb. (1.7 kg) unhopped, extra-light malt extract syrup

Bring to a boil, then add:

5 AAUs Hallertau hops

Boil 60 minutes, then remove from heat. Cool, then top up to 5¼ gallons (20 L) with chilled, preboiled water. Cool to 65°F (18°C), then pitch:

Munich lager yeast (Wyeast 2308 or equivalent)

Ferment at 60°F (16°C) for 4 to 5 days, then move to a colder location (45°F [7°C]) and continue fermentation for 2 weeks. Rack to secondary fermenter and condition cold (35–38°F [2–3°C]) for 4 to 6 weeks. Prime with:

¾ cup (177 ml) corn sugar

Bottle and age at 40°F (4°C) for 6 weeks.

 Serve at 40°F (4°C) in a tall-stemmed glass or a stein.

 **Alternate Methods**

All-extract: Steep 8 oz. (227 g) Pilsner malt and the Munich and caramunich malts as in main recipe in 2½ gallons (9.5 L) water at 150°F (66°C) for 45 minutes. Increase malt extract syrup to 5 lb. (2.3 kg). Follow directions from beginning of boil.

All-grain: Mash 5 lb. (2.3 kg) Pilsner malt, 2 lb. (907 g) Munich malt, and 1 lb. (454 g) each caramunich malt and crystal malt (30°L). Steep in 2 gallons (7.6 L) water at 130°F (55°C) for 30 minutes. Add 2 more gallons (7.6 L) water at 180°F (82°C) and steep for 45 more minutes at 150°F (66°C). Sparge with 3 gallons (11 L) water. Omit malt extract syrup and proceed as in main recipe, reducing wort volume to 5¼ gallons (20 L) or less. (Advanced brewers may wish to use a decoction-mash procedure to develop more fully the malty character.)

Old Brown Dog Ale

Smuttynose Brewing Co., Portsmouth, New Hampshire

This relatively complex and sweet brown ale has a reddish copper color and notes of raisins, figs, almonds, toffee, and chocolate. It's a smooth and easy-to-drink, English-style brown ale with minimal hop bitterness — just enough to keep the malt from being too sweet.

Original gravity: 1050 • **Final gravity: 1015** • **4.4% abv** • **20 IBU**

Heat 1¼ gallons (4.7 L) water to 164°F (73°C). Crush:

1 lb. (454 g) mild ale malt
8 oz. (227 g) brown malt
4 oz. (113 g) chocolate malt
8 oz. (227 g) toasted pale malt
8 oz. (227 g) dark (90°L) crystal malt

Add to liquor and steep at 152°F (67°C) for 90 minutes. Sparge with 2 gallons (7.6 L) water at 168°F (76°C). Add to runnings:

4 lb. (1.8 kg) unhopped, amber dry malt extract (DME)

Bring to a boil, then add:

5 AAUs Willamette hops

Boil 75 minutes, then remove from heat. Cool, then top up to 5¼ gallons (20 L) with chilled, preboiled water. Cool to 68°F (20°C), then pitch:

London ale yeast (Wyeast 1028, 1968, or equivalent)

Ferment at 68°F (20°C) for 2 weeks, then transfer to secondary fermenter and condition cool (50–55°F [10–13°C]) for 3 to 4 weeks. Prime with:

⅔ cup (158 ml) dark brown sugar

Bottle and age at 55–60°F (13–16°C) for 3 weeks.

Alternate Methods

All-extract: Steep the chocolate, toasted, and crystal malts as in main recipe in 2½ gallons (9.5 L) water at 150°F (66°C) for 45 minutes. Omit mild ale and brown malts and increase DME to 5 lb. (2.3 kg). Follow directions from beginning of boil.

All-grain: Mash 6 lb. (2.7 kg) mild ale malt, 1¼ lb. (567 g) brown malt, and the chocolate, toasted, and crystal malts as in main recipe in 3½ gallons (13.2 L) water at 152°F (67°C). Sparge with 4 gallons (15.1 L) water. Omit DME and proceed as in main recipe, reducing wort volume to 5¼ gallons (20 L) or less.

 Serve at 50°F (10°C) in a traditional pint glass.

Smuttynose Imperial Stout

Smuttynose Brewing Co., Portsmouth, New Hampshire

This is a very rich, dark brown, full-bodied stout, although perhaps a little light for an imperial stout. There is an intense dark malt and burnt sugar flavor that lingers long after the last sip.

Original gravity: 1070 • Final gravity: 1020 • 6.4% abv • 45 IBU

Heat 1¼ gallons (4.7 L) water to 164°F (73°C). Crush:

2 lb. (907 g) pale malt
8 oz. (227 g) dark (90°L) crystal malt
8 oz. (227 g) roasted barley

Add to liquor and steep at 152°F (67°C) for 90 minutes. Sparge with 2 gallons (7.6 L) water at 168°F (76°C). Add to runnings:

7 lb. (3.2 kg) unhopped, dark malt extract syrup
1 lb. (454 g) unhopped, amber dry malt extract (DME)
8 AAUs Challenger hops

Boil 70 minutes, then add:

8 AAUs Fuggles hops

Boil 20 minutes, then remove from heat. Cool, then top up to 5¼ gallons (20 L) with chilled, preboiled water. Cool to 68°F (20°C), then pitch:

British ale yeast (Wyeast 1098 or equivalent)
⅕ oz. (5.7 g) dry champagne yeast

Ferment at 68°F (20°C) for 3 weeks, then transfer to secondary fermenter and add:

4 AAUs Fuggles hops

Condition cool (50–55°F [10–13°C]) for 4 to 6 weeks. Prime with:

1 cup (237 ml) pale dry malt extract

Bottle and age at 55–60°F (13–16°C) for 8 weeks.

Alternate Methods

All-extract: Steep the crystal malt and roasted barley as in main recipe in 2½ gallons (9.5 L) water at 150°F (66°C) for 45 minutes. Omit pale malt, add malt extract syrup as in main recipe, and increase DME to 2½ lb. (1.1 kg). Follow directions from beginning of boil.

All-grain: Mash 11½ lb. (5.2 kg) pale malt and the crystal malt and roasted barley as in main recipe in 3¾ gallons (14.2 L) water at 152°F (67°C). Sparge with 3¾ gallons (14.2 L) water. Omit malt extract syrup and first DME and proceed as in main recipe, reducing wort volume to 5¼ gallons (20 L) or less.

 Serve at 50°F (10°C) in a traditional pint glass.

Smuttynose Scotch-Style Ale

Smuttynose Brewing Co., Portsmouth, New Hampshire
This warming, malty beer has a big hop burst in the aftertaste. Smuttynose brews this beer as part of its "Big Beers" series, rotating seasonally. This ale is reddish brown, alcoholic, and full of fruity, toffee, and smoky flavors and aromas.

Original gravity: 1068 • **Final gravity: 1015** • **6.8% abv** • **30 IBU**

Heat 1¾ gallons (6.6 L) water to 164°F (73°C). Crush:

3 lb. (1.4 kg) pale malt
8 oz. (227 g) dark (120°L) crystal malt
1 lb. (454 g) amber malt
2 oz. (57 g) roasted barley

Add to liquor and steep at 152°F (67°C) for 90 minutes. Sparge with 2½ gallons (9.5 L) water at 168°F (76°C). Separate 2 quarts (1.9 L) of the mixture and boil down to 1 quart (946 ml) to partially caramelize. Add this to runnings along with:

6 lb. (2.7 kg) unhopped, light malt extract syrup

Bring to a boil, then add:

7 AAUs Fuggles hops

Boil 90 minutes, then remove from heat. Cool, then top up to 5¼ gallons (20 L) with chilled, preboiled water. Cool to 68°F (20°C), then pitch:

Scottish ale yeast (Wyeast 1728 or equivalent)

Ferment at 62°F (17°C) for 2 weeks, then transfer to secondary fermenter and condition cold (40°F [4°C]) for 4 weeks. Prime with:

1 cup (237 ml) pale dry malt extract (DME)

Bottle and age at 45–50°F (7–10°C) for 3 weeks.

Alternate Methods

All-extract: Steep the crystal and amber malts and the roasted barley as in main recipe in 2½ gallons (9.5 L) water at 150°F (66°C) for 45 minutes. Omit pale malt and increase malt extract syrup to 8½ lb. (3.9 kg). Follow directions from beginning of boil.

All-grain: Mash 10 lb. (4.5 kg) pale malt and the crystal and amber malts and the roasted barley as in main recipe in 3¾ gallons (14.2 L) water at 152°F (67°C). Sparge with 3¾ gallons (14.2 L) water. Separate and caramelize 1 gallon (3.8 L) mixture as in main recipe. Omit malt extract syrup and proceed as in main recipe, reducing wort volume to 5¼ gallons (20 L) or less.

Serve at 50°F (10°C) in a Scottish thistle glass.

Flying Fish Belgian-Style Dubbel

Flying Fish Brewing Co., Cherry Hill, New Jersey

This is a bottle-conditioned Belgian dubbel that boasts a triple fermentation process using three strains of yeast. It is malty, sweet, grainy, and relatively full bodied with nice fruity notes in the finish.

Original gravity: 1064 • **Final gravity: 1007** • **7.3% abv** • **20 IBU**

Heat 3 gallons (11 L) water to 164°F (73°C). Crush:

5½ lb. (2.5 kg) Belgian pale malt
1 lb. (454 g) dark (120°L) crystal malt
1 lb. (454 g) Belgian Special B malt
8 oz. (227 g) malted wheat

Add to liquor and steep at 152°F (67°C) for 90 minutes. Sparge with 3¾ gallons (14.2 L) water at 168°F (76°C). Add to runnings:

2 lb. (907 g) unhopped, amber dry malt extract (DME)

Bring to a boil, then add:

4 AAUs Northern Brewer hops

Boil 60 minutes, then add:

4 AAUs Goldings hops

Boil 30 minutes, then remove from heat. Cool, then top up to 5¼ gallons (20 L) with chilled, preboiled water. Cool to 68°F (20°C), then pitch:

Recultured Flying Fish yeast or a blend of English and Belgian ale yeasts (Wyeast 1214, 3787, 1098, or equivalent)

Ferment at 65°F (18°C) for 2 weeks, then transfer to secondary fermenter and condition cool (50–55°F [10–13°C]) for 3 to 4 weeks. Prime with:

1 cup (237 ml) pale dry malt extract

Bottle and age at 55–60°F (13–16°C) for 3 weeks.

 **Alternate Methods**

All-extract: Steep 2½ lb. (1.1 kg) Belgian pale malt and the crystal and Special B malts and malted wheat as in main recipe in 2½ gallons (9.5 L) water at 150°F (66°C) for 45 minutes. Increase DME to 4 lb. (1.8 kg). Follow directions from beginning of boil.

All-grain: Mash 8½ lb. (3.9 kg) Belgian pale malt and the crystal and Special B malts and malted wheat as in main recipe in 3¼ gallons (12.3 L) water at 152°F (67°C). Sparge with 4 gallons (15.1 L) water. Omit first DME and proceed as in main recipe, reducing wort volume to 5¼ gallons (20 L) or less.

 Serve at 50°F (10°C) in a Trappist-style goblet.

Adirondack Amber

Saranac Brewing and F. X. Matt Brewing Co., Utica, New York

F. X. Matt is one of the largest contract brewers for other products in the eastern United States, but it also makes the Saranac line for its own label. Adirondack Amber is a nice example of an American-style amber lager: It's richer than a Pilsner, not quite as robust as a Märzen, and very smooth and drinkable.

Original gravity: 1055 • Final gravity: 1015 • 5.1% abv • 25 IBU

Heat 1½ gallons (5.7 L) water to 164°F (73°C). Crush:

2 lb. (907 g) Pilsner malt
1 lb. (454 g) Munich malt
8 oz. (227 g) medium (50°L) crystal malt

Add to liquor and steep at 152°F (67°C) for 90 minutes. Sparge with 2¼ gallons (8.5 L) water at 168°F (76°C). Add to runnings:

4 lb. (1.8 kg) unhopped, pale dry malt extract (DME)

Bring to a boil, then add:

4 AAUs Cascade hops

Boil 30 minutes, then add:

4 AAUs Hallertau hops

Boil 30 minutes, then remove from heat. Add:

2 AAUs Hallertau hops

Steep 30 minutes, then remove from heat. Cool, then top up to 5¼ gallons (20 L) with chilled, preboiled water. Cool to 68°F (20°C), then pitch:

Munich or Bavarian lager yeast (Wyeast 2308, 2206, or equivalent)

Ferment at 50°F (10°C) for 2 weeks, then transfer to secondary fermenter and condition cold (40°F [4°C]) for 5 to 6 weeks. Prime with:

1 cup (237 ml) pale dry malt extract

Bottle and age at 45–50°F (7–10°C) for 6 weeks.

Alternate Methods

All-extract: Steep the Munich and crystal malts as in main recipe, plus 8 oz. (227 g) carapils malt, in 2½ gallons (9.5 L) water at 150°F (66°C) for 45 minutes. Omit Pilsner malt and increase DME to 5½ lb. (2½ kg). Follow directions from beginning of boil.

All-grain: Mash 5½ lb. (2.5 kg) Pilsner malt, 3 lb. (1.4 kg) Munich malt, 8 oz. (227 g) carapils malt, and the crystal malt as in main recipe in 3¼ gallons (12.3 L) water at 152°F (67°C). Sparge with 4 gallons (15.1 L) water. Omit DME and proceed as in main recipe, reducing wort volume to 5¼ gallons (20 L) or less.

 Serve at 40°F (4°C) in a tall Pilsner-style glass.

Black Chocolate Stout

Brooklyn Brewery, Brooklyn, New York; Utica, New York

This is an imperial stout brewed as a winter seasonal. The beer is bottle conditioned, rich, dark, alcoholic, and filling. It has flavors and aromas of chocolate, raisins, coffee, treacle, and burnt sugar.

Original gravity: 1075 • Final gravity: 1020 • 7% abv • 45 IBU

Heat 2 gallons (7.6 L) water to 164°F (73°C). Crush:

2 lb. (907 g) pale malt
1 lb. (454 g) roasted barley
8 oz. (227 g) chocolate malt
8 oz. (227 g) black malt
8 oz. (227 g) kilncoffee malt
8 oz. (227 g) dark (90°L) crystal malt

Add to liquor and steep at 152°F (67°C) for 90 minutes. Sparge with 3 gallons (11 L) water at 168°F (76°C). Add to runnings:

5½ lb. (2½ kg) unhopped, dark dry malt extract (DME)

Bring to a boil, then add:

8 AAUs Northern Brewer hops

Boil 60 minutes, then add:

4 AAUs Fuggles hops

Boil 30 minutes, then remove from heat. Cool, then top up to 5¼ gallons (20 L) with chilled, preboiled water. Cool to 68°F (20°C), then pitch:

Irish ale yeast (recultured Brooklyn, Wyeast 1084, or equivalent)

Ferment at 68°F (20°C) for 2 weeks, then transfer to secondary fermenter and condition cool (50–55°F [10–13°C]) for 3 to 4 weeks. Prime with:

1 cup (237 ml) pale dry malt extract

Bottle and age at 55–60°F (13–16°C) for 8 weeks.

 **Alternate Methods**

All-extract: Steep the roasted barley and the chocolate, black, kilncoffee, and crystal malts as in main recipe in 2½ gallons (9.5 L) water at 150°F (66°C) for 45 minutes. Omit pale malt and add 7 lb. (3.2 kg) dark malt extract syrup and 1 lb. (454 g) dark DME. Follow directions from beginning of boil.

All-grain: Mash 9½ lb. (4.3 kg) pale malt and the roasted barley, chocolate, black, kilncoffee, and crystal malts in 2½ gallons (9.5 L) water at 152°F (67°C). Sparge with 3 gallons (11 L) water. Omit first DME and proceed as in main recipe, reducing wort volume to 5¼ gallons (20 L) or less.

 Serve at 50°F (10°C) in a traditional pint glass.

Fat Bear Stout

Ten Springs Brewing Co., Saratoga, New York
A smooth, full-bodied stout, Fat Bear is loaded with roasted malt aroma and English hop bitterness. Chocolate and coffee notes dominate, with balance provided by spicy hops.

Original gravity: 1048 • Final gravity: 1010 • 4.8% abv • 35 IBU

Heat 2¼ gallons (8.5 L) water to 164°F (73°C). Crush:

4 lb. (1.8 kg) pale malt
8 oz. (227 g) roasted barley
8 oz. (227 g) dark (90°L) crystal malt
4 oz. (113 g) chocolate malt

Add to liquor and steep at 152°F (67°C) for 90 minutes. Sparge with 3 gallons (11 L) water at 168°F (76°C). Add to runnings:

2 lb. (907 g) unhopped, dark dry malt extract (DME)

Bring to a boil, then add:

5 AAUs Target hops

Boil 30 minutes, then add:

5 AAUs Fuggles hops

Boil 30 minutes, then remove from heat and add:

4 AAUs Fuggles hops

Steep 15 minutes. Cool, then top up to 5¼ gallons (20 L) with chilled, preboiled water. Cool to 68°F (20°C), then pitch:

Irish ale yeast (Wyeast 1084 or equivalent)

Ferment at 68°F (20°C) for 2 weeks, then transfer to secondary fermenter and condition cool (50–55°F [10–13°C]) for 3 to 4 weeks. Prime with:

1 cup (237 ml) dark dry malt extract

Bottle and age at 55°F (13°C) for 3 weeks.

Alternate Methods

All-extract: Steep 8 oz. (227 g) pale malt and the roasted barley and crystal and chocolate malts as in main recipe in 2½ gallons (9.5 L) water at 150°F (66°C) for 45 minutes. Increase DME to 4½ lb. (2 kg). Follow directions from beginning of boil.

All-grain: Mash 7 lb. (3.2 kg) pale malt and the roasted barley and crystal and chocolate malts as in main recipe in 3 gallons (11 L) water at 152°F (67°C). Sparge with 3¾ gallons (14.2 L) water. Omit first DME and proceed as in main recipe, reducing wort volume to 5¼ gallons (20 L) or less.

Serve at 50°F (10°C) in a traditional pint glass.

Longshore Lager

Longshore Brewing, Garden City, New York

This traditional Bohemian-style Pilsner comes from Long Island. A rich golden color, a big, tight white head, and a distinct Saaz nose put this beer right on target.

Original gravity: 1042 • Final gravity: 1008 • 4.3% abv • 25 IBU

Heat 1½ gallons (5.7 L) water to 164°F (73°C). Crush:

2 lb. (907 g) lager malt
1 lb. (454 g) light Munich malt
1¼ lb. (567 g) carapils malt

Add to liquor and steep at 152°F (67°C) for 90 minutes. Sparge with 2¼ gallons (8.5 L) water at 168°F (76°C). Add to runnings:

2 lb. (907 g) unhopped, extra-light dry malt extract (DME)

Bring to a boil, then add:

5 AAUs Spalt hops

Boil 30 minutes, then add:

3 AAUs Saaz hops

Boil 30 minutes, then remove from heat. Cool, then top up to 5¼ gallons (20 L) with chilled, preboiled water. Cool to 60°F (16°C), then pitch:

Bohemian or Czech Pilsner yeast (Wyeast 2278 or equivalent)

Ferment at 50°F (10°C) for 2 weeks, then transfer to secondary fermenter and add:

4 AAUs Saaz hops

Condition cold (38–40°F [3–4°C]) for 3 to 4 weeks. Prime with:

1 cup (237 ml) extra-light dry malt extract

Bottle and age at 40°F (4°C) for 6 weeks.

Alternate Methods

All-extract: Steep 8 oz. (227 g) Munich malt and 12 oz. (340 g) carapils malt in 2½ gallons (9.5 L) water at 150°F (66°C) for 45 minutes. Omit lager malt and increase DME to 4 lb. (1.8 kg). Follow directions from beginning of boil.

All-grain: Mash 5 lb. (2.3 kg) lager malt and the Munich and carapils malts as in main recipe in 2¾ gallons (10.2 L) water at 152°F (67°C). Sparge with 3½ gallons (13.2 L) water. Omit first DME and proceed as in main recipe, reducing wort volume to 5¼ gallons (20 L) or less.

Serve at 40°F (4°C) in a tall, footed Pilsner glass.

Michael Shea's Black & Tan

Highfalls Brewing Co., Rochester, New York

A somewhat nontraditional variation on the theme, Michael Shea's Black & Tan is a blend of porter (instead of stout) and lager. This one is best brewed as two separate batches — 2½ gallons (9.5 L) each — and blended in the secondary fermenter.

Original gravity: 1050 (each batch) • Final gravity: 1010 (combined) • 5.1% abv • 30 IBU

Lager:

Heat 1 gallon (3.8 L) water to 164°F (73°C). Crush:

- **1 lb. (454 g) lager malt**
- **1 lb. (454 g) carapils malt**

Add to liquor and steep at 152°F (67°C) for 90 minutes. Sparge with 1½ gallons (5.7 L) water at 168°F (76°C). Add to runnings:

- **1½ lb. (680 g) unhopped, extra-light dry malt extract (DME)**

Bring to a boil, then add:

- **3 AAUs Saaz hops**

Boil 50 minutes, then add:

- **2 AAUs Hallertau hops**

Boil 10 minutes, then remove from heat. Cool, then top up to 2¾ gallons (10.2 L) with chilled, preboiled water. Cool to 60°F (16°C), then pitch:

- **Bohemian lager yeast (Wyeast 2206 or equivalent)**

Ferment at 50°F (10°C) for 2 weeks, then start the porter.

Porter:

Heat 1 gallon (3.8 L) water to 164°F (73°C). Crush:

- **1 lb. (454 g) pale malt**
- **8 oz. (227 g) black malt**
- **8 oz. (227 g) chocolate malt**

Add to liquor and steep at 152°F (67°C) for 90 minutes. Sparge with 1½ gallons (5.7 L) water at 168°F (76°C). Add to runnings:

- **1½ lb. (680 g) unhopped, amber dry malt extract (DME)**

Bring to a boil, then add:

- **3 AAUs Fuggles hops**

Boil 60 minutes, then add:

- **2 AAUs Goldings hops**

Remove from heat and steep 15 minutes. Cool, then top up to 2¾ gallons (10.2 L) with chilled, preboiled water. Cool to 65°F (18°C), then pitch:

- **London ale yeast (Wyeast 1968 or equivalent)**

Ferment at 65°F (18°C) for 2 weeks. Transfer to secondary fermenter, blending with lager (now 4 weeks old). Condition cool (50°F [10°C]) for 3 to 4 weeks. Prime with:

- **1 cup (237 ml) pale dry malt extract**

Bottle and age at 50°F (10°C) for 3 weeks.

Alternate Methods

All-extract (applies to lager and porter): Steep the specialty grains (carapils or black and chocolate malts) as in main recipe in 2½ gallons (9.5 L) water at 150°F (66°C) for 45 minutes. Omit lager or pale malt and increase DME to 2 lb. (907 g). Follow directions from beginning of boil.

All-grain (applies to lager and porter): Mash 3 lb. (1.4 kg) lager or pale malt and the specialty grains (carapils or black and chocolate malts) as in main recipe in 1½ gallons (5.7 L) water at 152°F (67°C). Sparge with 2¼ gallons (8.5 L) water. Omit first DME and proceed as in main recipe, reducing wort volume to 2¾ gallons (10.2 L) or less.

 Serve at 50°F (10°C) in a traditional pint glass.

New Amsterdam IPA

New Amsterdam Brewing, Utica, New York

An IPA for lovers of Cascade hop aroma, this copper ale has a complex fruity and grainy flavor profile and loads of hop flavor, bitterness, and aroma.

Original gravity: 1060 • Final gravity: 1015 • 5.7% abv • 55 IBU

Heat 2 gallons (7.6 L) water to 164°F (73°C). Crush:
- **3 lb. (1.4 kg) pale malt**
- **1 lb. (454 g) dark (90°L) crystal malt**
- **8 oz. (227 g) light (20°L) crystal malt**
- **8 oz. (227 g) amber malt**
- **4 oz. (113 g) roasted barley**

Add to liquor and steep at 152°F (67°C) for 90 minutes. Sparge with 2½ gallons (9.5 L) water at 168°F (76°C). Add to runnings:
- **4¼ lb. (1.9 kg) light malt extract syrup**

Bring to a boil, then add:
- **6 AAUs Centennial hops**

Boil 30 minutes, then add:
- **4 AAUs Centennial hops**

Boil 30 minutes, then add:
- **4 AAUs Cascade hops**

Boil 25 minutes, then add:
- **4 AAUs Cascade hops**

Boil 5 minutes, then remove from heat. Cool, then top up to 5¼ gallons (20 L) with chilled, preboiled water. Cool to 68°F (20°C), then pitch:
- **English ale yeast (Wyeast 1098 or equivalent)**

Ferment at 68°F (20°C) for 2 weeks, then transfer to secondary fermenter and add:
- **4 AAUs Cascade hops**

Condition cool (50–55°F [10–13°C]) for 3 to 4 weeks. Prime with:
- **1 cup (237 ml) pale dry malt extract (DME)**

Bottle and age at 50°F (10°C) for 6 weeks.

 Serve at 50°F (10°C) in a traditional pint glass.

 **Alternate Methods**

All-extract: Steep the dark and light crystal and amber malts and roasted barley as in main recipe in 2½ gallons (9.5 L) water at 150°F (66°C) for 45 minutes. Omit pale malt and increase malt extract syrup to 6¾ lb. (3.1 kg). Follow directions from beginning of boil.

All-grain: Mash 8 lb. (3.6 kg) pale malt, the dark and light crystal and amber malts, and the roasted barley as in main recipe in 3¼ gallons (12.3 L) water at 152°F (67°C). Sparge with 4 gallons (15.1 L) water. Omit malt extract syrup and proceed as in main recipe, reducing wort volume to 5¼ gallons (20 L) or less.

Ommegang

Brewery Ommegang, Cooperstown, New York

A real Belgian brewery in the hometown of the Baseball Hall of Fame? Yes, indeed. The product of a partnership between U.S. importers Vanberg & DeWulf and a major Belgian brewery, this dubbel ale is earthy, rich, yeasty, and full of Belgian flavor and aroma.

Original gravity: 1082 • Final gravity: 1015 • 8.5% abv • 30 IBU

Heat 2½ gallons (9.5 L) water to 164°F (73°C). Crush:

5 lb. (2.3 kg) Belgian pale malt
1 lb. (454 g) Munich malt
1 lb. (454 g) Belgian Special B malt

Add to liquor and steep at 152°F (67°C) for 90 minutes. Sparge with 3 gallons (11 L) water 168°F (76°C). Add to runnings:

4 lb. (1.8 kg) unhopped, amber dry malt extract (DME)
1 lb. (454 g) amber candi sugar

Bring to a boil, then add:

6 AAUs Hallertau hops

Boil 75 minutes, then add:

3 AAUs Hallertau hops

Boil 15 minutes, then remove from heat. Cool, then top up to 5¼ gallons (20 L) with chilled, preboiled water. Cool to 68°F (20°C), then pitch:

Belgian strong ale or Trappist yeast (recultured Ommegang, Wyeast 1214, 1388, or equivalent)

Ferment at 68°F (20°C) for 2 weeks, then transfer to secondary fermenter and condition cool (50–55°F [10–13°C]) for 5 to 6 weeks. Prime with:

1 cup (237 ml) pale dry malt extract

Bottle (cork finish, if possible) and age at 50°F (10°C) for 8 to 10 weeks. This beer will keep for more than a year in a cool, dark place.

Alternate Methods

All-extract: Steep 8 oz. (227 g) Belgian pale malt and the Munich and Belgian Special B malts as in main recipe in 2½ gallons (9.5 L) water at 150°F (66°C) for 45 minutes. Increase DME to 7 lb. (3.2 kg). Add the amber candi sugar and follow directions from beginning of boil.

All-grain: Mash 11 lb. (5 kg) Belgian pale malt and the Munich and Belgian Special B malts as in main recipe in 3½ gallons (13.2 L) water at 152°F (67°C). Sparge with 4 gallons (15.1 L) water. Omit first DME, but add the candi sugar and proceed as in main recipe, reducing wort volume to 5¼ gallons (20 L) or less.

Serve at 50°F (10°C) in a widemouthed goblet.

Saranac Black Forest Lager

F. X. Matt Brewing Co., Utica, New York

A dark lager deriving from both the Bavarian dunkels and the more northerly
schwarzbiers, Black Forest is rich and semisweet. It has a nice, deep, roasty color and
the bitter notes associated with roasted barley and dark malts.

Original gravity: 1050 • Final gravity: 1012 • 4.8% abv • 32 IBU

Heat 2¼ gallons (8.5 L) water to 164°F (73°C). Crush:

3 lb. (1.4 kg) lager malt
1 lb. (454 g) Munich malt
8 oz. (227 g) carapils malt
8 oz. (227 g) black malt
8 oz. (227 g) roasted barley

Add to liquor and steep at 152°F (67°C) for 90 minutes. Sparge with 3 gallons (11 L) water at 168°F (76°C). Add to runnings:

2 lb. (907 g) unhopped, amber dry malt extract (DME)

Bring to a boil, then add:

6 AAUs Tettnang hops

Boil 60 minutes, then add:

3 AAUs Perle hops

Boil 30 minutes, then remove from heat. Cool, then top up to 5¼ gallons (20 L) with chilled, preboiled water. Cool to 60°F (16°C), then pitch:

Munich lager yeast (Wyeast 2308 or equivalent)

Ferment at 38°F (3°C) for 2 weeks, then transfer to secondary fermenter and condition cold (40°F [4°C]) for 4 to 6 weeks. Prime with:

1 cup (237 ml) pale dry malt extract

Bottle and age at 40°F (4°C) for 3 weeks.

Alternate Methods

All-extract: Steep the Munich, carapils, and black malts and roasted barley as in main recipe in 2½ gallons (9.5 L) water at 150°F (66°C) for 45 minutes. Omit lager malt and increase DME to 4 lb. (1.8 kg). Follow directions from beginning of boil.

All-grain: Mash 6 lb. (2.7 kg) lager malt and the Munich, carapils, and black malts and roasted barley as in main recipe in 3 gallons (11 L) water at 152°F (67°C). Sparge with 3¾ gallons (14.2 L) water. Omit first DME and proceed as in main recipe, reducing wort volume to 5¼ gallons (20 L) or less.

 Serve at 40°F (4°C) in a tall, fluted Pilsner glass.

Double Eagle Scotch Ale

Pinehurst Village Brewing, Aberdeen, North Carolina

*Double Eagle is a rich, malty Scotch ale, a little hoppier than you might find
in the old country, but still quite enjoyable. The brewery sits within
driving distance of many of the best fairways and greens on the East Coast.*

Original gravity: 1072 • **Final gravity: 1016** • **5.8% abv** • **20 IBU**

Heat 3 gallons (11 L) water to 164°F (73°C). Crush:

3½ lb. (1.6 kg) pale malt
1 lb. (454 g) amber malt
1 lb. (454 g) carapils malt
8 oz. (227 g) black malt
8 oz. (227 g) flaked oats
1 lb. (454 g) torrefied wheat
4 oz. (113 g) roasted barley

Add to liquor and steep at 152°F (67°C) for 90 minutes. Sparge with
3¾ gallons (14.2 L) water at 168°F (76°C). Add to runnings:

3 lb. (1.4 kg) unhopped, pale dry malt extract (DME)

Bring to a boil, then add:

3 AAUs Nugget hops

Boil 30 minutes, then add:

3 AAUs Willamette hops

Boil 30 minutes, then add:

3 AAUs Styrian Goldings hops

Remove from heat. Cool, then top up to 5¼ gallons (20 L) with chilled,
preboiled water. Cool to 68°F (20°C), then pitch:

Scottish ale yeast (Wyeast 1728 or equivalent)

Ferment at 65°F (18°C) for 2 weeks, then transfer to secondary fermenter
and condition cool (50–55°F [10–13°C]) for 3 to 4 weeks. Prime with:

½ cup (118 ml) pale dry malt extract
½ cup (118 ml) brown sugar

Bottle and age at 55–60°F (13–16°C) for 6 weeks.

 Serve at 50°F (10°C) in a traditional Scottish thistle glass.

 **Alternate Methods**

All-extract: Steep 8 oz.
(227 g) pale malt and the
amber, carapils, and black
malts, flaked oats, torrefied
wheat, and roasted barley
as in main recipe in
2½ gallons (9.5 L) water
at 150°F (66°C) for 45
minutes. Remove grains,
then add 6⅔ lb. (3 kg)
malt extract syrup. Follow
directions from beginning
of boil.

All-grain: Mash 8 lb.
(3.6 kg) pale malt and the
amber, carapils, and black
malts, flaked oats, torrefied
wheat, and roasted barley
as in main recipe in 2½
gallons (9.5 L) water at
152°F (67°C). Sparge with
3 gallons (11 L) water.
Omit first DME and pro-
ceed as in main recipe,
reducing wort volume to
5¼ gallons (20 L) or less.

Black Honey Ale

Devil Mountain Brewing Co., Cincinnati, Ohio

With the bitterness of black and chocolate malts softened by the addition of honey, this black ale is something like a robust porter. The brewer uses "exotic African black honey," but the flavor of any good wildflower honey will do the trick.

Original gravity: 1050 • Final gravity: 1015 • 4.5% abv • 20 IBU

Heat 1½ gallons (5.7 L) water to 164°F (73°C). Crush:
- **2 lb. (907 g) pale malt**
- **8 oz. (227 g) black malt**
- **8 oz. (227 g) chocolate malt**
- **8 oz. (227 g) dark (90°L) crystal malt**

Add to liquor and steep at 152°F (67°C) for 90 minutes. Sparge with 2¼ gallons (8.5 L) water at 168°F (76°C). Add to runnings:
- **3⅓ lb. (1.5 kg) unhopped, amber malt extract syrup**
- **1 lb. (454 g) dark honey**

Bring to a boil, then add:
- **4 AAUs Willamette hops**

Boil 90 minutes, then add:
- **2 AAUs Willamette hops**

Remove from heat and steep 15 minutes. Cool, then top up to 5¼ gallons (20 L) with chilled, preboiled water. Cool to 68°F (20°C), then pitch:
- **London ale yeast (Wyeast 1968 or equivalent)**

Ferment at 65°F (18°C) for 3 weeks, then transfer to secondary fermenter and condition cool (50°F [10°C]) for 3 to 4 weeks. Prime with:
- **1 cup (237 ml) pale dry malt extract (DME)**

Bottle and age at 50°F (10°C) for 3 weeks.

Alternate Methods

All-extract: Steep 8 oz. (227 g) pale malt and the black, chocolate, and crystal malts as in main recipe in 2½ gallons (9.5 L) water at 150°F (66°C) for 45 minutes. Increase malt extract syrup to 5 lb. (2.3 kg) and add the honey. Follow directions from beginning of boil.

All-grain: Mash 6 lb. (2.7 kg) pale malt and the black, chocolate, and crystal malts as in main recipe in 2½ gallons (9.5 L) water at 152°F (67°C). Sparge with 3 gallons (11 L) water. Omit malt extract syrup, but add the honey and proceed as in main recipe, reducing wort volume to 5¼ gallons (20 L) or less.

 Serve at 50°F (10°C) in a traditional pint glass.

Edmund Fitzgerald Porter

Great Lakes Brewing Co., Cleveland, Ohio

I think this may be the best porter in the United States (and there are many very good ones), although it has many of the characteristics of a stout. It is dark, bitter, and malty-sweet at the same time. The flavor is also roasty, hoppy, and full bodied.

Original gravity: 1057 • Final gravity: 1012 • 5.7% abv • 55–60 IBU

Heat 2½ gallons (9.5 L) water to 164°F (73°C). Crush:

5 lb. (2.3 kg) pale malt
12 oz. (340 g) medium (50°L) crystal malt
8 oz. (227 g) chocolate malt
8 oz. (227 g) roasted barley

Add to liquor and steep at 152°F (67°C) for 90 minutes. Sparge with 3¼ gallons (12.3 L) water at 168°F (76°C). Add to runnings:

2 lb. (907 g) unhopped, dark dry malt extract (DME)

Bring to a boil, then add:

7 AAUs Northern Brewer hops

Boil 30 minutes, then add:

4 AAUs Fuggles hops

Boil 30 minutes, then add:

4 AAUs Cascade hops

Boil 30 minutes, then add:

4 AAUs Cascade hops

Remove from heat. Cool, then top up to 5¼ gallons (20 L) with chilled, preboiled water. Cool to 65°F (18°C), then pitch:

London ale yeast (Wyeast 1968 or equivalent)

Ferment at 62°F (17°C) for 2 weeks, then transfer to secondary fermenter and condition cool (50–55°F [10–13°C]) for 3 to 4 weeks. Prime with:

1 cup (237 ml) pale dry malt extract

Bottle and age at 50°F (10°C) for 3 weeks.

Alternate Methods

All-extract: Steep 2 lb. (907 g) pale malt and the crystal and chocolate malts and roasted barley as in main recipe in 2½ gallons (9.5 L) water at 150°F (66°C) for 45 minutes. Increase DME to 4 lb. (1.8 kg). Follow directions from beginning of boil.

All-grain: Mash 8 lb. (3.6 kg) pale malt and the crystal and chocolate malts and roasted barley as in main recipe in 3¼ gallons (12.3 L) water at 152°F (67°C). Sparge with 4 gallons (15.2 L) water. Omit first DME and proceed as in main recipe, reducing wort volume to 5¼ gallons (20 L) or less.

Serve at 50°F (10°C) in a traditional pint glass.

Oregon Original India Pale Ale

Oregon Ale & Beer Co., Cincinnati, Ohio; Portland, Oregon
This floral and aromatic IPA is creamy smooth and dry, light in body for the style,
pleasantly bitter, and well balanced. It's deep gold to pale copper in color,
with a thick off-white head that clings to the glass.

Original gravity: 1060 • Final gravity: 1015 • 5.7% abv • 45 IBU

Heat 1¾ gallons (6.6 L) water to 164°F (73°C). Crush:
- **3 lb. (1.4 kg) pale malt**
- **1 lb. (454 g) light (20°L) crystal malt**
- **4 oz. (113 g) biscuit malt**

Add to liquor and steep at 152°F (67°C) for 90 minutes. Sparge with 2½ gallons (9.5 L) water at 168°F (76°C). Add to runnings:
- **4 lb. (1.8 kg) unhopped, pale dry malt extract (DME)**

Bring to a boil, then add:
- **8 AAUs Chinook hops**

Boil 30 minutes, then add:
- **4 AAUs Cascade hops**

Boil 30 minutes, then remove from heat. Cool, then top up to 5¼ gallons (20 L) with chilled, preboiled water. Cool to 68°F (20°C), then pitch:
- **American ale yeast (Wyeast 1056 or equivalent)**

Ferment at 68°F (20°C) for 2 weeks, then transfer to secondary fermenter and add:
- **6 AAUs Cascade hops**

Condition-cool (50–55°F [10–13°C]) for 3 to 4 weeks. Prime with:
- **1 cup (237 ml) pale dry malt extract**

Bottle and age at 55–60°F (13–16°C) for 3 weeks.

Alternate Methods

All-extract: Steep 1 lb. (454 g) pale malt and the crystal and biscuit malts as in main recipe in 2½ gallons (9.5 L) water at 150°F (66°C) for 45 minutes. Increase DME to 5½ lb. (2½ kg). Follow directions from beginning of boil.

All-grain: Mash 9 lb. (4.1 kg) pale malt and the crystal and biscuit malts as in main recipe in 3¼ gallons (12.3 L) water at 152°F (67°C). Sparge with 3¾ gallons (14.2 L) water. Omit first DME and proceed as in main recipe, reducing wort volume to 5¼ gallons (20 L) or less.

 Serve at 50°F (10°C) in a traditional pint glass.

Blue Heron Pale Ale

Bridgeport Brewing Co., Portland, Oregon

This relatively light and crisp pale ale is deep gold and very hoppy. The flavor is mellow, malty, and not at all bitter. Blue Heron has an outstanding hoppy aftertaste.

Original gravity: 1050 • Final gravity: 1012 • 4.8% abv • 40 IBU

Heat 1½ gallons (5.7 L) water to 164°F (73°C). Crush:

2 lb. (907 g) pale malt
1 lb. (454 g) medium (50°L) crystal malt
8 oz. (227 g) malted wheat

Add to liquor and steep at 152°F (67°C) for 90 minutes. Sparge with 2¼ gallons (8.5 L) water at 168°F (76°C). Add to runnings:

4¼ lb. (1.9 kg) unhopped, pale malt extract syrup

Bring to a boil, then add:

6 AAUs Willamette hops

Boil 30 minutes, then add:

4 AAUs Willamette hops
4 AAUs Cascade hops

Boil 30 minutes, then remove from heat. Cool, then top up to 5¼ gallons (20 L) with chilled, preboiled water. Cool to 68°F (20°C), then pitch:

American ale yeast (Wyeast 1056 or equivalent)

Ferment at 68°F (20°C) for 2 weeks, then transfer to secondary fermenter and add:

4 AAUs Willamette hops

Condition-cool (50–55°F [10–13°C]) for 3 to 4 weeks. Prime with:

1 cup (237 ml) pale dry malt extract

Bottle and age at 50°F (10°C) for 3 weeks.

Alternate Methods

All-extract: Steep the crystal malt and malted wheat as in main recipe in 2½ gallons (9.5 L) water at 150°F (66°C) for 45 minutes. Omit pale malt and increase malt extract syrup to 6 lb. (2.7 kg). Follow directions from beginning of boil.

All-grain: Mash 7 lb. (3.2 kg) pale malt and the crystal malt and malted wheat as in main recipe in 3 gallons (11 L) water at 152°F (67°C). Sparge with 3¾ gallons (14.2 L) water. Omit malt extract syrup and proceed as in main recipe, reducing wort volume to 5¼ gallons (20 L) or less.

 Serve at 50°F (10°C) in a traditional pint glass.

Fred

Hair of the Dog Brewing Co., Portland, Oregon

Brewed in honor of legendary beer writer Fred Eckhardt, this "Special Ale" has an unusual combination of ingredients and a deliciously uncommon blend of aromas and flavors. The brewers boast of using 10 hops from five countries in the making of Fred.

Original gravity: 1098 • Final gravity: 1020 • 10% abv • 80 IBU

Heat 3¾ gallons (14.2 L) water to 164°F (73°C). Crush:

6 lb. (2.7 kg) pale malt
2 lb. (907 g) aromatic malt
2 lb. (907 g) malted rye
12 oz. (340 g) light (20°L) crystal malt

Add to liquor and steep at 152°F (67°C) for 90 minutes. Sparge with 4½ gallons (17 L) water at 168°F (76°C). Add to runnings:

4 lb. (1.8 kg) unhopped, pale dry malt extract (DME)

Bring to a boil, then add:

2 AAUs *each* of Bramling Cross hops, Fuggles hops, Hallertau hops, and Willamette hops
4 AAUs Eroica hops

Boil 30 minutes, then add:

3 AAUs *each* of Target hops, Northern Brewer hops, and B. C. Goldings hops

Boil 55 minutes, then add:

4 AAUs Saaz hops

Boil 5 minutes, then add:

4 AAUs Cascade hops

Remove from heat. Cool, then top up to 5¼ gallons (20 L) with chilled, preboiled water. Cool to 68°F (20°C), then pitch:

English ale yeast (Wyeast 1098 or equivalent)
½ oz. (14 g) dry champagne yeast

Ferment at 68°F (20°C) for 3 weeks, then transfer to secondary fermenter and condition cool (50–55°F [10–13°C]) for 5 to 6 weeks. Prime with:

¾ cup (177 ml) pale dry malt extract

Bottle and age at 55–60°F (13–16°C) for 6 months.

 Serve at 50°F (10°C) in a brandy snifter.

 **Alternate Methods**

All-extract: Steep 3 lb. (1.4 kg) pale malt and the aromatic malt, malted rye, and crystal malt as in main recipe in 2½ gallons (9.5 L) water at 150°F (66°C) for 45 minutes. Increase DME to 6 lb. (2.7 kg). Follow directions from beginning of boil.

All-grain: Mash 12 lb. (5.4 kg) pale malt and the aromatic malt, malted rye, and crystal malt as in main recipe in 2½ gallons (9.5 L) water at 152°F (67°C). Sparge with 3 gallons (11 L) water. Omit first DME and proceed as in main recipe, reducing wort volume to 5¼ gallons (20 L) or less.

Haystack Black Ale

Portland Brewing Co., Portland, Oregon

This is a big, creamy, bitter porter with a floral hop nose. Haystack Black, named for a huge offshore rock at Cannon Beach on the beautiful Oregon coast, is as impressive and robust as its namesake.

Original gravity: 1050 • Final gravity: 1012 • 4.8% abv • 40 IBU

Heat 1¾ gallons (6.6 L) water to 164°F (73°C). Crush:
- **3 lb. (1.4 kg) pale malt**
- **8 oz. (227 g) black malt**
- **8 oz. (227 g) chocolate malt**
- **8 oz. (227 g) dark (120°L) crystal malt**

Add to liquor and steep at 152°F (67°C) for 90 minutes. Sparge with 2½ gallons (9.5 L) water at 168°F (76°C). Add to runnings:
- **3⅓ lb. (1.5 kg) unhopped, amber malt extract syrup**

Bring to a boil, then add:
- **6 AAUs Galena hops**

Boil 30 minutes, then add:
- **4 AAUs Fuggles hops**

Boil 15 minutes, then add:
- **4 AAUs Cascade hops**

Boil 15 minutes, then remove from heat. Cool, then top up to 5¼ gallons (20 L) with chilled, preboiled water. Cool to 68°F (20°C), then pitch:
- **London ale yeast (Wyeast 1968 or equivalent)**

Ferment at 65°F (18°C) for 2 weeks, then transfer to secondary fermenter and add:
- **4 AAUs Cascade hops**

Condition-cool (50–55°F [10–13°C]) for 3 to 4 weeks. Prime with:
- **1 cup (237 ml) pale dry malt extract**

Bottle and age at 55–60°F (13–16°C) for 3 weeks.

Alternate Methods

All-extract: Steep the black, chocolate, and crystal malts as in main recipe in 2½ gallons (9.5 L) water at 150°F (66°C) for 45 minutes. Omit pale malt and increase malt extract syrup to 6 lb. (2.7 kg). Follow directions from beginning of boil.

All-grain: Mash 7 lb. (3.2 kg) pale malt and the black, chocolate, and crystal malts as in main recipe in 3 gallons (11 L) water at 152°F (67°C). Sparge with 3¾ gallons (14.2 L) water. Omit malt extract syrup and proceed as in main recipe, reducing wort volume to 5¼ gallons (20 L) or less.

 Serve at 50°F (10°C) in a traditional pint glass.

Honey Weizen

Nor'wester Brewing Co., Portland, Oregon

Brewed with a special honey malt and fermented with clover honey, this wheat ale has lots of flavor. The Mt. Hood hops give it a pleasant grassy, floral aroma, and the wheat contributes a toasted biscuit flavor.

Original gravity: 1042 • Final gravity: 1010 • 4% abv • 20 IBU

Heat 1½ gallons (5.7 L) water to 164°F (73°C). Crush:
- **1 lb. (454 g) pale malt**
- **8 oz. (227 g) light (20°L) crystal malt**
- **1 lb. (454 g) honey malt**
- **8 oz. (227 g) toasted pale malt**
- **1 lb. (454 g) malted wheat**

Add to liquor and steep at 152°F (67°C) for 90 minutes. Sparge with 2¼ gallons (8.5 L) water at 168°F (76°C). Add to runnings:
- **1½ lb. (680 g) unhopped, wheat dry malt extract (DME)**

Bring to a boil, then add:
- **4 AAUs Mt. Hood hops**

Boil 30 minutes, then add:
- **1 lb. (454 g) clover honey**
- **2 AAUs Mt. Hood hops**

Boil 30 minutes, then remove from heat. Cool, then top up to 5¼ gallons (20 L) with chilled, preboiled water. Cool to 68°F (20°C), then pitch:
- **American ale yeast (Wyeast 1056 or equivalent)**
- **or**
- **German wheat beer yeast (Wyeast 3333 — not a Bavarian or Weihenstephen weizen yeast)**

Ferment at 68°F (20°C) for 2 weeks, then transfer to secondary fermenter and condition cool (50–55°F [10–13°C]) for 3 to 4 weeks. Prime with:
- **⅞ cup (202 ml) corn sugar**

Bottle and age at 55–60°F (13–16°C) for 3 weeks.

Alternate Methods

All-extract: Steep 4 oz. (113 g) crystal malt, 8 oz. (227 g) honey malt, and the toasted malt and malted wheat as in main recipe in 2½ gallons (9.5 L) water at 150°F (66°C) for 45 minutes. Omit pale malt and increase DME to 2½ lb. (1.1 kg). Follow directions from first boil.

All-grain: Mash 2 lb. (907 g) pale malt and the crystal, honey, toasted, and pale malts as in main recipe, plus 2 lb. (907 g) malted wheat, in 2½ gallons (9.5 L) water at 152°F (67°C). Sparge with 3 gallons (11 L) water. Omit DME, but add the honey as in main recipe, and proceed from beginning of boil, reducing wort volume to 5¼ gallons (20 L) or less.

 Serve at 48°F (9°C) in a tall wheat-beer glass.

Mercator Doppelbock

Full Sail Brewing Co., Hood River, Oregon; Portland, Oregon
*Mercator is a rich, well-rounded doppelbock with a gorgeous red color and
a cheering alcoholic warmth. With bready and sweet malt along
with tangy and spicy hops, this is a complex beer.*

Original gravity: 1076 • Final gravity: 1015 • 7.8% abv • 40 IBU

Heat 3 gallons (11 L) water to 164°F (73°C). Crush:

5 lb. (2.3 kg) lager malt
1 lb. (454 g) Vienna malt
1 lb. (454 g) Munich malt
8 oz. (227 g) caravienne malt
8 oz. (227 g) medium (50°L) crystal malt

Add to liquor and steep at 152°F (67°C) for 90 minutes. Sparge with
3¾ gallons (14.2 L) water at 168°F (76°C). Add to runnings:

3½ lb. (1.6 kg) unhopped, pale dry malt extract (DME)

Bring to a boil, then add:

4 AAUs Tettnang hops

Boil 30 minutes, then add:

4 AAUs Hallertau hops

Boil 45 minutes, then add:

4 AAUs Spalt hops

Boil 15 minutes, then remove from heat. Cool, then top up to 5¼ gallons
(20 L) with chilled, preboiled water. Cool to 62°F (17°C), then pitch:

Munich lager yeast (Wyeast 2308 or equivalent)

Ferment at 55°F (13°C) for 2 weeks, then transfer to secondary fermenter
and condition cold (40°F [4°C]) for 3 to 4 months. Prime with:

1 cup (237 ml) pale dry malt extract

Bottle and age at 45°F (7°C) for 3 months.

Alternate Methods

All-extract: Steep the
Vienna, Munich, caravi-
enne, and crystal malts as
in main recipe in 2½ gal-
lons (9.5 L) water at 150°F
(66°C) for 45 minutes. Omit
lager malt and increase
DME to 7 lb. (3.2 kg).
Follow directions from
beginning of boil.

All-grain: Mash 10 lb.
(4.5 kg) lager malt and the
Vienna, Munich, caravi-
enne, and crystal malts as
in main recipe in 4 gallons
(15.1 L) water at 152°F
(67°C). Sparge with 4½
gallons (17 L) water. Omit
first DME and proceed as
in main recipe, reducing
wort volume to 5¼ gallons
(20 L) or less. (Advanced
brewers may wish to try a
triple decoction on this
brew.)

 Serve at 40°F (4°C) in a glass or ceramic stein.

Mirror Pond Pale Ale

Deschutes Brewery, Bend, Oregon

*This deep golden, crisp, and pleasantly dry pale ale carries a fresh
Cascade hop aroma and a big, clean flavor.*

Original gravity: 1044 • Final gravity: 1008 • 4.6% abv • 35–40 IBU

Heat 1¼ gallons (4.7 L) water to 164°F (73°C). Crush:

2 lb. (907 g) pale malt
1 lb. (454 g) light (20°L) crystal malt

Add to liquor and steep at 152°F (67°C) for 90 minutes. Sparge with
2 gallons (7.6 L) water at 168°F (76°C). Add to runnings:

3 lb. (1.4 kg) unhopped, pale dry malt extract (DME)

Bring to a boil, then add:

6 AAUs Cascade hops

Boil 45 minutes, then add:

6 AAUs Cascade hops

Boil 15 minutes, then remove from heat. Cool, then top up to 5¼ gallons
(20 L) with chilled, preboiled water. Cool to 68°F (20°C), then pitch:

American ale yeast (Wyeast 1056 or equivalent)

Ferment at 68°F (20°C) for 2 weeks, then transfer to secondary fermenter
and add:

10 AAUs Cascade hops

Condition-cool (50–55°F [10–13°C]) for 3 to 4 weeks. Prime with:

1 cup (237 ml) pale dry malt extract

Bottle and age at 55–60°F (13–16°C) for 3 weeks.

Alternate Methods

All-extract: Steep the crystal malt as in main recipe in 2½ gallons (9.5 L) water at 150°F (66°C) for 45 minutes. Omit pale malt and increase DME to 4½ lb. (2 kg). Follow directions from beginning of boil.

All-grain: Mash 6½ lb. (3 kg) pale malt and the crystal malt in 2½ gallons (9.5 L) water at 152°F (67°C). Sparge with 3 gallons (11 L) water. Omit first DME and proceed as in main recipe, reducing wort volume to 5¼ gallons (20 L) or less.

Serve at 50°F (10°C) in a traditional pint glass.

Rogue Mocha Porter

Oregon Brewing Co., Newport, Oregon

This is a rich, dark brown porter with big malt flavor and hints of smoky coffee, chocolate, and fruit. Don't be deceived by its creamy head and stoutlike opaqueness: This clean, refreshing beer is lighter than it looks.

Original gravity: 1050 • Final gravity: 1012 • 4.8% abv • 38 IBU

Heat 1½ gallons (5.7 L) water to 164°F (73°C). Crush:

2 lb. (907 g) pale malt
1 lb. (454 g) Munich malt
8 oz. (227 g) chocolate malt
8 oz. (227 g) medium (50°L) crystal malt

Add to liquor and steep at 152°F (67°C) for 90 minutes. Sparge with 2¼ gallons (8.5 L) water at 168°F (76°C). Add to runnings:

3 lb. (1.4 kg) unhopped, amber dry malt extract (DME)

Bring to a boil, then add:

6 AAUs Perle hops

Boil 45 minutes, then add:

6 AAUs Centennial hops

Boil 45 minutes, then remove from heat. Cool, then top up to 5¼ gallons (20 L) with chilled, preboiled water. Cool to 68°F (20°C), then pitch:

Recultured Rogue Pacman ale yeast (or London ale yeast, Wyeast 1968, or equivalent)

Ferment at 68°F (20°C) for 2 weeks, then transfer to secondary fermenter and condition cool (50–55°F [10–13°C]) for 3 to 4 weeks. Prime with:

1 cup (237 ml) pale dry malt extract

Bottle and age at 55–60°F (13–16°C) for 3 weeks.

Alternate Methods

All-extract: Steep 8 oz. (227 g) pale malt, 1 lb. (454 g) Munich malt, and the chocolate and crystal malts as in main recipe in 2½ gallons (9.5 L) water at 150°F (66°C) for 45 minutes. Increase DME to 4 lb. (1.8 kg). Follow directions from beginning of boil.

All-grain: Mash 6½ lb. (3 kg) pale malt and the Munich, chocolate, and crystal malts as in main recipe in 3 gallons (11 L) water at 152°F (67°C). Sparge with 3¾ gallons (14.2 L) water. Omit first DME and proceed as in main recipe, reducing wort volume to 5¼ gallons (20 L) or less.

 Serve at 50°F (10°C) in a traditional pint glass.

Rogue XS Smoke Ale

Oregon Brewing Co., Newport, Oregon

This is an unfiltered, unfined, very smoky amber ale from the cellars of John Maier. Unlike many other smoked beers, this one actually has some beer flavor under all the smoke — a sweet, malty base with a pleasant hop bitterness and a roasty bite in the background.

Original gravity: 1058 • Final gravity: 1010 • 6.1% abv • 48 IBU

Heat 2 gallons (7.6 L) water to 164°F (73°C). Crush:

- **3 lb. (1.4 kg) pale malt**
- **1 lb. (454 g) Munich malt**
- **1 lb. (454 g) alder- or beech-smoked malt**
- **1 lb. (454 g) medium (60°L) crystal malt**

Add to liquor and steep at 152°F (67°C) for 90 minutes. Sparge with 2¾ gallons (10.2 L) water at 168°F (76°C). Add to runnings:

- **3⅓ lb. (1.5 kg) unhopped, amber malt extract syrup**

Bring to a boil, then add:

- **4 AAUs Perle hops**
- **4 AAUs Saaz hops**

Boil 60 minutes, then add:

- **4 AAUs Saaz hops**

Boil 15 minutes, then add:

- **3 AAUs Perle hops**

Boil 15 minutes, then remove from heat. Cool, then top up to 5¼ gallons (20 L) with chilled, preboiled water. Cool to 68°F (20°C), then pitch:

- **American ale yeast (recultured Rogue Pacman, Wyeast 1056, or equivalent)**

Ferment at 68°F (20°C) for 2 weeks, then transfer to secondary fermenter and condition cool (50–55°F [10–13°C]) for 3 to 4 weeks. Prime with:

- **1 cup (237 ml) pale dry malt extract**

Bottle and age at 55–60°F (13–16°C) for 3 weeks.

Alternate Methods

All-extract: Steep the Munich, smoked, and crystal malts as in main recipe in 2½ gallons (9.5 L) water at 150°F (66°C) for 45 minutes. Omit pale malt and increase malt extract syrup to 6 lb. (2.7 kg). Follow directions from beginning of boil.

All-grain: Mash 7 lb. (3.2 kg) pale malt and the Munich, smoked, and crystal malts as in main recipe in 3 gallons (11 L) water at 152°F (67°C). Sparge with 3¾ gallons (14.2 L) water. Omit malt extract syrup and proceed as in main recipe, reducing wort volume to 5¼ gallons (20 L) or less.

 Serve at 50°F (10°C) in a traditional pint glass.

Widmer Summerbräu

Widmer Bros. Brewing Co., Portland, Oregon

A golden Kölsch-style summer seasonal beer, this one is crisp and clean tasting, thirst quenching, and refreshing. Mild hops, some sulfur notes, and a light but firm body make this American version pretty close to the original model.

Original gravity: 1045 • **Final gravity: 1012** • **4.2% abv** • **20 IBU**

Heat 1¾ gallons (6.6 L) water to 164°F (73°C). Crush:
- **2 lb. (907 g) lager malt**
- **1 lb. (454 g) carapils malt**
- **1 lb. (454 g) Vienna malt**
- **12 oz. (340 g) malted wheat**

Add to liquor and steep at 152°F (67°C) for 90 minutes. Sparge with 2½ gallons (9.5 L) water at 168°F (76°C). Add to runnings:
- **2 lb. (907 g) unhopped, extra-light dry malt extract (DME)**

Bring to a boil, then add:
- **4 AAUs Spalt hops**

Boil 50 minutes, then add:
- **4 AAUs Tettnang hops**

Boil 10 minutes, then remove from heat. Cool, then top up to 5¼ gallons (20 L) with chilled, preboiled water. Cool to 68°F (20°C), then pitch:
- **German ale or Kölsch yeast (Wyeast 1007, 2565, or equivalent)**

Ferment at 65°F (18°C) for 2 weeks, then transfer to secondary fermenter and condition cool (50–55°F [10–13°C]) for 3 to 4 weeks. Prime with:
- **¾ cup (177 ml) corn sugar**

Bottle and age at 50°F (10°C) for 3 weeks.

Alternate Methods

All-extract: Steep 8 oz. (227 g) lager malt and the carapils and Vienna malts and malted wheat as in main recipe in 2½ gallons (9.5 L) water at 150°F (66°C) for 45 minutes. Increase DME to 3 lb. (1.4 kg). Follow directions from beginning of boil.

All-grain: Mash 5 lb. (2.3 kg) lager malt and the carapils and Vienna malts and malted wheat as in main recipe in 2½ gallons (9.5 L) water at 152°F (67°C). Sparge with 3 gallons (11 L) water. Omit DME and proceed as in main recipe, reducing wort volume to 5¼ gallons (20 L) or less.

Serve at 50°F (10°C) in a cylindrical Kölsch glass.

Caramel Porter

Brewery Hill Brewing Co., Wilkes-Barre, Pennsylvania
Try this robust porter with a decidedly English malt and hop profile. The caramel and dark malt notes are well balanced by Goldings hop flavor and bitterness. There is a mild syrupy, molasses aftertaste that is anything but unpleasant, especially in combination with the beer's roasty notes.

Original gravity: 1055 • Final gravity: 1020 • 4.5% abv • 30 IBU

Heat 2½ gallons (9.5 L) water to 164°F (73°C). Crush:
4 lb. (1.8 kg) pale malt
1 lb. (454 g) dark (120°L) crystal malt
8 oz. (227 g) chocolate malt
8 oz. (227 g) black malt
8 oz. (227 g) roasted barley

Add to liquor and steep at 152°F (67°C) for 90 minutes. Sparge with 3 gallons (11 L) water at 168°F (76°C). Add to runnings:
2 lb. (907 g) unhopped, amber dry malt extract (DME)

Bring to a boil, then add:
6 AAUs Target hops

Boil 30 minutes, then add:
4 AAUs Goldings hops

Boil 25 minutes, then add:
4 AAUs Goldings hops

Boil 5 minutes, then remove from heat. Cool, then top up to 5¼ gallons (20 L) with chilled, preboiled water. Cool to 68°F (20°C), then pitch:
London ale yeast (Wyeast 1028 or equivalent)

Ferment at 62°F (17°C) for 2 weeks, then transfer to secondary fermenter and condition cool (50–55°F [10–13°C]) for 3 to 4 weeks. Prime with:
1 cup (237 ml) pale dry malt extract

Bottle and age at 50°F (10°C) for 3 weeks.

 **Alternate Methods**

All-extract: Steep 1 lb. (454 g) pale malt and the crystal, chocolate, and black malts and roasted barley as in main recipe in 2½ gallons (9.5 L) water at 150°F (66°C) for 45 minutes. Increase DME to 4 lb. (1.8 kg). Follow directions from beginning of boil.

All-grain: Mash 7 lb. (3.2 kg) pale malt and the crystal, chocolate, and black malts and roasted barley as in main recipe in 3¼ gallons (12.3 L) water at 152°F (67°C). Sparge with 3¾ gallons (14.2 L) water. Omit first DME and proceed as in main recipe, reducing wort volume to 5¼ gallons (20 L) or less.

 Serve at 50°F (10°C) in a traditional pint glass.

Festbier

Stoudt's Brewing Co., Wilkes-Barre, Pennsylvania

*This well-respected brewery makes primarily German-influenced beers and holds
several festivals throughout the year at its main facility in Adamstown,
a Bavarian-style biergarten, restaurant, theme park, and all-around fun place.
This is the featured beer at its Oktoberfest celebration. It's a rich amber lager
that's aromatic and malty in the nose, smooth and clean on the palate.*

Original gravity: 1060 • Final gravity: 1015 • 5.7% abv • 35–40 IBU

Heat 1¾ gallons (6.6 L) water to 164°F (73°C). Crush:

2 lb. (907 g) lager malt
1 lb. (454 g) Vienna malt
8 oz. (227 g) Munich malt
8 oz. (227 g) medium (50°L) crystal malt
4 oz. (113 g) black malt

Add to liquor and steep at 152°F (67°C) for 90 minutes. Sparge with
2½ gallons (9.5 L) water at 168°F (76°C). Add to runnings:

4 lb. (1.8 kg) unhopped, pale dry malt extract (DME)

Bring to a boil, then add:

6 AAUs Saaz hops

Boil 60 minutes, then add:

4 AAUs Tettnang hops

Boil 30 minutes, then add:

4 AAUs Spalt hops

Remove from heat. Steep 15 minutes, then remove hops. Cool, then top
up to 5¼ gallons (20 L) with chilled, preboiled water. Cool to 60°F
(16°C), then pitch:

**Munich lager yeast (recultured Stoudt's, Wyeast 2308, or
equivalent)**

Ferment at 55°F (13°C) for 2 weeks, then transfer to secondary fermenter
and condition cold (35–40°F [2–4°C]) for 5 to 6 weeks. Prime with:

1 cup (237 ml) pale dry malt extract

Bottle and age at 45°F (7°C) for 6 weeks.

 Serve at 45°F (7°C) in a glass or ceramic stein.

Alternate Methods

All-extract: Steep 8 oz.
(227 g) Vienna malt and
the Munich, crystal, and
black malts as in main
recipe in 2½ gallons (9.5 L)
water at 150°F (66°C) for
45 minutes. Omit lager
malt and increase DME
to 5¾ lb. (2.6 kg). Follow
directions from beginning
of boil.

All-grain: Mash 8 lb.
(3.6 kg) lager malt and the
Vienna, Munich, crystal,
and black malts as in main
recipe in 3 gallons (11 L)
water at 152°F (67°C).
Sparge with 3¾ gallons
(14.2 L) water. Omit first
DME and proceed as in
main recipe, reducing wort
volume to 5¼ gallons
(20 L) or less.

Prima Pils

Victory Brewing Co., Downington, Pennsylvania

A northern German–style Pilsner, Prima packs a spritzy hop aroma along with a pleasant, buttery diacetyl flavor and aroma profile that blend well. This is a nice, clean beer with very little aftertaste.

Original gravity: 1050 • Final gravity: 1012 • 4.8% abv • 30 IBU

Heat 1¾ gallons (6.6 L) water to 164°F (73°C). Crush:

4 lb. (1.8 kg) lager malt
1 lb. (454 g) carapils malt
8 oz. (227 g) Vienna malt

Add to liquor and steep at 152°F (67°C) for 90 minutes. Sparge with 2½ gallons (9.5 L) water at 168°F (76°C). Add to runnings:

2 lb. (907 g) unhopped, extra-light dry malt extract (DME)

Bring to a boil, then add:

6 AAUs Hallertau hops

Boil 45 minutes, then add:

4 AAUs Spalt hops

Boil 15 minutes, then remove from heat. Cool, then top up to 5¼ gallons (20 L) with chilled, preboiled water. Cool to 60°F (16°C), then pitch:

Czech or Bohemian lager yeast (Wyeast 2278, 2124, or equivalent)

Ferment at 55°F (13°C) for 2 weeks, then transfer to secondary fermenter and condition cold (40°F [4°C]) for 6 weeks. Prime with:

1¼ cups extra-light dry malt extract

Bottle and age at 40°F (4°C) for 6 weeks.

Alternate Methods

All-extract: Steep 1 lb. (454 g) lager malt and the carapils and Vienna malts as in main recipe in 2½ gallons (9.5 L) water at 150°F (66°C) for 45 minutes. Increase DME to 4 lb. (1.8 kg). Follow directions from beginning of boil.

All-grain: Mash 7 lb. (3.2 kg) lager malt and the carapils and Vienna malts as in main recipe in 3 gallons (11 L) water at 152°F (67°C). Sparge with 3¾ gallons (14.2 L) water. Omit first DME and proceed as in main recipe, reducing wort volume to 5¼ gallons (20 L) or less.

Serve at 50°F (10°C) in a traditional Pilsner glass.

Rolling Rock Beer

Latrobe Brewing Co., Latrobe, Pennsylvania

Here's a crisp, clean, slightly sweet take on the standard American lager style by a small (comparatively), regional brewery. Rolling Rock's recipe and taste have not changed in generations, making it a true American classic. It's very pale with a big white head and a distinct aroma of corn and German hops.

Original gravity: 1040 • Final gravity: 1008 • 4% abv • 35–30 IBU

Heat 1½ gallons (5.7 L) water to 164°F (73°C). Crush:

2 lb. (907 g) lager malt
1 lb. (454 g) carapils malt
1 lb. (454 g) flaked maize

Add to liquor and steep at 152°F (67°C) for 90 minutes. Sparge with 2¼ gallons (8.5 L) water at 168°F (76°C). Add to runnings:

2 lb. (907 g) unhopped, extra-light dry malt extract (DME)

Bring to a boil, then add:

6 AAUs Hallertau hops

Boil 50 minutes, then add:

3 AAUs Hallertau hops

Boil 15 minutes, then remove from heat. Cool, then top up to 5¼ gallons (20 L) with chilled, preboiled water. Cool to 60°F (16°C), then pitch:

American lager yeast (Wyeast 2035 or equivalent)

Ferment at 50°F (10°C) for 2 weeks, then transfer to secondary fermenter and condition cold (35°F [2°C]) for 4 to 6 weeks. Prime with:

⅞ cup (202 ml) corn sugar

Bottle and age at 40°F (4°C) for 5 weeks.

Alternate Methods

All-extract: Steep 8 oz. (227 g) lager malt and the carapils malt and maize as in main recipe in 2½ gallons (9.5 L) water at 150°F (66°C) for 45 minutes. Increase DME to 3 lb. (1.4 kg). Follow directions from beginning of boil.

All-grain: Mash 5 lb. (2.3 kg) lager malt and the carapils malt and maize as in main recipe in 2½ gallons (9.5 L) water at 152°F (67°C). Sparge with 3 gallons (11 L) water. Omit DME and proceed as in main recipe, reducing wort volume to 5¼ gallons (20 L) or less.

Serve at 40°F (4°C) in a traditional Pilsner glass or pub mug.

Celis White Beer

Celis Brewery, Austin, Texas

It's well known that Pierre Celis revived the Belgian witbier style, first at Hoegaarden in Belgium, then in the United States with his own brewery in Texas hill country. Like the best of the Belgian products, this white ale is silky smooth, spicy, and very thirst quenching.

Original gravity: 1050 • **Final gravity: 1012** • **4.8% abv** • **20 IBU**

Heat 1½ gallons (5.7 L) water to 164°F (73°C). Crush:

3 lb. (1.4 kg) malted wheat
1 lb. (454 g) Pilsner malt
8 oz. (227 g) carapils malt

Add to liquor and steep at 152°F (67°C) for 90 minutes. Sparge with 2¼ gallons (8.5 L) water at 168°F (76°C). Add to runnings:

3 lb. (1.4 kg) unhopped, extra-light malt extract syrup
8 oz. (227 g) corn sugar

Bring to a boil, then add:

2 AAUs Cascade hops
2 AAUs Willamette hops

Boil 45 minutes, then add:

2 AAUs Cascade hops
2 AAUs Willamette hops

Boil 15 minutes, then remove from heat. Add:

¼ oz. (7 g) cracked coriander seed
¼ oz. (7 g) dried curaçao (bitter) orange peel

Steep 30 minutes, then remove orange peel. Cool, then top up to 5¼ gallons (20 L) with chilled, preboiled water. Cool to 68°F (20°C), then pitch:

Belgian witbier yeast (recultured Celis or Hoegaarden, or Wyeast 3944 or equivalent)

Ferment at 68°F (20°C) for 2 weeks, then transfer to secondary fermenter and condition cool (50–55°F [10–13°C]) for 3 to 4 weeks. Prime with:

1 cup (237 ml) corn sugar

Bottle and age at 50°F (10°C) for 3 weeks.

 Serve at 50°F (10°C) in a Belgian chalice or goblet.

Alternate Methods

All-extract: Steep 1 lb. (454 g) malted wheat, 8 oz. (227 g) flaked wheat, and the carapils malt as in main recipe in 2½ gallons (9.5 L) water at 150°F (66°C) for 45 minutes. Omit Pilsner malt and add 3 lb. (1.4 kg) unhopped, extra-light DME, 1 lb. (454 g) wheat DME, and 8 oz. (227 g) corn sugar. Follow directions from beginning of boil.

All-grain: Mash 4¼ lb. (1.9 kg) Pilsner malt, 3¼ lb. (1.5 kg) malted wheat, and the carapils malt as in main recipe in 3 gallons (11 L) water at 152°F (67°C). Sparge with 3¾ gallons (14.2 L) water. Omit malt extract syrup, but add the corn sugar and proceed as in main recipe, reducing wort volume to 5¼ gallons (20 L) or less.

Honcho Grande Brown Ale

Yellow Rose Brewing Co., San Antonio, Texas
*Try this deep amber, not-quite-brown ale from deep in the heart of Texas.
It's bottle conditioned and has a big head, big malt flavor,
and loads of diacetyl butterscotch sweetness.*

Original gravity: 1048 • Final gravity: 1015 • 4.2% abv • 18 IBU

Heat 1½ gallons (5.7 L) water to 164°F (73°C). Crush:
- **2 lb. (907 g) pale malt**
- **1 lb. (454 g) medium (50°L) crystal malt**
- **4 oz. (113 g) black malt**
- **4 oz. (113 g) chocolate malt**

Add to liquor and steep at 152°F (67°C) for 90 minutes. Sparge with 2¼ gallons (8.5 L) water at 168°F (76°C). Add to runnings:
- **4 lb. (1.8 kg) unhopped, amber malt extract syrup**

Bring to a boil, then add:
- **4 AAUs Willamette hops**

Boil 90 minutes, then remove from heat. Cool, then top up to 5¼ gallons (20 L) with chilled, preboiled water. Cool to 68°F (20°C), then pitch:
- **Recultured Honcho Grande yeast or American ale yeast (Wyeast 1056 or equivalent)**

Ferment at 68°F (20°C) for 2 weeks, then transfer to secondary fermenter and condition cool (50–55°F [10–13°C]) for 3 to 4 weeks. Prime with:
- **1 cup (237 ml) pale dry malt extract (DME)**

Bottle and age at 55–60°F (13–16°C) for 3 weeks.

 **Alternate Methods**

All-extract: Steep the crystal, black, and chocolate malts as in main recipe in 2½ gallons (9.5 L) water at 150°F (66°C) for 45 minutes. Omit pale malt and increase malt extract syrup to 6 lb. (2.7 kg). Follow directions from beginning of boil.

All-grain: Mash 6¾ lb. (3.1 kg) pale malt and the crystal, black, and chocolate malts as in main recipe in 3 gallons (11 L) water at 152°F (67°C). Sparge with 3½ gallons (13.2 L) water. Omit malt extract syrup and proceed as in main recipe, reducing wort volume to 5¼ gallons (20 L) or less.

 Serve at 50°F (10°C) in a traditional pint glass.

Shiner Bock

Spoetzl Brewery, Shiner, Texas

A light, thirst-quenching bock, not as hearty or rich (or alcoholic) as a traditional bock, but a well-rounded, smooth beer, Shiner is more sweet than bitter. It is bright copper and has a definite caramel and fruit aroma.

Original gravity: 1060 • **Final gravity: 1015** • **5.7% abv** • **30 IBU**

Heat 2¼ gallons (8.5 L) water to 164°F (73°C). Crush:

4 lb. (1.8 kg) lager malt
1 lb. (454 g) carapils malt
1 lb. (454 g) Munich malt
4 oz. (113 g) black malt

Add to liquor and steep at 152°F (67°C) for 90 minutes. Sparge with 3 gallons (11 L) water at 168°F (76°C). Add to runnings:

3⅓ lb. (1.5 kg) unhopped, light malt extract syrup

Bring to a boil, then add:

6 AAUs Northern Brewer hops

Boil 75 minutes, then add:

3 AAUs Hallertau hops

Boil 15 minutes, then remove from heat. Cool, then top up to 5¼ gallons (20 L) with chilled, preboiled water. Cool to 62°F (17°C), then pitch:

Munich lager yeast (Wyeast 2308 or equivalent)

Ferment at 50°F (10°C) for 2 weeks, then transfer to secondary fermenter and condition cold (40°F [4°C]) for 5 to 6 weeks. Prime with:

1 cup (237 ml) pale dry malt extract (DME)

Bottle and age at 50°F (10°C) for 3 weeks.

Alternate Methods

All-extract: Steep the carapils, Munich, and black malts as in main recipe in 2½ gallons (9.5 L) water at 150°F (66°C) for 45 minutes. Omit lager malt and increase malt extract syrup to 6⅔ lb. (3 kg). Follow directions from beginning of boil.

All-grain: Mash 8 lb. (3.6 kg) lager malt and the carapils, Munich, and black malts as in main recipe in 3 gallons (11 L) water at 152°F (67°C). Sparge with 3¾ gallons (14.2 L) water. Omit malt extract syrup and proceed as in main recipe, reducing wort volume to 5¼ gallons (20 L) or less.

Serve at 50°F (10°C) in a glass or ceramic stein.

King's Peak Porter

Uinta Brewing, Salt Lake City, Utah

A nice mild, brown porter, King's Peak has a sweet, malty aroma but a dry, roasty flavor profile. The aftertaste is roasty and nutty with minimal hop bitterness.

Original gravity: 1052 • Final gravity: 1012 • 5.1% abv • 32 IBU

Heat 1¾ gallons (6.6 L) water to 164°F (73°C). Crush:
2½ lb. (1.1 kg) pale malt
1 lb. (454 g) medium (50°L) crystal malt
8 oz. (227 g) Munich malt
4 oz. (113 g) chocolate malt
2 oz. (56.7 g) black malt
2 oz. (56.7 g) roasted barley

Add to liquor and steep at 152°F (67°C) for 90 minutes. Sparge with 2½ gallons (9.5 L) water at 168°F (76°C). Add to runnings:
3 lb. (1.4 kg) unhopped, amber dry malt extract (DME)

Bring to a boil, then add:
6 AAUs Chinook hops

Boil 30 minutes, then add:
3 AAUs Willamette hops

Boil 15 minutes, then remove from heat. Add:
4 AAUs Tettnang hops

Steep 30 minutes, then remove hops. Cool, then top up to 5¼ gallons (20 L) with chilled, preboiled water. Cool to 68°F (20°C), then pitch:
London ale yeast (Wyeast 1968 or equivalent)

Ferment at 65°F (18°C) for 2 weeks, then transfer to secondary fermenter and condition cool (50°F [10°C]) for 3 to 4 weeks. Prime with:
1 cup (237 ml) pale dry malt extract

Bottle and age at 55–60°F (13–16°C) for 3 weeks.

Alternate Methods

All-extract: Steep 8 oz. (227 g) crystal malt and the Munich, chocolate, and black malts and the roasted barley as in main recipe in 2½ gallons (9.5 L) water at 150°F (66°C) for 45 minutes. Omit pale malt and increase DME to 5 lb. (2.3 kg). Follow directions from beginning of boil.

All-grain: Mash 7 lb. (3.2 kg) pale malt and the crystal, Munich, chocolate, and black malts and the roasted barley as in main recipe in 3 gallons (11 L) water at 152°F (67°C). Sparge with 3¾ gallons (14.2 L) water. Omit DME and proceed as in main recipe, reducing wort volume to 5¼ gallons (20 L) or less.

 Serve at 50°F (10°C) in a traditional pint glass.

Brueghel Blonde Ale

Kross Brewing Co., Morrisville, Vermont

This blond brew is a Belgian-style witbier that's tart, spicy, and hazy gold. It's light in body but has significant malt flavor underlying all the other tastes.

Original gravity: 1048 • Final gravity: 1010 • 4.8% abv • 15–18 IBU

Heat 2 gallons (7.6 L) water to 164°F (73°C). Crush:

2 lb. (907 g) Belgian Pilsner malt
1½ lb. (680 g) malted wheat
8 oz. (227 g) flaked wheat
1 lb. (454 g) light (20°L) crystal malt
4 oz. (113 g) caravienne malt

Add to liquor and steep at 152°F (67°C) for 90 minutes. Sparge with 3 gallons (11 L) water at 168°F (76°C). Add to runnings:

2 lb. (907 g) unhopped, wheat dry malt extract (DME)

Bring to a boil, then add:

4 AAUs Willamette hops

Boil 60 minutes, then add:

¼ tablespoon (3.8 ml) coarsely crushed (not ground) coriander seed

Remove from heat and steep 30 minutes. Cool, then top up to 5¼ gallons (20 L) with chilled, preboiled water. Cool to 65°F (18°C), then pitch:

Recultured Kross yeast or Belgian witbier yeast (Wyeast 3944 or equivalent)

Ferment at 65°F (18°C) for 2 weeks, then transfer to secondary fermenter and condition cool (50–55°F [10–13°C]) for 3 to 4 weeks. Prime with:

1 cup (237 ml) wheat dry malt extract

Bottle and age at 50°F (10°C) for 3 weeks.

 **Alternate Methods**

All-extract: Steep 8 oz. (227 g) Belgian Pilsner malt, 8 oz. (227 g) flaked wheat, and the crystal and caravienne malts as in main recipe in 2½ gallons (9.5 L) water at 150°F (66°C) for 45 minutes. Omit the malted wheat and increase DME to 4 lb. (1.8 kg). Follow directions from beginning of boil.

All-grain: Mash 4 lb. (1.8 kg) Belgian Pilsner malt, 2 lb. (907 g) malted wheat, 1 lb. (454 g) flaked wheat, and the crystal and caravienne malts as in main recipe in 3¼ gallons (12.3 L) water at 152°F (67°C). Sparge with 4 gallons (15.2 L) water. Omit first DME and proceed as in main recipe, reducing wort volume to 5¼ gallons (20 L) or less.

 Serve at 40°F (4°C) in a tall weizen glass.

Catamount Porter

Catamount Brewing Co., Windsor, Vermont

A rich, robust porter, Catamount is considered by beer writer Michael Jackson to be the best porter on the East Coast. This beer is full and dark with roasty, chocolatey flavors, a nice hop bite, and a pleasant dryness in the finish.

Original gravity: 1044 • Final gravity: 1012 • 4% abv • 30 IBU

Heat 1½ gallons (5.7 L) water to 164°F (73°C). Crush:

2 lb. (907 g) pale malt
8 oz. (227 g) black patent malt
4 oz. (113 g) chocolate malt
12 oz. (340 g) dark (90°L) crystal malt

Add to liquor and steep at 152°F (67°C) for 90 minutes. Sparge with 2¼ gallons (8.5 L) water at 168°F (76°C). Add to runnings:

2½ lb. (1.1 kg) unhopped, amber dry malt extract (DME)

Bring to a boil, then add:

6 AAUs Galena hops

Boil 45 minutes, then add:

4 AAUs Cascade hops

Boil 15 minutes, then remove from heat. Cool, then top up to 5¼ gallons (20 L) with chilled, preboiled water. Cool to 68°F (20°C), then pitch:

London ale yeast (Wyeast 1028, 1968, or equivalent)

Ferment at 68°F (20°C) for 2 weeks, then transfer to secondary fermenter and condition cool (50–55°F [10–13°C]) for 3 to 4 weeks. Prime with:

1 cup (237 ml) amber dry malt extract

Bottle and age at 50°F (10°C) for 3 weeks.

Alternate Methods

All-extract: Steep the black and chocolate malts as in main recipe, 8 oz. (227 g) crystal malt, and 12 oz. (340 g) toasted pale malt in 2½ gallons (9.5 L) water at 150°F (66°C) for 45 minutes. Increase DME to 3½ lb. (1.6 kg), then follow directions from beginning of boil.

All-grain: Mash 5½ lb. (2.5 kg) pale malt and the black, chocolate, and crystal malts as in main recipe in 2½ gallons (9.5 L) water at 152°F (67°C). Sparge with 3 gallons (11 L) water. Omit first DME and proceed as in main recipe, reducing wort volume to 5¼ gallons (20 L) or less.

Serve at 50°F (10°C) in a traditional pint glass.

Firehouse Amber Ale

McNeill's Brewery, Brattleboro, Vermont

With deep gold to reddish amber color and a strong hop aroma backed by big malty notes, this ale seems to be a cross between an altbier and an IPA. The maltiness is clean and the hop flavor and aroma are at IPA levels, but the hop bitterness is subdued and the body is less full, like a Dusseldorf-style alt.

Original gravity: 1050 • **Final gravity: 1012** • **4.8% abv** • **40 IBU**

Heat 1¼ gallons (4.7 L) water to 164°F (73°C). Crush:

2 lb. (907 g) pale malt
1 lb. (454 g) medium (60°L) crystal malt

Add to liquor and steep at 152°F (67°C) for 90 minutes. Sparge with 2 gallons (7.6 L) water at 168°F (76°C). Add to runnings:

4½ lb. (2 kg) unhopped, pale malt extract syrup

Bring to a boil, then add:

6 AAUs Northern Brewer hops

Boil 60 minutes, then add:

6 AAUs Northern Brewer hops

Boil 30 minutes, then remove from heat. Add:

4 AAUs Cascade hops

Steep 5 minutes, then cool and top up to 5¼ gallons (20 L) with chilled, preboiled water. Cool to 68°F (20°C), then pitch:

English ale yeast (Wyeast 1098 or equivalent)
German ale yeast (Wyeast 1338)

Ferment at 65°F (18°C) for 2 weeks, then transfer to secondary fermenter and add:

4 AAUs Cascade hops

Condition-cool (50–55°F [10–13°C]) for 3 to 4 weeks. Prime with:

1 cup (237 ml) pale dry malt extract (DME)

Bottle and age at 55–60°F (13–16°C) for 3 weeks.

Alternate Methods

All-extract: Steep 1 lb. (454 g) toasted pale malt (toast at 350°F [177°C] for 30 minutes) and the crystal malt as in main recipe in 2½ gallons (9.5 L) water at 150°F (66°C) for 45 minutes. Increase malt extract syrup to 5½ lb. (2½ kg), then follow directions from beginning of boil.

All-grain: Mash 7½ lb. (3.4 kg) pale malt and the crystal malt as in main recipe in 3 gallons (11 L) water at 152°F (67°C). Sparge with 3¾ gallons (14.2 L) water. Omit malt extract syrup and proceed as in main recipe, reducing wort volume to 5¼ gallons (20 L) or less.

Serve at 50°F (10°C) in a traditional pint glass.

Heart of Darkness Stout

Magic Hat Brewing Co., South Burlington, Vermont

Here's a deep, dark, hearty Irish-style stout from one of the most eclectic and interesting breweries on the East Coast. The label art alone is worth the price of the beer, but the beer is also remarkably well made. This stout has notes of burnt sugar, smoke, rich malt, buttery diacetyl, roasted barley, and hop bitterness balanced by a bittersweet finish.

Original gravity: 1050 • Final gravity: 1014 • 4.6% abv • 30 IBU

Heat 1¼ gallons (4.7 L) water to 164°F (73°C). Crush:

2 lb. (907 g) pale malt
4 oz. (113 g) dark (90°L) crystal malt
8 oz. (227 g) roasted barley

Add to liquor and steep at 152°F (67°C) for 90 minutes. Sparge with 2 gallons (7.6 L) water at 168°F (76°C). Add to runnings:

4 lb. (1.8 kg) unhopped, amber dry malt extract (DME)

Boil 30 minutes, then add:

6 AAUs Northern Brewer hops

Boil 30 minutes, then add:

4 AAUs Northern Brewer hops

Boil 15 minutes, then remove from heat. Cool, then top up to 5¼ gallons (20 L) with chilled, preboiled water. Cool to 68°F (20°C), then pitch:

Irish ale yeast (Wyeast 1084 or equivalent)

Ferment at 65°F (18°C) for 2 weeks, then transfer to secondary fermenter and condition cool (45–50°F [7–10°C]) for 3 to 4 weeks. Prime with:

1 cup (237 ml) dark dry malt extract

Bottle and age at 50–55°F (10–13°C) for 3 weeks.

Alternate Methods

All-extract: Steep 8 oz. (227 g) each dark crystal malt and roasted barley in 2½ gallons (9.5 L) water at 150°F (66°C) for 45 minutes. Omit pale malt and increase DME to 5 lb. (2.3 kg). Follow directions from beginning of boil.

All-grain: Mash 7 lb. (3.2 kg) pale malt and 8 oz. (227 g) each dark crystal malt, roasted barley, and Munich malt in 3 gallons (11 L) water at 152°F (67°C). Sparge with 3¾ gallons (14.2 L) water. Omit first DME and proceed as in main recipe, reducing wort volume to 5¼ gallons (20 L) or less.

 Serve at 50°F (10°C) in a traditional pint glass or Irish-style tulip glass.

Long Trail Ale

Long Trail Brewing Co., Bridgewater Corners, Vermont

A nice crisp, clean, German alt-style beer, Long Trail is brewed in the traditional Dusseldorf manner with fresh Vermont water. It's full flavored and has a distinctive bitterness that cuts the malty sweetness and balances all the elements.

Original gravity: 1046 • **Final gravity: 1010** • **4.6% abv** • **32 IBU**

Heat 1½ gallons (5.7 L) water to 164°F (73°C). Crush:

2 lb. (907 g) Pilsner malt
8 oz. (227 g) Munich malt
8 oz. (227 g) malted wheat
8 oz. (227 g) medium (50°L) crystal malt

Add to liquor and steep at 152°F (67°C) for 90 minutes. Sparge with 2¼ gallons (8.5 L) water at 168°F (76°C). Add to runnings:

3 lb. (1.4 kg) unhopped, light dry malt extract (DME)

Bring to a boil, then add:

4 AAUs Tettnang hops

Boil 30 minutes, then add:

2 AAUs Tettnang hops

Boil 30 minutes, then add:

2 AAUs Tettnang hops

Boil 30 minutes, then remove from heat. Cool, then top up to 5¼ gallons (20 L) with chilled, preboiled water. Cool to 68°F (20°C), then pitch:

European or German ale yeast (Wyeast 1338 or equivalent)
or
California lager yeast (Wyeast 2112)

Ferment at 62–65°F (17–18°C) for 2 weeks, then transfer to secondary fermenter and condition cold (40°F [4°C]) for 3 to 4 weeks. Prime with:

1 cup (237 ml) light dry malt extract

Bottle and age at 45–50°F (7–10°C) for 3 weeks.

Alternate Methods

All-extract: Steep the Munich and crystal malts and malted wheat as in main recipe in 2½ gallons (9.5 L) water at 150°F (66°C) for 45 minutes. Omit Pilsner malt and increase DME to 5½ lb. (2½ kg). Follow directions from beginning of boil.

All-grain: Mash 5 lb. (2.3 kg) Pilsner malt, 2 lb. (907 g) Munich malt, and the malted wheat and crystal malt as in main recipe in 3 gallons (11 L) water at 152°F (67°C). Sparge with 3¾ gallons (14.2 L) water. Omit first DME and proceed as in main recipe, reducing wort volume to 5¼ gallons (20 L) or less.

 Serve at 45°F (7°C) in a narrow, cylindrical altbier glass.

Long Trail Kölsch

Long Trail Brewing Co., Bridgewater Corners, Vermont

In 1998 Long Trail became Vermont's largest, most successful brewery. This Kölsch is a deep golden, buttery-sweet ale with a fresh German noble hop character. The clean diacetyl and hop flavors linger.

Original gravity: 1046 • Final gravity: 1010 • 4.6% abv • 30 IBU

Heat 1¾ gallons (6.6 L) water to 164°F (73°C). Crush:
- **3 lb. (1.4 kg) lager malt**
- **1 lb. (454 g) malted wheat**
- **4 oz. (113 g) carapils malt**

Add to liquor and steep at 152°F (67°C) for 90 minutes. Sparge with 2½ gallons (9.5 L) water at 168°F (76°C). Add to runnings:
- **3 lb. (1.4 kg) unhopped, extra-light malt extract syrup**

Bring to a boil, then add:
- **4 AAUs Tettnang hops**

Boil 30 minutes, then add:
- **6 AAUs Spalt hops**

Boil 30 minutes, then remove from heat. Cool, then top up to 5¼ gallons (20 L) with chilled, preboiled water. Cool to 68°F (20°C), then pitch:
- **Kölsch or German ale yeast (Wyeast 2565, 1007, or equivalent)**

Ferment at 65°F (18°C) for 2 weeks, then transfer to secondary fermenter and condition cool (48–50°F [8–10°C]) for 3 to 4 weeks. Prime with:
- **⅞ cup (202 ml) corn sugar**

Bottle and age at 50–55°F (10–13°C) for 3 weeks.

Alternate Methods

All-extract: Steep 8 oz. (227 g) lager malt, 8 oz. (227 g) malted wheat, and the carapils malt as in main recipe in 2½ gallons (9.5 L) water at 150°F (66°C) for 45 minutes. Increase malt extract syrup to 5½ lb. (2.5 kg), then follow directions from beginning of boil.

All-grain: Mash 6½ lb. (3 kg) lager malt and the wheat and carapils malts as in main recipe in 3 gallons (11 L) water at 152°F (67°C). Sparge with 3¾ gallons (14.2 L) water. Omit malt extract syrup and proceed as in main recipe, reducing wort volume to 5¼ gallons (20 L) or less.

 Serve at 48°F (9°C) in a cylindrical Alt or Kölsch glass.

Stovepipe Porter

Otter Creek Brewing Co., Middlebury, Vermont

*This black porter is rich with dark malt flavor and herbal, floral hop aroma.
Stovepipe finishes dry and pleasantly bitter, with roasted malt
and burnt-sugar notes in the aftertaste.*

Original gravity: 1055 • Final gravity: 1015 • 5.1% abv • 40 IBU

Heat 2 gallons (7.6 L) water to 164°F (73°C). Crush:

3 lb. (1.4 kg) pale malt
8 oz. (227 g) black malt
8 oz. (227 g) chocolate malt
8 oz. (227 g) Munich malt
8 oz. (227 g) dark (120°L) crystal malt

Add to liquor and steep at 152°F (67°C) for 90 minutes. Sparge with
3 gallons (11 L) water at 168°F (76°C). Add to runnings:

3 lb. (1.4 kg) unhopped, amber dry malt extract (DME)

Bring to a boil, then add:

6 AAUs Nugget hops

Boil 30 minutes, then add:

4 AAUs Galena hops

Boil 30 minutes, then add:

4 AAUs Willamette hops

Remove from heat and steep hops for 15 minutes. Cool, then top up to
5¼ gallons (20 L) with chilled, preboiled water. Cool to 65°F (18°C),
then pitch:

London ale yeast (Wyeast 1968 or equivalent)

Ferment at 65°F (18°C) for 2 weeks, then transfer to secondary fermenter
and condition cool (50°F [10°C]) for 3 to 4 weeks. Prime with:

1 cup (237 ml) pale dry malt extract

Bottle and age at 50°F (10°C) for 3 weeks.

Alternate Methods

All-extract: Steep the
black, chocolate, Munich,
and crystal malts as in
main recipe in 2½ gallons
(9.5 L) water at 150°F
(66°C) for 45 minutes. Omit
pale malt and increase
DME to 5 lb. (2.3 kg).
Follow directions from
beginning of boil.

All-grain: Mash 7½ lb.
(3.4 kg) pale malt and the
black, chocolate, Munich,
and crystal malts as in
main recipe in 3 gallons
(11 L) water at 152°F
(67°C). Sparge with 3¾
gallons (14.2 L) water. Omit
first DME and proceed as
in main recipe, reducing
wort volume to 5¼ gallons
(20 L) or less.

 Serve at 50°F (10°C) in a traditional pint glass.

Tunbridge Sap Brew

Jigger Hill Brewery, Tunbridge, Vermont; South Royalton, Vermont
*This springtime golden ale is brewed by a small but growing microbrewery in my
hometown. It's a modern adaptation of a legendary country beer. It uses fresh maple
sap as mash liquor and maple syrup as a kettle addition and as a priming sugar.
I've adapted the recipe for those without access to fresh sap, but don't use
commercial maple-flavored corn sugar syrup in place of the real thing!*

Original gravity: 1040 • **Final gravity: 1006** • **4.3% abv** • **14 IBU**

Heat 1¼ gallons (4.7 L) water (or fresh maple sap) to 164°F (73°C).
Crush:

2 lb. (907 g) pale malt
8 oz. (227 g) carapils malt
8 oz. (227 g) biscuit malt

Add to liquor and steep at 152°F (67°C) for 90 minutes. Sparge with
2 gallons (7.6 L) water at 168°F (76°C). Add to runnings:

2 lb. (907 g) unhopped, pale dry malt extract (DME)
1 quart (946 ml) pure (preferably Vermont) maple syrup

Bring to a boil, then add:

3 AAUs Willamette hops

Boil 60 minutes, then remove from heat. Cool, then top up to 5¼ gallons
(20 L) with chilled, preboiled water. Cool to 68°F (20°C), then pitch:

**American ale yeast (recultured Tunbridge, Wyeast 1056, or
equivalent)**

Ferment at 68°F (20°C) for 2 weeks, then transfer to secondary fermenter
and condition cool (50–55°F [10–13°C]) for 3 to 4 weeks. Prime with:

1¼ cups (300 ml) maple syrup

Bottle and age at 50°F (10°C) for 3 weeks.

 Serve at 50°F (10°C) in a traditional pint glass.

Alternate Methods

All-extract: Steep 8 oz.
(227 g) toasted pale malt
(toast at 350°F [177°C] for
30 minutes) and the cara-
pils and biscuit malts as in
main recipe in 2½ gallons
(9.5 L) water or sap at
150°F (66°C) for 45 min-
utes. Increase DME to 3 lb.
(1.4 kg) and add 1 quart
(946 ml) maple syrup.
Follow directions from
beginning of boil.

All-grain: Mash 5 lb.
(2.3 kg) pale malt and the
carapils and biscuit malts
as in main recipe in 2½
gallons (9.5 L) water at
152°F (67°C). Sparge with
3 gallons (11 L) water.
Omit DME, but add maple
syrup. Proceed as in main
recipe, reducing wort volume to 5¼ gallons (20 L)
or less.

Whistling Pig Red Ale

Jasper Murdoch's Alehouse, Norwich, Vermont

This rich, reddish amber Irish ale is brewed by what may be the smallest brewery on the East Coast. Whistling Pig is a mild, malty ale with spicy, peppery notes in the aftertaste. It's a nice session beer with good solid flavor.

Original gravity: 1048 • **Final gravity: 1016** • **4.1% abv** • **25 IBU**

Heat 1½ gallons (5.7 L) water to 164°F (73°C). Crush:

- **2 lb. (907 g) pale malt**
- **8 oz. (227 g) medium (50°L) crystal malt**
- **4 oz. (113 g) brown malt**
- **8 oz. (227 g) carapils malt**

Add to liquor and steep at 152°F (67°C) for 90 minutes. Sparge with 2¼ gallons (8.5 L) water at 168°F (76°C). Add to runnings:

- **3½ lb. (1.6 kg) unhopped, amber dry malt extract (DME)**

Bring to a boil, then add:

- **3 AAUs Fuggles hops**
- **3 AAUs Goldings hops**

Boil 60 minutes, then add:

- **3 AAUs Goldings hops**

Remove from heat. Cool, then top up to 5¼ gallons (20 L) with chilled, preboiled water. Cool to 68°F (20°C), then pitch:

- **Irish ale yeast (Wyeast 1084 or equivalent)**

Ferment at 65°F (18°C) for 2 weeks, then transfer to secondary fermenter and condition cool (50°F [10°C]) for 3 to 4 weeks. Prime with:

- **1 cup (237 ml) pale dry malt extract**

Bottle and age at 50°F (10°C) for 3 weeks.

Alternate Methods

All-extract: Steep the crystal, brown, and carapils malts as in main recipe in 2½ gallons (9.5 L) water at 150°F (66°C) for 45 minutes. Omit pale malt and DME, but add 6 lb. (2.7 kg) amber malt extract syrup. Follow directions from beginning of boil.

All-grain: Mash 7 lb. (3.2 kg) pale malt and the crystal, brown, and carapils malts as in main recipe in 3 gallons (11 L) water at 152°F (67°C). Sparge with 3¾ gallons (14.2 L) water. Omit first DME and proceed as in main recipe, reducing wort volume to 5¼ gallons (20 L) or less.

Serve at 50°F (10°C) in a traditional pint glass.

Devil's Elbow IPA

Rock Creek Brewing Co., Richmond, Virginia

Bottle conditioned and dry hopped, this IPA is reminiscent of the best bottled English IPAs. It has a wonderful balance of malt and hop bitterness and a lingering hop aroma that is remarkable.

Original gravity: 1070　•　Final gravity: 1014　•　5.8% abv　•　45–50 IBU

Heat 2¼ gallons (8.5 L) water to 164°F (73°C). Crush:

4 lb. (1.8 kg) pale malt
1 lb. (454 g) light (20°L) crystal malt
8 oz. (227 g) biscuit malt
8 oz. (227 g) malted wheat

Add to liquor and steep at 152°F (67°C) for 90 minutes. Sparge with 3 gallons (11 L) water at 168°F (76°C). Add to runnings:

4 lb. (1.8 kg) unhopped, pale dry malt extract (DME)

Bring to a boil, then add:

4 AAUs Fuggles hops

Boil 30 minutes, then add:

4 AAUs Kent Goldings hops

Boil 30 minutes, then add:

4 AAUs Fuggles hops

Boil 30 minutes, then add:

4 AAUs Kent Goldings hops

Remove from heat. Cool, then top up to 5¼ gallons (20 L) with chilled, preboiled water. Cool to 68°F (20°C), then pitch:

Recultured Rock Creek yeast or British ale yeast (Wyeast 1098 or equivalent)

Ferment at 68°F (20°C) for 2 weeks, then transfer to secondary fermenter and add:

3 AAUs Kent Goldings hops

Condition-cool (50–55°F [10–13°C]) for 3 to 4 weeks. Prime with:

1 cup (237 ml) pale dry malt extract

Bottle and age at 55–60°F (13–16°C) for 3 weeks.

 Serve at 50°F (10°C) in a traditional pint glass.

 **Alternate Methods**

All-extract: Steep 1 lb. (454 g) pale malt and the crystal and biscuit malts and the malted wheat as in main recipe in 2½ gallons (9.5 L) water at 150°F (66°C) for 45 minutes. Increase DME to 6 lb. (2.7 kg). Follow directions from beginning of boil.

All-grain: Mash 10 lb. (4.5 kg) pale malt and the crystal and biscuit malts and malted wheat as in main recipe in 3¾ gallons (14.2 L) water at 152°F (67°C). Sparge with 4½ gallons (7.6 L) water. Omit first DME and proceed as in main recipe, reducing wort volume to 5¼ gallons (20 L) or less.

Dominion Lager

Old Dominion Brewing Co., Ashburn, Virginia

This Dortmund-style lager has a rich golden color, a sweet malty aroma, and a maltiness balanced by spritzy hop flavor. It is medium bodied, smooth, and clean with a dry aftertaste.

Original gravity: 1052 • Final gravity: 1010 • 5.4% abv • 25 IBU

Heat 1½ gallons (5.7 L) water to 164°F (73°C). Crush:

2 lb. (907 g) lager malt
10 oz. (.28 kg) Munich malt
8 oz. (227 g) carapils malt
8 oz. (227 g) light (20°L) crystal malt

Add to liquor and steep at 152°F (67°C) for 90 minutes. Sparge with 2¼ gallons (8.5 L) water at 168°F (76°C). Add to runnings:

3½ lb. (1.6 kg) unhopped, extra-light dry malt extract (DME)

Bring to a boil, then add:

2 AAUs Perle hops
2 AAUs Hallertau hops

Boil 45 minutes, then add:

2 AAUs Tettnang hops
2 AAUs Hallertau hops

Boil 15 minutes, then remove from heat. Add:

5 AAUs Saaz hops

Steep 30 minutes, then cool and top up to 5¼ gallons (20 L) with chilled, preboiled water. Cool to 65°F (18°C), then pitch:

Danish lager yeast (Wyeast 2042 or equivalent)

Ferment at 52°F (11°C) for 2 weeks, then transfer to secondary fermenter and condition cold (32–34°F [0–1°C]) for 4 to 6 weeks. Prime with:

¾ cup (177 ml) corn sugar

Bottle and age at 55–60°F (13–16°C) for 6 weeks.

Alternate Methods

All-extract: Steep 4 oz. (113 g) lager malt and the Munich, carapils, and crystal malts as in main recipe in 2½ gallons (9.5 L) water at 150°F (66°C) for 45 minutes. Omit DME and add 6 lb. (2.7 kg) extra-light malt extract syrup. Follow directions from beginning of boil.

All-grain: Mash 7¼ lb. (3.3 kg) lager malt and the Munich, carapils, and crystal malts as in main recipe in 3 gallons (11 L) water at 152°F (67°C). Sparge with 3¾ gallons (14.2 L) water. Omit DME and proceed as in main recipe, reducing wort volume to 5¼ gallons (20 L) or less. (Use a double or triple decoction mash procedure, if you prefer, to increase the malty character.)

 Serve at 40°F (4°C) in a tall Pilsner glass.

Rapahannock Red Ale

Potomac River Brewing Co., Chantilly, Virginia

Try this pale ale with a nice reddish amber glow and a big spicy hop profile.
Aromas range from pepper to cinnamon over a faintly astringent malt bouquet,
and the flavor is on the dry side of caramel and butter.

Original gravity: 1048 • Final gravity: 1010 • 4.8% abv • 40 IBU

Heat 2 gallons (7.6 L) water to 164°F (73°C). Crush:

3½ lb. (1.6 kg) pale malt
1 lb. (454 g) medium (50°L) crystal malt
4 oz. (113 g) black malt
8 oz. (227 g) malted wheat

Add to liquor and steep at 152°F (67°C) for 90 minutes. Sparge with 2¾ gallons (10.2 L) water at 168°F (76°C). Add to runnings:

2 lb. (907 g) unhopped, pale dry malt extract (DME)

Bring to a boil, then add:

4 AAUs Chinook hops

Boil 30 minutes, then add:

4 AAUs Cascade hops

Boil 45 minutes, then add:

4 AAUs Cascade hops

Remove from heat, then steep 15 minutes. Cool, then top up to 5¼ gallons (20 L) with chilled, preboiled water. Cool to 68°F (20°C), then pitch:

British ale yeast (Wyeast 1098 or equivalent)

Ferment at 68°F (20°C) for 2 weeks, then transfer to secondary fermenter and condition cool (50–55°F [10–13°C]) for 3 to 4 weeks. Prime with:

1 cup (237 ml) pale dry malt extract

Bottle and age at 55–60°F (13–16°C) for 3 weeks.

Alternate Methods

All-extract: Steep 8 oz. (227 g) pale malt and the crystal and black malts and malted wheat as in main recipe in 2½ gallons (9.5 L) water at 150°F (66°C) for 45 minutes. Increase DME to 4 lb. (1.8 kg). Follow directions from beginning of boil.

All-grain: Mash 6½ lb. (3 kg) pale malt and the crystal and black malts and the malted wheat as in main recipe in 3 gallons (11 L) water at 152°F (67°C). Sparge with 3¾ gallons (14.2 L) water. Omit first DME and proceed as in main recipe, reducing wort volume to 5¼ gallons (20 L) or less.

 Serve at 50°F (10°C) in a traditional pint glass.

River City ESB

Rock Creek Brewing Co., Richmond, Virginia

A traditional English-style extra special bitter, River City has a very English hop and malt blend in the bouquet. It is bottle conditioned, making it soft and full feeling in the mouth. Sweet notes are balanced by a bitter and nutty aftertaste.

Original gravity: 1050 • Final gravity: 1012 • 5.0% abv • 35 IBU

Heat 1¾ gallons (6.6 L) water to 164°F (73°C). Crush:

2 lb. (907 g) pale malt
8 oz. (227 g) light (20°L) crystal malt
12 oz. (340 g) medium (50°L) crystal malt
8 oz. (227 g) toasted pale malt (toast at 350°F [177°C] for 15 minutes)
4 oz. (113 g) black malt
8 oz. (227 g) malted wheat

Add to liquor and steep at 152°F (67°C) for 90 minutes. Sparge with 2½ gallons (9.5 L) water at 168°F (76°C). Add to runnings:

2¾ lb. (1.3 kg) unhopped, pale dry malt extract (DME)

Bring to a boil, then add:

5 AAUs Fuggles hops

Boil 60 minutes, then add:

5 AAUs Fuggles hops

Boil 30 minutes, then remove from heat. Add:

4 AAUs Goldings hops

Steep 30 minutes. Cool, then top up to 5¼ gallons (20 L) with chilled, preboiled water. Cool to 68°F (20°C), then pitch:

English or London ale yeast (Wyeast 1098, 1028, or equivalent)

Ferment at 68°F (20°C) for 2 weeks, then transfer to secondary fermenter and condition cool (50–55°F [10–13°C]) for 3 to 4 weeks. Prime with:

1 cup (237 ml) pale dry malt extract

Bottle and age at 50°F (10°C) for 3 weeks.

 Serve at 50°F (10°C) in a traditional pint glass.

 **Alternate Methods**

All-extract: Steep the crystal, toasted, and black malts and the malted wheat as in main recipe in 2½ gallons (9.5 L) water at 150°F (66°C) for 45 minutes. Omit pale malt and increase DME to 4 lb. (1.8 kg). Follow directions from beginning of boil.

All-grain: Mash 6 lb. (2.7 kg) pale malt and the crystal, toasted, and black malts and malted wheat as in main recipe in 3 gallons (11 L) water at 152°F (67°C). Sparge with 3¾ gallons (14.2 L) water. Omit first DME and proceed as in main recipe, reducing wort volume to 5¼ gallons (20 L) or less.

Stony Man Stout

Shenandoah Brewing Co., Alexandria, Virginia

This is a dry stout emphasizing dark malts and roasted barley with little interference from hops, except in the aftertaste. The taste and aroma of burnt sugar and the slight grainy sourness of black malt work well together in the main flavor of Stony Man.

Original gravity: 1050 • **Final gravity: 1015** • **4.5% abv** • **30 IBU**

Heat 2 gallons (7.6 L) water to 164°F (73°C). Crush:

4 lb. (1.8 kg) pale malt
8 oz. (227 g) dark (120°L) crystal malt
8 oz. (227 g) roasted barley
4 oz. (113 g) black malt
4 oz. (113 g) chocolate malt

Add to liquor and steep at 152°F (67°C) for 90 minutes. Sparge with 3 gallons (11 L) water at 168°F (76°C). Add to runnings:

2 lb. (907 g) unhopped, pale dry malt extract (DME)

Bring to a boil, then add:

7 AAUs Northern Brewer hops

Boil 45 minutes, then add:

4 AAUs Willamette hops

Boil 15 minutes, then remove from heat. Cool, then top up to 5¼ gallons (20 L) with chilled, preboiled water. Cool to 68°F (20°C), then pitch:

Irish ale yeast (Wyeast 1084 or equivalent)

Ferment at 68°F (20°C) for 2 weeks, then transfer to secondary fermenter and condition cool (50–55°F [10–13°C]) for 3 to 4 weeks. Prime with:

1 cup (237 ml) pale dry malt extract

Bottle and age at 50°F (10°C) for 3 weeks.

Alternate Methods

All-extract: Steep the crystal malt, roasted barley, and black and chocolate malts as in main recipe in 2½ gallons (9.5 L) water at 150°F (66°C) for 45 minutes. Omit pale malt and increase DME to 4 lb. (1.8 kg). Follow directions from beginning of boil.

All-grain: Mash 7 lb. (3.2 kg) pale malt and the crystal malt, roasted barley, and black and chocolate malts as in main recipe in 3 gallons (11 L) water at 152°F (67°C). Sparge with 3¾ gallons (14.2 L) water. Omit first DME and proceed as in main recipe, reducing wort volume to 5¼ gallons (20 L) or less.

Serve at 50°F (10°C) in a traditional pint glass.

Tupper's Hop Pocket Ale

Tupper's Hop Pocket Brewing Co.
(brewed by Old Dominion Brewing Co., Ashburn, Virginia)

A harvest ale, somewhere between an IPA and an Oktoberfest, this krausened and bottle-conditioned ale is rich in malt flavor and hop aroma and bitterness. It has a malty and butterscotch nose, along with the obvious Cascade hops. A portion of the proceeds from this beer goes to help the homeless.

Original gravity: 1055 • Final gravity: 1010 • 5.7% abv • 55 IBU

Heat 1½ gallons (5.7 L) water to 164°F (73°C). Crush:

2 lb. (907 g) pale malt
1 lb. (454 g) light (20°L) crystal malt
8 oz. (227 g) malted wheat

Add to liquor and steep at 152°F (67°C) for 90 minutes. Sparge with 2¼ gallons (8.5 L) water at 168°F (76°C). Add to runnings:

4 lb. (1.8 kg) unhopped, pale dry malt extract (DME)

Bring to a boil, then add:

6 AAUs Mt. Hood hops

Boil 30 minutes, then add:

3 AAUs Mt. Hood hops
3 AAUs Cascade hops

Boil 60 minutes, then remove from heat. Cool, then top up to 5¼ gallons (20 L) with chilled, preboiled water. Cool to 68°F (20°C), then pitch:

American ale yeast (recultured Tupper's, Wyeast 1056, or equivalent)

Ferment at 68°F (20°C) for 2 weeks, then transfer to secondary fermenter and add:

6 AAUs Cascade hops

Condition-cool (50–55°F [10–13°C]) for 3 to 4 weeks. Prime with:

1 cup (237 ml) pale dry malt extract

Bottle and age at 50°F (10°C) for 3 weeks.

Alternate Methods

All-extract: Steep the crystal malt and malted wheat as in main recipe in 2½ gallons (9.5 L) water at 150°F (66°C) for 45 minutes. Omit pale malt and increase DME to 5½ lb. (2½ kg). Follow directions from beginning of boil.

All-grain: Mash 8 lb. (3.6 kg) pale malt and the crystal malt and malted wheat as in main recipe in 3 gallons (11 L) water at 152°F (67°C). Sparge with 3¾ gallons (14.2 L) water. Omit first DME and proceed as in main recipe, reducing wort volume to 5¼ gallons (20 L) or less.

 Serve at 50°F (10°C) in a traditional pint glass.

Bert Grant's Hefeweizen

Yakima Brewing and Malting Co., Yakima, Washington

This unfiltered wheat ale is full of spritzy, citrusy, yeasty flavor. It's a very enjoyable and refreshing German-style weizenbier: thirst quenching and satisfying.

Original gravity: 1045 • Final gravity: 1012 • 4.2% abv • 20 IBU

Heat 1½ gallons (5.7 L) water to 164°F (73°C). Crush:

- **2 lb. (907 g) malted wheat**
- **8 oz. (227 g) light (30°L) crystal malt**
- **8 oz. (227 g) carapils malt**
- **1 lb. (454 g) light Pilsner malt**

Add to liquor and steep at 152°F (67°C) for 90 minutes. Sparge with 2½ gallons (9.5 L) water at 168°F (76°C). Add to runnings:

- **2½ lb. (1.1 kg) unhopped, wheat dry malt extract (DME)**

Bring to a boil, then add:

- **4 AAUs Hallertau hops**

Boil 45 minutes, then add:

- **4 AAUs Hallertau hops**

Boil 15 minutes, then remove from heat. Cool, then top up to 5¼ gallons (20 L) with chilled, preboiled water. Cool to 68°F (20°C), then pitch:

- **Recultured yeast from a bottle of Bert Grant's Hefeweizen**
  or
- **German wheat beer yeast (Wyeast 3333 or equivalent)**

Ferment at 68°F (20°C) for 2 weeks, then transfer to secondary fermenter and condition cool (50–55°F [10–13°C]) for 3 to 4 weeks. Prime with:

- **¾ cup (177 ml) corn sugar**

Bottle and age at 55–60°F (13–16°C) for 3 weeks.

Alternate Methods

All-extract: Steep 1 lb. (454 g) malted wheat and the crystal and carapils malts as in main recipe in 2½ gallons (9.5 L) water at 150°F (66°C) for 45 minutes. Omit Pilsner malt and increase DME to 4 lb. (1.8 kg). Follow directions from beginning of boil.

All-grain: Mash 3½ lb. (1.6 kg) malted wheat, 3¼ lb. (1.5 kg) Pilsner malt, and the carapils and crystal malts as in main recipe in 3 gallons (11 L) water at 152°F (67°C). Sparge with 3½ gallons (13.2 L) water. Omit DME and proceed as in main recipe, reducing wort volume to 5¼ gallons (20 L) or less.

Serve at 40–45°F (4–7°F) in a traditional, tall weizen glass.

Old Bawdy 1998

Pike Brewery, Seattle, Washington

*A traditional barleywine, vintage dated and worth saving for a couple of years,
Old Bawdy is big, rich, smoky, and warming.*

Original gravity: 1095 • Final gravity: 1015 • 10.2% abv • 85–90 IBU

Heat 3¾ gallons (14.2 L) water to 164°F (73°C). Crush:

7 lb. (3.2 kg) pale malt (Maris Otter 2-row)
1¼ lb. (567 g) dark (120°L) crystal malt
2 lb. (907 g) peat-smoked malt

Add to liquor and steep at 152°F (67°C) for 90 minutes. Sparge with
4½ gallons (17 L) water at 168°F (76°C). Add to runnings:

4 lb. (1.8 kg) unhopped, amber dry malt extract (DME)

Bring to a boil, then add:

8 AAUs Magnum hops

Boil 30 minutes, then add:

8 AAUs Chinook hops

Boil 30 minutes, then add:

6 AAUs Cascade hops

Boil 25 minutes, then add:

4 AAUs Cascade hops

Boil 5 minutes, then remove from heat. Cool, then top up to 5¼ gallons
(20 L) with chilled, preboiled water. Cool to 68°F (20°C), then pitch:

English ale yeast (Wyeast 1098 or equivalent)
½ oz. (14 g) dry champagne yeast

Ferment at 65°F (18°C) for 3 weeks, then transfer to secondary fermenter
and condition cool (50–55°F [10–13°C]) for 8 weeks. Prime with:

¾ cup (177 ml) pale dry malt extract

Bottle and age at 55–60°F (13–16°C) for 3 weeks.

Alternate Methods

All-extract: Steep 1 lb.
(454 g) pale malt and the
crystal and peat-smoked
malts as in main recipe in
2½ gallons (9.5 L) water at
150°F (66°C) for 45 min-
utes. Increase DME to 8 lb.
(3.6 kg). Follow directions
from beginning of boil.

All-grain: Mash 13 lb.
(5.9 kg) pale malt and the
crystal and peat-smoked
malts as in main recipe in
4½ gallons (17 L) water at
152°F (67°C). Sparge with
3¾ gallons (14.2 L) water.
Omit first DME and pro-
ceed as in main recipe,
reducing wort volume to
5¼ gallons (20 L) or less.

 Serve at 50°F (10°C) in a brandy snifter.

Pike India Pale Ale

Pike Brewing Co., Seattle, Washington

The IPA by Pike Brewing is considered by many to be the best example of the American or West Coast IPA. Pike uses a combination of five malts and three different hops to achieve a full-bodied, malty beer with a complex hop flavor and aroma that come across as floral, herbal, spicy, and fruity. I swear I've detected basil, pear, pineapple, mint, and other aromas in there.

Original gravity: 1062 • Final gravity: 1014 • 6.3% abv • 64 IBU

Heat 2 gallons (7.6 L) water to 164°F (73°C). Crush:

- **2 lb. (907 g) pale malt**
- **1 lb. (454 g) amber malt**
- **8 oz. (227 g) Munich malt**
- **8 oz. (227 g) carapils malt**
- **1 lb. (454 g) medium (50°L) crystal malt**

Add to liquor and steep at 152°F (67°C) for 90 minutes. Sparge with 3 gallons (11 L) water at 168°F (76°C). Add to runnings:

- **4 lb. (1.8 kg) unhopped, pale dry malt extract (DME)**

Bring to a boil, then add:

- **6 AAUs Magnum hops**

Boil 30 minutes, then add:

- **6 AAUs Chinook hops**

Boil 30 minutes, then add:

- **4 AAUs Chinook hops**

Boil 30 minutes, then add:

- **3 AAUs Goldings hops**

Remove from heat, then steep 15 minutes. Top up to 5¼ gallons (20 L) with chilled, preboiled water. Cool to 68°F (20°C), then pitch:

- **American ale yeast (Wyeast 1056 or equivalent)**

Ferment at 68°F (20°C) for 2 weeks, then transfer to secondary fermenter and add:

- **3 AAUs Goldings hops**

Condition-cool (50–55°F [10–13°C]) for 3 to 4 weeks. Prime with:

- **1 cup (237 ml) pale dry malt extract**

Bottle and age at 55–60°F (13–16°C) for 3 weeks.

 Serve at 50°F (10°C) in a traditional pint glass.

Alternate Methods

All-extract: Steep the amber, Munich, carapils, and crystal malts as in main recipe in 2½ gallons (9.5 L) water at 150°F (66°C) for 45 minutes. Omit pale malt and increase DME to 5½ lb. (2½ kg). Follow directions from beginning of boil.

All-grain: Mash 8 lb. (3.6 kg) pale malt and the amber, Munich, carapils, and crystal malts as in main recipe in 3½ gallons (13.2 L) water at 152°F (67°C). Sparge with 4 gallons (15.1 L) water. Omit first DME and proceed as in main recipe, reducing wort volume to 5¼ gallons (20 L) or less.

Weizen-berry

Thomas Kemper Brewing Co., Seattle, Washington
This unique wheat lager has a subtle, crisp, raspberry flavor. It is hazy and golden colored with lots of fruit in both the nose and flavor. The raspberry doesn't overwhelm the wheat beer underneath, however, and there is a nice bready, malty character to this light, refreshing brew.

Original gravity: 1045 • Final gravity: 1012 • 4.2% abv • 20 IBU

Heat 1¾ gallons (6.6 L) water to 164°F (73°C). Crush:

2 lb. (907 g) lager malt
1½ lb. (680 g) malted wheat
8 oz. (227 g) carapils malt
4 oz. (113 g) light (20°L) crystal malt

Add to liquor and steep at 152°F (67°C) for 90 minutes. Sparge with 2½ gallons (9.5 L) water at 168°F (76°C). Add to runnings:

2½ lb. (1.1 kg) unhopped, wheat dry malt extract (DME)

Bring to a boil, then add:

4 AAUs Hallertau hops

Boil 45 minutes, then add:

4 AAUs Hallertau hops

Boil 15 minutes, then remove from heat. Cool, then top up to 5¼ gallons (20 L) with chilled, preboiled water. Cool to 62°F (17°C), then pitch a blend of:

German wheat yeast (Wyeast 3333 or equivalent)
and
Munich lager yeast (Wyeast 2308 or equivalent)

Ferment at 58°F (15°C) for 2 weeks, then transfer to secondary fermenter onto:

4 lb. (1.8 kg) crushed fresh raspberries

Condition cold (45–50°F [7–10°C]) for 3 to 4 weeks. Rerack to a clean carboy for 2 weeks to clarify. Prime with:

1 cup (237 ml) pale dry malt extract

Bottle and age at 50°F (10°C) for 3 weeks.

 Serve at 50°F (10°C) in a traditional, tall weizen glass.

 **Alternate Methods**

All-extract: Steep 1 lb. (454 g) lager malt, 1 lb. (454 g) malted wheat, and the carapils and crystal malts as in main recipe in 2½ gallons (9.5 L) water at 150°F (66°C) for 45 minutes. Increase DME to 3½ lb. (1.6 kg). Follow directions from beginning of boil.

All-grain: Mash 4 lb. (1.8 kg) lager malt, 3 lb. (1.4 kg) malted wheat, and the carapils and crystal malts as in main recipe in 3 gallons (11 L) water at 152°F (67°C). Sparge with 3¾ gallons (14.2 L) water. Omit first DME and proceed as in main recipe, reducing wort volume to 5¼ gallons (20 L) or less.

Ballantine XXX Ale

Falstaff Brewing Co., Milwaukee, Wisconsin

This is "America's largest-selling ale" and a legend from the golden age of American brewing. Reportedly, it's not like it used to be (what is?), but it is still a pleasantly refreshing, spicy, hoppy ale, nicely balanced and finishing dry and clean.

Original gravity: 1045 • Final gravity: 1010 • 4.5% abv • 44 IBU

Heat 1½ gallons (5.7 L) water to 164°F (73°C). Crush:

3 lb. (1.4 kg) pale malt
12 oz. (340 g) medium (50°L) crystal malt

Add to liquor and steep at 152°F (67°C) for 90 minutes. Sparge with 2 gallons (7.6 L) water at 168°F (76°C). Add to runnings:

3⅓ lb. (1.5 kg) unhopped, light malt extract syrup

Bring to a boil, then add:

3 AAUs Cascade hops
4 AAUs Nugget hops

Boil 60 minutes, then add:

5 AAUs Cascade hops

Boil 30 minutes, then remove from heat. Cool, then top up to 5¼ gallons (20 L) with chilled, preboiled water. Cool to 68°F (20°C), then pitch:

American ale yeast (Wyeast 1056 or equivalent)

Ferment at 68°F (20°C) for 2 weeks, then transfer to secondary fermenter and add:

3 AAUs Cascade hops

Condition-cool (50–55°F [10–13°C]) for 3 to 4 weeks. Prime with:

1 cup (237 ml) pale dry malt extract (DME)

Bottle and age at 50°F (10°C) for 3 weeks.

Alternate Methods

All-extract: Steep the crystal malt as in main recipe in 2½ gallons (9.5 L) water at 150°F (66°C) for 45 minutes. Omit pale malt and increase malt extract syrup to 6 lb. (2.7 kg). Follow directions from beginning of boil.

All-grain: Mash 7 lb. (3.2 kg) pale malt and the crystal malt as in main recipe in 2½ gallons (9.5 L) water at 152°F (67°C). Sparge with 3 gallons (11 L) water. Omit malt extract syrup and proceed as in main recipe, reducing wort volume to 5¼ gallons (20 L) or less.

Serve at 50°F (10°C) in a traditional pint glass.

Berghoff Dark

Joseph Huber Brewing Co., Monroe, Wisconsin

This dark lager is more or less in the Munich dunkel or continental dark style, although it's a bit closer to amber than to dark brown or black. Nevertheless, it is a satisfyingly crisp and light-bodied beer with a pleasant hop bite in the background.

Original gravity: 1045 • **Final gravity: 1012** • **4.2% abv** • **28–30 IBU**

Heat 1¾ gallons water to 164°F (73°C). Crush:

3 lb. (1.4 kg) lager malt
1 lb. (454 g) dark (20°L) Munich malt
4 oz. (113 g) black malt
8 oz. (227 g) carapils malt

Add to liquor and steep at 152°F (67°C) for 90 minutes. Sparge with 2½ gallons (9.5 L) water at 168°F (76°C). Add to runnings:

2 lb. (907 g) unhopped, amber dry malt extract (DME)

Bring to a boil, then add:

6 AAUs Tettnang hops

Boil 45 minutes, then add:

3 AAUs Tettnang hops

Boil 15 minutes, then remove from heat. Cool, then top up to 5¼ gallons (20 L) with chilled, preboiled water. Cool to 65°F (18°C), then pitch:

Munich lager yeast (Wyeast 2308 or equivalent)

Ferment at 45°F (7°C) for 2 weeks, then transfer to secondary fermenter and condition cold (40°F [4°C]) for 5 to 6 weeks. Prime with:

1 cup (237 ml) pale dry malt extract

Bottle and age at 45°F (7°C) for 6 weeks.

Alternate Methods

All-extract: Steep the Munich, black, and carapils malts as in main recipe in 2½ gallons (9.5 L) water at 150°F (66°C) for 45 minutes. Omit lager malt and increase DME to 4 lb. (1.8 kg). Follow directions from beginning of boil.

All-grain: Mash 6 lb. (2.7 kg) lager malt and the Munich, black, and carapils malts as in main recipe in 3 gallons (11 L) water at 152°F (67°C). Sparge with 3¾ gallons (14.2 L) water. Omit first DME and proceed as in main recipe, reducing wort volume to 5¼ gallons (20 L) or less.

Serve at 40°F (4°C) in a tall Pilsner-style glass.

Black Bavarian-Style Lager

Sprecher Brewing, Milwaukee, Wisconsin

This is a dark, Kulmbacher-style lager that's light and refreshing despite its rich black color and roasty, malty nose. Notes of burnt sugar, raisins, chocolate, and caramel blend with the hints of bitterness from both hops and roasted grains in a smooth, clean finish.

Original gravity: 1055 • Final gravity: 1010 • 5.7% abv • 30 IBU

Heat 1¾ gallons (6.6 L) water to 164°F (73°C). Crush:

2 lb. (907 g) lager malt
8 oz. (227 g) chocolate malt
8 oz. (227 g) black malt
8 oz. (227 g) Munich malt
1 lb. (454 g) dark (120°L) crystal malt

Add to liquor and steep at 152°F (67°C) for 90 minutes. Sparge with 2½ gallons (9.5 L) water at 168°F (76°C). Add to runnings:

3½ lb. (1.6 kg) unhopped, amber dry malt extract (DME)

Bring to a boil, then add:

4 AAUs Hallertau hops

Boil 30 minutes, then add:

6 AAUs Tettnang hops

Boil 30 minutes, then remove from heat. Cool, then top up to 5¼ gallons (20 L) with chilled, preboiled water. Cool to below 60°F (16°C), then pitch:

Bavarian lager yeast (Wyeast 2206 or equivalent)

Ferment at 48°F (9°C) for 2 weeks, then transfer to secondary fermenter and condition cold (35°F [2°C]) for 5 to 6 weeks. Prime with:

1 cup (237 ml) pale dry malt extract

Bottle and age at 45–50°F (7–10°C) for 8 weeks.

Alternate Methods

All-extract: Steep the chocolate, black, Munich, and crystal malts as in main recipe in 2½ gallons (9.5 L) water at 150°F (66°C) for 45 minutes. Omit lager malt and increase DME to 4¾ lb. (2.2 kg). Follow directions from beginning of boil.

All-grain: Mash 7 lb. (3.2 kg) lager malt and the chocolate, black, Munich, and crystal malts in 3 gallons (11 L) water at 152°F (67°C). Sparge with 3¾ gallons (14.2 L) water. Omit first DME and proceed as in main recipe, reducing wort volume to 5¼ gallons (20 L) or less.

 Serve at 50°F (10°C) in a tall, footed Pilsner glass.

Capital Summerfest

Capital Brewing, Middleton, Wisconsin; Stevens Point, Wisconsin
*A deep copper lager with reddish hues, this is more like a California Common beer
than a Märzen or a Festbier. It's relatively light in body and has a dry, clean aftertaste.*

Original gravity: 1052 • Final gravity: 1012 • 5.1% abv • 40 IBU

Heat 1¼ gallons (4.7 L) water to 164°F (73°C). Crush:

1 lb. (454 g) lager malt
1 lb. (454 g) Munich malt
1 lb. (454 g) carapils malt
8 oz. (227 g) malted wheat

Add to liquor and steep at 152°F (67°C) for 90 minutes. Sparge with
2 gallons (7.6 L) water at 168°F (76°C). Add to runnings:

4 lb. (1.8 kg) unhopped, amber dry malt extract (DME)

Bring to a boil, then add:

6 AAUs Saaz hops

Boil 60 minutes, then add:

4 AAUs Spalt hops
4 AAUs Hallertau hops

Boil 30 minutes, then remove from heat. Cool, then top up to 5¼ gallons
(20 L) with chilled, preboiled water. Cool to 60°F (16°C), then pitch:

**California lager ("steam") yeast (Wyeast 2112 or
equivalent)**

Ferment at 60°F (16°C) for 2 weeks, then transfer to secondary fermenter
and condition cool (50°F [10°C]) for 3 to 4 weeks. Prime with:

1 cup (237 ml) pale dry malt extract

Bottle and age at 50°F (10°C) for 4 weeks.

Alternate Methods

All-extract: Steep 8 oz.
(227 g) Munich malt, 8 oz.
(227 g) carapils malt, and
the malted wheat as in
main recipe in 2½ gallons
(9.5 L) water at 150°F
(66°C) for 45 minutes.
Omit lager malt and
increase DME to 5½ lb.
(2½ kg). Follow directions
from beginning of boil.

All-grain: Mash 6 lb.
(2.7 kg) lager malt and
2 lb. (907 g) Munich malt
and the carapils malt and
malted wheat as in main
recipe in 3 gallons (11 L)
water at 152°F (67°C).
Sparge with 3¾ gallons
(14.2 L) water. Omit first
DME and proceed as in
main recipe, reducing wort
volume to 5¼ gallons
(20 L) or less.

Serve at 50°F (10°C) in a traditional pint or Pilsner glass.

Dempsey's Extra Stout

Joseph Huber Brewing Co., Monroe, Wisconsin

Dempsey's is a smoky, roasty, semisweet black stout that's dry, bitter, thirst quenching, and delicious. This stout is very complex, with echoes of bread and crackers under the bitterness of the dark grains and the fresh hop aroma.

Original gravity: 1050 • Final gravity: 1012 • 4.8% abv • 38–40 IBU

Heat 2¼ gallons (8.5 L) water to 164°F (73°C). Crush:

3½ lb. (1.6 kg) pale malt
8 oz. (227 g) dark (20°L) crystal malt
1 lb. (454 g) roasted barley
8 oz. (227 g) Munich malt

Add to liquor and steep at 152°F (67°C) for 90 minutes. Sparge with 3 gallons (11 L) water at 168°F (76°C). Add to runnings:

2 lb. (907 g) unhopped, amber dry malt extract (DME)

Bring to a boil, then add:

6 AAUs Cluster hops

Boil 30 minutes, then add:

4 AAUs Willamette hops

Boil 60 minutes, then remove from heat. Cool, then top up to 5¼ gallons (20 L) with chilled, preboiled water. Cool to 68°F (20°C), then pitch:

Irish ale yeast (Wyeast 1084 or equivalent)

Ferment at 65°F (18°C) for 2 weeks, then transfer to secondary fermenter and condition cool (50–55°F [10–13°C]) for 3 to 4 weeks. Prime with:

1 cup (237 ml) pale dry malt extract

Bottle and age at 55–60°F (13–16°C) for 3 weeks.

Alternate Methods

All-extract: Steep 8 oz. (227 g) pale malt and the crystal malt, roasted barley, and Munich malt as in main recipe in 2½ gallons (9.5 L) water at 150°F (66°C) for 45 minutes. Increase DME to 4 lb. (1.8 kg). Follow directions from beginning of boil.

All-grain: Mash 6½ lb. (3 kg) pale malt and the crystal malt, roasted barley, and Munich malt as in main recipe in 3 gallons (11 L) water at 152°F (67°C). Sparge with 3¾ gallons (14.2 L) water. Omit first DME and proceed as in main recipe, reducing wort volume to 5¼ gallons (20 L) or less.

 Serve at 50°F (10°C) in a traditional pint glass.

Gray's Imperial Stout

Gray's Brewing Co., Janesville, Wisconsin

This is a big, rich, seasonal stout, warming and alcoholic, perfect for cold winter nights in Wisconsin (or elsewhere). Black and opaque, with both bitter and sweet flavors, it has lots of roasted barley aroma, a silky smooth finish, and a dry and bitter aftertaste.

Original gravity: 1070 • **Final gravity: 1020** • **6.4% abv** • **40 IBU**

Heat 2¼ gallons (8.5 L) water to 164°F (73°C). Crush:
- **3 lb. (1.4 kg) pale malt**
- **1 lb. (454 g) Munich malt**
- **8 oz. (227 g) black malt**
- **1 lb. (454 g) dark (120°L) crystal malt**
- **8 oz. (227 g) roasted barley**

Add to liquor and steep at 152°F (67°C) for 90 minutes. Sparge with 3 gallons (11 L) water at 168°F (76°C). Add to runnings:
- **4 lb. (1.8 kg) unhopped, dark dry malt extract (DME)**

Bring to a boil, then add:
- **4 AAUs Willamette hops**
- **4 AAUs Tettnang hops**

Boil 85 minutes, then add:
- **6 AAUs Willamette hops**

Boil 5 minutes, then remove from heat. Cool, then top up to 5¼ gallons (20 L) with chilled, preboiled water. Cool to 68°F (20°C), then pitch:
- **English ale yeast (Wyeast 1098 or equivalent)**

Ferment at 68°F (20°C) for 2 weeks, then transfer to secondary fermenter and condition cool (50–55°F [10–13°C]) for 5 to 6 weeks. Prime with:
- **1 cup (237 ml) pale dry malt extract**

Bottle and age at 55–60°F (13–16°C) for 6 weeks.

Alternate Methods

All-extract: Steep 8 oz. (227 g) pale malt and the Munich, black, and crystal malts and roasted barley as in main recipe in 2½ gallons (9.5 L) water at 150°F (66°C) for 45 minutes. Increase DME to 6 lb. (2.7 kg). Follow directions from beginning of boil.

All-grain: Mash 9 lb. (4.1 kg) pale malt and the Munich, black, and crystal malts and roasted barley as in main recipe in 3¾ gallons (14.2 L) water at 152°F (67°C). Sparge with 4½ gallons (17 L) water. Omit first DME and proceed as in main recipe, reducing wort volume to 5¼ gallons (20 L) or less.

Serve at 50°F (10°C) in a traditional pint glass.

Gray's Oatmeal Stout

Gray's Brewing Co., Janesville, Wisconsin

A dark, robust stout — smooth and creamy because of the oats, roasty and bitter because of roasted barley. This brew has a pleasant burnt sugar smokiness and hints of coffee, chocolate, and toasted oatmeal bread.

Original gravity: 1045 • Final gravity: 1010 • 4.5% abv • 30 IBU

Heat 1½ gallons (5.7 L) water to 164°F (73°C). Crush:

2 lb. (907 g) pale malt
1 lb. (454 g) flaked oats
8 oz. (227 g) roasted barley
8 oz. (227 g) dark (120°L) crystal malt

Add to liquor and steep at 152°F (67°C) for 90 minutes. Sparge with 2¼ gallons (8.5 L) water at 168°F (76°C). Add to runnings:

2½ lb. (1.1 kg) unhopped, dark dry malt extract (DME)

Bring to a boil, then add:

6 AAUs Goldings hops

Boil 30 minutes, then add:

3 AAUs Northern Brewer hops

Boil 30 minutes, then remove from heat. Cool, then top up to 5¼ gallons (20 L) with chilled, preboiled water. Cool to 68°F (20°C), then pitch:

English or Irish ale yeast (Wyeast 1098, 1084, or equivalent)

Ferment at 68°F (20°C) for 2 weeks, then transfer to secondary fermenter and condition cool (50°F [10°C]) for 3 to 4 weeks. Prime with:

1 cup (237 ml) pale dry malt extract

Bottle and age at 50°F (10°C) for 3 weeks.

Alternate Methods

All-extract: Steep the oats, roasted barley, and crystal malt as in main recipe in 2½ gallons (9.5 L) water at 150°F (66°C) for 45 minutes. Omit pale malt and increase DME to 4 lb. (1.8 kg). Follow directions from beginning of boil.

All-grain: Mash 5¾ lb. (2.6 kg) pale malt and the oats, roasted barley, and crystal malt as in main recipe in 2½ gallons (9.5 L) water at 152°F (67°C). Sparge with 3¼ gallons (12.3 L) water. Omit first DME and proceed as in main recipe, reducing wort volume to 5¼ gallons (20 L) or less.

Serve at 50°F (10°C) in a traditional pint glass.

Hearty Hop Ale

New Glarus Brewing Co., New Glarus, Wisconsin

Big and hoppy, this IPA-style ale comes from a brewery perhaps better known for Belgian-style fruit beers. Dry hopped in the secondary fermenter, this beer is full of caramel, grapefruit, cracker, and herb flavors; it's nicely balanced and clean.

Original gravity: 1060　•　Final gravity: 1015　•　5.7% abv　•　60–65 IBU

Heat 1½ gallons (5.7 L) water to 164°F (73°C). Crush:

3 lb. (1.4 kg) pale malt
1¼ lb. (567 g) medium (50°L) crystal malt

Add to liquor and steep at 152°F (67°C) for 90 minutes. Sparge with 2¼ gallons (8.5 L) water at 168°F (76°C). Add to runnings:

4 lb. (1.8 kg) unhopped, pale dry malt extract (DME)

Bring to a boil, then add:

6 AAUs Cascade hops
4 AAUs Goldings hops

Boil 60 minutes, then add:

4 AAUs Cascade hops

Boil 30 minutes, then remove from heat. Cool, then top up to 5¼ gallons (20 L) with chilled, preboiled water. Cool to 68°F (20°C), then pitch:

English ale yeast (Wyeast 1098 or equivalent)

Ferment at 68°F (20°C) for 2 weeks, then transfer to secondary fermenter and add:

4 AAUs Cascade hops
4 AAUs Goldings hops

Condition-cool (50–55°F [10–13°C]) for 3 to 4 weeks. Prime with:

1 cup (237 ml) pale dry malt extract

Bottle and age at 55–60°F (13–16°C) for 3 weeks.

Alternate Methods

All-extract: Steep 1 lb. (454 g) pale malt and the crystal malt as in main recipe in 2½ gallons (9.5 L) water at 150°F (66°C) for 45 minutes. Increase DME to 5½ lb. (2.5 kg). Follow directions from beginning of boil.

All-grain: Mash 9 lb. (4.1 kg) pale malt and the crystal malt as in main recipe in 3 gallons (11 L) water at 152°F (67°C). Sparge with 3¾ gallons (14.2 L) water. Omit first DME and proceed as in main recipe, reducing wort volume to 5¼ gallons (20 L) or less.

 Serve at 50°F (10°C) in a traditional pint glass.

Point Amber

Stevens Point Brewery, Stevens Point, Wisconsin

*A rich lager that is somewhere between a Märzenbier and a Vienna in style,
Point Amber is full flavored and nicely balanced. It has a decent
hop character and a real malty sweetness.*

Original gravity: 1048 • Final gravity: 1014 • 4.3% abv • 25 IBU

Heat 2 gallons (7.6 L) water to 164°F (73°C). Crush:
- **4 lb. (1.8 kg) lager malt**
- **1 lb. (454 g) Vienna malt**
- **4 oz. (113 g) medium (50°L) crystal malt**

Add to liquor and steep at 152°F (67°C) for 90 minutes. Sparge with
3 gallons (11 L) water at 168°F (76°C). Add to runnings:
- **2 lb. (907 g) unhopped, pale dry malt extract (DME)**

Bring to a boil, then add:
- **4 AAUs Perle hops**

Boil 30 minutes, then add:
- **4 AAUs Mt. Hood hops**

Boil 20 minutes, then add:
- **4 AAUs Hallertau hops**

Boil 10 minutes, then remove from heat. Cool, then top up to 5¼ gallons
(20 L) with chilled, preboiled water. Cool to 68°F (20°C), then pitch:
- **Munich or Bavarian lager yeast (Wyeast 2038, 2206, or
  equivalent)**

Ferment at 58°F (15°C) for 2 weeks, then transfer to secondary fermenter
and condition cold (40°F [4°C]) for 5 to 6 weeks. Prime with:
- **1 cup (237 ml) pale dry malt extract**

Bottle and age at 35–40°F (2–4°C) for 8 weeks.

Alternate Methods

All-extract: Steep 1 lb.
(454 g) toasted lager malt
(toast at 350°F [177°C] for
30 minutes) and the Vienna
and crystal malts as in
main recipe in 2½ gallons
(9.5 L) water at 150°F
(66°C) for 45 minutes.
Increase DME to 4 lb.
(1.8 kg). Follow directions
from beginning of boil.

All-grain: Mash 7 lb.
(3.2 kg) lager malt and
the Vienna and crystal
malts as in main recipe in
3 gallons (11 L) water at
152°F (67°C). Sparge with
3¾ gallons (14.2 L) water.
Omit first DME and pro-
ceed as in main recipe,
reducing wort volume to
5¼ gallons (20 L) or less.

Serve at 40°F (4°C) in a glass or ceramic stein.

Wisconsin Belgian Red

New Glarus Brewing Co., New Glarus, Wisconsin
This is a huge, Belgian-style wheat ale with cherries. Not a lambic, it is instead a sweet, fruity beer with hints of tartness, spiciness, and an overwhelming cherry aroma and flavor. Even the head is reddish pink.

Original gravity: 1065 • Final gravity: 1020 • 5.7% abv • 25–30 IBU

Heat 2¼ gallons (8.5 L) water to 164°F (73°C). Crush:
- **3 lb. (1.4 kg) pale malt**
- **2 lb. (907 g) malted wheat**
- **1 lb. (454 g) medium (50°L) crystal malt**

Add to liquor and steep at 152°F (67°C) for 90 minutes. Sparge with 3 gallons (11 L) water at 168°F (76°C). Add to runnings:
- **4½ lb. (2 kg) unhopped, malted wheat extract syrup**

Bring to a boil, then add:
- **6 AAUs aged hops, any variety**

Boil 90 minutes, then remove from heat. Cool, then top up to 5¼ gallons (20 L) with chilled, preboiled water. Cool to 68°F (20°C), then pitch:
- **Recultured New Glarus yeast, Belgian strong ale yeast (Wyeast 3787), or wheat yeast (Wyeast 3942)**

Ferment at 65°F (18°C) for 2 weeks, then transfer to secondary fermenter on:
- **6 lb. (2.7 kg) whole sweet cherries (frozen and then thawed)**

Condition-cool (50–55°F [10–13°C]) for 3 to 4 weeks. Rack to another vessel to clarify for 2 weeks. Prime with:
- **⅞ cup (202 ml) corn sugar**

Bottle and age at 55–60°F (13–16°C) for 3 weeks.

Alternate Methods

All-extract: Steep 1 lb. (454 g) each pale, wheat, and crystal malts in 2½ gallons (9.5 L) water at 150°F (66°C) for 45 minutes. Increase malt extract syrup to 6¾ lb. (3.1 kg). Follow directions from beginning of boil.

All-grain: Mash 6 lb. (2.7 kg) pale malt, 4 lb. (1.8 kg) malted wheat, and the crystal malt as in main recipe in 3¼ gallons (12.3 L) water at 152°F (67°C). Sparge with 3¾ gallons (14.2 L) water. Omit malt extract syrup and proceed as in main recipe, reducing wort volume to 5¼ gallons (20 L) or less.

Serve at 50°F (10°C) in a traditional lambic tumbler.

Moose Juice Stout

Otto Bros. Brewing Co., Jackson Hole, Wyoming; Victor, Idaho

*A bottle-conditioned, sweet stout, Moose Juice has a roasty, roasty, roasty nose and
flavor. Oh, by the way, there's also some Cascade aroma there, too.
Well rounded and chewy, this is a big stout.*

Original gravity: 1055 • Final gravity: 1012 • 5.5% abv • 45 IBU

Heat 1¾ gallons (6.6 L) water to 164°F (73°C). Crush:

3 lb. (1.4 kg) pale malt
8 oz. (227 g) dark (120°L) crystal malt
8 oz. (227 g) roasted barley
8 oz. (227 g) black malt

Add to liquor and steep at 152°F (67°C) for 90 minutes. Sparge with
2½ gallons (9.5 L) water at 168°F (76°C). Add to runnings:

3½ lb. (1.6 kg) unhopped, dark dry malt extract (DME)

Bring to a boil, then add:

6 AAUs Chinook hops

Boil 60 minutes, then add:

4 AAUs Chinook hops
4 AAUs Cascade hops

Boil 30 minutes, then remove from heat. Cool, then top up to 5¼ gallons
(20 L) with chilled, preboiled water. Cool to 65°F (18°C), then pitch:

**English or Scottish ale yeast (recultured Moose Juice or
    Wyeast 1098, 1728, or equivalent)**

Ferment at 65°F (18°C) for 2 weeks, then transfer to secondary fermenter
and condition cool (50–55°F [10–13°C]) for 3 to 4 weeks. Prime with:

1 cup (237 ml) pale dry malt extract

Bottle and age at 50°F (10°C) for 3 weeks.

Alternate Methods

All-extract: Steep 1 lb.
(454 g) pale malt and the
crystal malt, roasted barley,
and black malt as in main
recipe in 2½ gallons (9.5 L)
water at 150°F (66°C) for
45 minutes. Increase DME
to 5 lb. (2.3 kg). Follow
directions from beginning
of boil.

All-grain: Mash 8 lb.
(3.6 kg) pale malt and the
crystal malt, roasted barley,
and black malt as in main
recipe in 3 gallons (11 L)
water at 152°F (67°C).
Sparge with 3¾ gallons
(14.2 L) water. Omit first
DME and proceed as in
main recipe, reducing wort
volume to 5¼ gallons
(20 L) or less.

 Serve at 50°F (10°C) in a traditional pint glass.

Clone Recipes
for
Canadian Beers

Moosehead Lager

Moosehead Breweries Ltd., St. John, New Brunswick; Dartmouth, Nova Scotia
Moosehead is a grainy-sweet golden lager from Canada's oldest independent brewery.
Mild, German-style hopping gives this brew a crisp flavor
with low bitterness and a clean aftertaste.

Original gravity: 1045 • Final gravity: 1010 • 4.5% abv • 30 IBU

Heat 1¾ gallons (6.6 L) water to 164°F (73°C). Crush:

3 lb. (1.4 kg) lager malt
1 lb. (454 g) flaked maize
12 oz. (340 g) carapils malt

Add to liquor and steep at 152°F (67°C) for 90 minutes. Sparge with 2½ gallons (9.5 L) water at 168°F (76°C). Add to runnings:

2 lb. (907 g) unhopped, extra-light dry malt extract (DME)

Bring to a boil, then add:

4 AAUs Tettnang hops

Boil 30 minutes, then add:

3 AAUs Tettnang hops
3 AAUs Hallertau hops

Boil 30 minutes, then remove from heat. Cool, then top up to 5¼ gallons (20 L) with chilled, preboiled water. Cool to 62°F (17°C), then pitch:

American lager yeast (Wyeast 2305 or equivalent)

Ferment at 50°F (10°C) for 2 weeks, then transfer to secondary fermenter and condition cold (35°F [2°C]) for 5 to 6 weeks. Prime with:

⅞ cup (202 ml) corn sugar

Bottle and age at 45°F (7°C) for 6 weeks.

Alternate Methods

All-extract: Steep 1 lb. (454 g) lager malt and the flaked maize and carapils malt as in main recipe in 2½ gallons (9.5 L) water at 150°F (66°C) for 45 minutes. Increase DME to 3½ lb. (1.6 kg). Follow directions from beginning of boil.

All-grain: Mash 6 lb. (2.7 kg) lager malt and the maize and carapils malt as in main recipe in 2½ gallons (9.5 L) water at 152°F (67°C). Sparge with 3 gallons (11 L) water. Omit DME and proceed as in main recipe, reducing wort volume to 5¼ gallons (20 L) or less.

Serve at 40°F (4°C) in a traditional Pilsner glass.

County Ale

Wellington County Brewery, Guelph, Ontario

A pleasantly hoppy, "ordinary" bitter ale, County Ale is English in character and has a copper glow and dry finish.

Original gravity: 1052 • Final gravity: 1012 • 5% abv • 40 IBU

Heat 2¼ gallons (8.5 L) water to 164°F (73°C). Crush:

4 lb. (1.8 kg) pale malt
1 lb. (454 g) medium (50°L) crystal malt
8 oz. (227 g) chocolate malt
8 oz. (227 g) malted wheat

Add to liquor and steep at 152°F (67°C) for 90 minutes. Sparge with 3 gallons (11 L) water at 168°F (76°C). Add to runnings:

2 lb. (907 g) unhopped, pale dry malt extract (DME)

Bring to a boil, then add:

6 AAUs Willamette hops

Boil 30 minutes, then add:

4 AAUs Goldings hops

Boil 30 minutes, then remove from heat. Cool, then top up to 5¼ gallons (20 L) with chilled, preboiled water. Cool to 68°F (20°C), then pitch:

English ale yeast (Wyeast 1098 or equivalent)

Ferment at 68°F (20°C) for 2 weeks, then transfer to secondary fermenter and condition cool (50–55°F [10–13°C]) for 3 to 4 weeks. Prime with:

⅞ cup (202 ml) pale dry malt extract

Bottle and age at 50°F (10°C) for 3 weeks.

Alternate Methods

All-extract: Steep 1 lb. (454 g) pale malt and the crystal and chocolate malts and malted wheat as in main recipe in 2½ gallons (9.5 L) water at 150°F (66°C) for 45 minutes. Increase DME to 4 lb. (1.8 kg). Follow directions from beginning of boil.

All-grain: Mash 7 lb. (3.2 kg) pale malt and the crystal and chocolate malts and malted wheat as in main recipe in 3 gallons (11 L) water at 152°F (67°C). Sparge with 3¾ gallons (14.2 L) water. Omit first DME and proceed as in main recipe, reducing wort volume to 5¼ gallons (20 L) or less.

Serve at 50°F (10°C) in a traditional pint glass.

Creemore Springs Premium Lager

Creemore Springs Brewery, Creemore, Ontario

*Creemore Springs is an amber lager that seems to be closest to
a true Bohemian Pilsner than to anything else. However, the hoppy nose
and the malt profile are Bavarian, and the body is a bit lighter than usual.*

Original gravity: 1050 • Final gravity: 1010 • 5% abv • 35–40 IBU

Heat 2¼ gallons (8.5 L) water to 164°F (73°C). Crush:
- **4 lb. (1.8 kg) lager malt**
- **8 oz. (227 g) light carapils malt**
- **8 oz. (227 g) Munich malt**
- **8 oz. (227 g) Vienna malt**

Add to liquor and steep at 152°F (67°C) for 90 minutes. Sparge with
3 gallons (11 L) water at 168°F (76°C). Add to runnings:
- **2 lb. (907 g) unhopped, pale dry malt extract (DME)**

Bring to a boil, then add:
- **6 AAUs Hallertau hops**

Boil 45 minutes, then add:
- **4 AAUs Saaz hops**

Boil 15 minutes, then remove from heat. Cool, then top up to 5¼ gallons
(20 L) with chilled, preboiled water. Cool to 62°F (17°C), then pitch:
- **Czech or Bohemian lager yeast (Wyeast 2278, 2124, or
equivalent)**

Ferment at 40°F (4°C) for 3 weeks, then transfer to secondary fermenter
and condition cold (35°F [2°C]) for 5 to 6 weeks. Prime with:
- **⅞ cup (202 ml) corn sugar**

Bottle and age at 45°F (7°C) for 6 weeks.

Alternate Methods

All-extract: Steep 1 lb.
(454 g) lager malt and the
carapils, Munich, and
Vienna malts as in main
recipe in 2½ gallons (9.5 L)
water at 150°F (66°C) for
45 minutes. Increase DME
to 4 lb. (1.8 kg). Follow
directions from beginning
of boil.

All-grain: Mash 7 lb.
(3.2 kg) lager malt and
the carapils, Munich, and
Vienna malts as in main
recipe in 3 gallons (11 L)
water at 152°F (67°C).
Sparge with 3¾ gallons
(14.2 L) water. Omit DME
and proceed as in main
recipe, reducing wort volume to 5¼ gallons (20 L)
or less.

 Serve at 45°F (7°C) in a traditional Pilsner glass.

Maple Brown Ale

Upper Canada Brewing Co., Toronto, Ontario

*Here's a nicely bittersweet, copper-colored ale with a noticeable maple taste,
a clean malt sweetness, and underlying hop bitterness.*

Original gravity: 1056 • **Final gravity: 1014** • **5.4% abv** • **25 IBU**

Heat 2 gallons (7.6 L) water to 164°F (73°C). Crush:
- **3½ lb. (1.6 kg) mild ale malt**
- **1 lb. (454 g) medium (50°L) crystal malt**
- **8 oz. (227 g) chocolate malt**
- **8 oz. (227 g) Munich malt**

Add to liquor and steep at 152°F (67°C) for 90 minutes. Sparge with 3 gallons (11 L) water at 168°F (76°C). Add to runnings:
- **2 lb. (907 g) unhopped, amber dry malt extract (DME)**
- **1 pint (473 ml) pure maple syrup**

Bring to a boil, then add:
- **4 AAUs Fuggles hops**

Boil 45 minutes, then add:
- **4 AAUs Goldings hops**

Boil 15 minutes, then remove from heat. Cool, then top up to 5¼ gallons (20 L) with chilled, preboiled water. Cool to 68°F (20°C), then pitch:
- **English ale yeast (Wyeast 1098 or equivalent)**

Ferment at 68°F (20°C) for 2 weeks, then transfer to secondary fermenter and condition cool (50–55°F [10–13°C]) for 3 to 4 weeks. Prime with:
- **½ cup (118 ml) pale dry malt extract**
- **½ cup (118 ml) maple syrup**

Bottle and age at 55–60°F (13–16°C) for 3 weeks.

Alternate Methods

All-extract: Steep 8 oz. (227 g) mild ale malt and the crystal, chocolate, and Munich malts as in main recipe in 2½ gallons (9.5 L) water at 150°F (66°C) for 45 minutes. Increase DME to 4 lb. (1.8 kg). Add maple syrup, then follow directions from beginning of boil.

All-grain: Mash 6½ lb. (3 kg) mild ale malt and the crystal, chocolate, and Munich malts as in main recipe in 3 gallons (11 L) water at 152°F (67°C). Sparge with 3¾ gallons (14.2 L) water. Omit first DME, but add maple syrup. Proceed as in main recipe, reducing wort volume to 5¼ gallons (20 L) or less.

Serve at 50°F (10°C) in a traditional pint glass.

Sleeman Steam Beer

Sleeman Brewing and Malting Co., Guelph, Ontario

This brew is a pleasant, semisweet light ale that's slightly fruity, but with a dry finish and aftertaste. "Steam" beer, or California Common beer, is traditionally a cross between ale and lager, often using lager yeast at warmer fermenting temperatures.

Original gravity: 1048 • Final gravity: 1008 • 5% abv • 25 IBU

Heat 1½ gallons (5.7 L) water to 164°F (73°C). Crush:

3 lb. (1.4 kg) lager malt
12 oz. (340 g) carapils malt
1 lb. (454 g) brewer's flaked rice

Add to liquor and steep at 152°F (67°C) for 90 minutes. Sparge with 2¼ gallons (8.5 L) water at 168°F (76°C). Add to runnings:

2 lb. (907 g) unhopped, extra-light dry malt extract (DME)

Bring to a boil, then add:

4 AAUs Mt. Hood hops

Boil 30 minutes, then add:

4 AAUs Hallertau hops

Boil 15 minutes, then remove from heat. Cool, then top up to 5¼ gallons (20 L) with chilled, preboiled water. Cool to 62°F (17°C), then pitch:

California lager yeast (Wyeast 2112 or equivalent)

Ferment at 55°F (13°C) for 2 weeks, then transfer to secondary fermenter and condition cool (50°F [10°C]) for 3 to 4 weeks. Prime with:

⅞ cup (202 ml) corn sugar

Bottle and age at 50°F (10°C) for 3 weeks.

 **Alternate Methods**

All-extract: Steep 1 lb. (454 g) lager malt and the carapils malt as in main recipe in 2½ gallons (9.5 L) water at 150°F (66°C) for 45 minutes. Increase DME to 4 lb. (1.8 kg) and add 8 oz. (227 g) rice syrup solids. Follow directions from beginning of boil.

All-grain: Mash 6 lb. (2.7 kg) lager malt and the carapils malt and flaked rice as in main recipe in 2½ gallons (9.5 L) water at 152°F (67°C). Sparge with 3 gallons (11 L) water. Omit DME and proceed as in main recipe, reducing wort volume to 5¼ gallons (20 L) or less.

 Serve at 50°F (10°C) in a traditional pint glass.

Ambrée de Sarrasin

Bières de la Nouvelle France, Saint-Paulin, Québec

From an artisanal brewery in rural Québec (part museum, part bed-and-breakfast, and even a windmill), this all-natural beer is brewed from unmalted buckwheat, wheat, and oats. It is reddish brown, cloudy, and full of rich and complex flavors.

Original gravity: 1055 • Final gravity: 1016 • 5% abv • 35 IBU

Heat 1¾ gallons (6.6 L) water to 164°F (73°C). Crush:

1½ lb. (680 g) pale malt
8 oz. (227 g) dark (120°L) crystal malt
8 oz. (227 g) flaked oats
8 oz. (227 g) malted wheat
1 lb. (454 g) unmalted buckwheat

Add to liquor and steep at 152°F (67°C) for 90 minutes. Sparge with 2½ gallons (9.5 L) water at 168°F (76°C). Add to runnings:

2 lb. (907 g) unhopped, wheat dry malt extract (DME)
2 lb. (907 g) unhopped, pale dry malt extract

Bring to a boil, then add:

6 AAUs Saaz hops

Boil 30 minutes, then add:

4 AAUs Hallertau hops

Boil 30 minutes, then remove from heat. Cool, then top up to 5¼ gallons (20 L) with chilled, preboiled water. Cool to 68°F (20°C), then pitch:

Recultured Nouvelle France yeast or Belgian wheat beer yeast (Wyeast 3944 or equivalent)

Ferment at 68°F (20°C) for 2 weeks, then transfer to secondary fermenter and condition cool (50–55°F [10–13°C]) for 3 to 4 weeks. Prime with:

1 cup (237 ml) pale dry malt extract

Bottle and age at 55–60°F (13–16°C) for 3 weeks.

Alternate Methods

All-extract: Steep the crystal malt, flaked oats, malted wheat, and buckwheat as in main recipe in 2½ gallons (9.5 L) water at 150°F (66°C) for 45 minutes. Omit pale malt and increase wheat DME to 2 lb. (907 g) and the pale DME to 3 lb. (1.4 kg). Follow directions from beginning of boil.

All-grain: Mash 6 lb. (2.7 kg) pale malt, 2 lb. (907 g) malted wheat, and the crystal malt, flaked oats, and buckwheat as in main recipe in 3¼ gallons (12.3 L) water at 152°F (67°C). Sparge with 3¾ gallons (14.2 L) water. Omit both DMEs and proceed as in main recipe, reducing wort volume to 5¼ gallons (20 L) or less.

Serve at 50°F (10°C) in a weizen glass.

Boréale Noire

Les Brasseurs du Nord, Blainville, Québec

This is a northern stout, creamy and dark, with a rich, smooth finish and a sturdy, roasty character. Grain and hop bitterness are in balance with the malty sweetness.

Original gravity: 1055 • Final gravity: 1015 • 5.1% abv • 40 IBU

Heat 2½ gallons (9.5 L) water to 164°F (73°C). Crush:

- **4 lb. (1.8 kg) pale malt**
- **1 lb. (454 g) dark (120°L) crystal malt**
- **1 lb. (454 g) flaked oats**
- **8 oz. (227 g) roasted barley**
- **8 oz. (227 g) black malt**

Add to liquor and steep at 152°F (67°C) for 90 minutes. Sparge with 3¼ gallons (12.3 L) water at 168°F (76°C). Add to runnings:

- **2 lb. (907 g) unhopped, dark dry malt extract (DME)**

Bring to a boil, then add:

- **4 AAUs Goldings hops**

Boil 30 minutes, then add:

- **4 AAUs Northern Brewer hops**

Boil 45 minutes, then add:

- **4 AAUs Goldings hops**

Boil 15 minutes, then remove from heat. Cool, then top up to 5¼ gallons (20 L) with chilled, preboiled water. Cool to 68°F (20°C), then pitch:

- **Irish ale yeast (Wyeast 1084 or equivalent)**

Ferment at 65°F (18°C) for 2 weeks, then transfer to secondary fermenter and condition cool (50–55°F [10–13°C]) for 3 to 4 weeks. Prime with:

- **1 cup (237 ml) pale dry malt extract**

Bottle and age at 55–60°F (13–16°C) for 3 weeks.

Alternate Methods

All-extract: Steep 1 lb. (454 g) pale malt and the crystal malt, flaked oats, roasted barley, and black malt as in main recipe in 2 1/2 gallons (9.5 L) water at 150°F (66°C) for 45 minutes. Increase DME to 4 lb. (1.8 kg). Follow directions from beginning of boil.

All-grain: Mash 7 lb. (3.2 kg) pale malt and the crystal malt, flaked oats, roasted barley, and black malt as in main recipe in 3 1/4 gallons (12.3 L) water at 152°F (67°C). Sparge with 4 gallons (15.2 L) water. Omit first DME and proceed as in main recipe, reducing wort volume to 5 1/4 gallons (20 L) or less.

 Serve at 50°F (10°C) in a traditional pint glass.

La Fin du Monde

Unibroue, Chambly, Québec

More or less a Belgian tripel, la Fin du Monde is golden and strong, yeasty, fruity, and absolutely wonderful. This brewery outside of Montréal has gained an international reputation for its Belgian-style, bottle-conditioned beers as well as its clever label art — this one features an aerial photo of the province of Québec, the "end of the world."

Original gravity: 1086 • Final gravity: 1015 • 9% abv • 30–35 IBU

Heat 2½ gallons (9.5 L) water to 164°F (73°C). Crush:

4 lb. (1.8 kg) Belgian Pilsner malt
1 lb. (454 g) malted wheat
1 lb. (454 g) caravienne
1 lb. (454 g) light (20°L) crystal malt

Add to liquor and steep at 152°F (67°C) for 90 minutes. Sparge with 3 gallons (11 L) water at 168°F (76°C). Add to runnings:

6 lb. (2.7 kg) unhopped, extra-light malt extract syrup
8 oz. (227 g) clear candi sugar

Bring to a boil, then add:

6 AAUs Perle hops

Boil 30 minutes, then add:

4 AAUs Styrian Goldings hops

Boil 30 minutes, then remove from heat. Cool, then top up to 5¼ gallons (20 L) with chilled, preboiled water. Cool to 68°F (20°C), then pitch:

Belgian strong ale yeast (recultured Unibroue, Wyeast 1388, or equivalent)

Ferment at 65°F (18°C) for 2 weeks, then transfer to secondary fermenter and condition cool (50–55°F [10–13°C]) for 5 to 6 weeks. Prime with:

1 cup (237 ml) extra-light dry malt extract (DME)

Bottle and age at 50°F (10°C) for 8 weeks.

Alternate Methods

All-extract: Steep the malted wheat and the caravienne and crystal malts as in main recipe in 2½ gallons (9.5 L) water at 150°F (66°C) for 45 minutes. Omit Pilsner malt and add 7½ lb. (3.4 kg) extra-light DME. Add the candi sugar. Follow directions from beginning of boil.

All-grain: Mash 10 lb. (4.5 kg) Belgian Pilsner malt, 2 lb. (907 g) malted wheat, and the caravienne and crystal malts as in main recipe in 4 gallons (15.1 L) water at 152°F (67°C). Sparge with 4 gallons (15.1 L) water. Omit malt extract syrup, but add candi sugar and proceed as in main recipe, reducing wort volume to 5¼ gallons (20 L) or less.

 Serve at 50°F (10°C) in a Trappist-style goblet.

Griffon Brown Ale

McAuslan Brewery, Montréal, Québec

Griffon is brewed with an eye toward the French-speaking beer drinker by a decidedly English-style brewery in Montréal, Canada's largest Francophonic city. Griffon Brown is a sweet, nutty, fruity brown ale, much like an English southern brown style. This deep amber-colored beer exudes a prune and chocolate aroma and finishes crisp and clean.

Original gravity: 1040 • Final gravity: 1008 • 4% abv • 18 IBU

Heat 2 gallons (7.6 L) water to 164°F (73°C). Crush:

2 lb. (907 g) mild ale malt
8 oz. (227 g) carapils malt
4 oz. (113 g) chocolate malt

Add to liquor and steep at 152°F (67°C) for 90 minutes. Sparge with 3 gallons (11 L) water at 168°F (76°C). Add to runnings:

3 lb. (1.4 kg) unhopped, amber malt extract syrup
2 cups (460 ml) light brown sugar

Boil 60 minutes, then add:

3 AAUs Willamette hops

Boil 30 minutes, then add:

3 AAUs Willamette hops

Boil 30 minutes, then remove from heat. Cool, then top up to 5¼ gallons (20 L) with chilled, preboiled water. Cool to 68°F (20°C), then pitch:

British ale yeast (Wyeast 1098 or equivalent)

Ferment at 68°F (20°C) for 2 weeks, then transfer to secondary fermenter and condition cool (50–55°F [10–13°C]) for 3 to 4 weeks. Prime with:

½ cup (118 ml) pale dry malt extract
½ cup (118 ml) light brown sugar

Bottle and age at 55–60°F (13–16°C) for 3 weeks.

Alternate Methods

All-extract: Steep the carapils and chocolate malts as in main recipe in 2½ gallons (9.5 L) water at 150°F (66°C) for 45 minutes. Omit mild ale malt and increase malt extract syrup to 4 lb. (1.8 kg). Add brown sugar and follow directions from beginning of boil.

All-grain: Mash 6 lb. (2.7 kg) mild ale malt and the carapils and chocolate malts as in main recipe in 2½ gallons (9.5 L) water at 152°F (67°C). Sparge with 3¼ gallons (12.3 L) water. Omit malt extract syrup, but add the brown sugar and proceed as in main recipe, reducing wort volume to 5¼ gallons (20 L) or less.

Serve at 50°F (10°C) in a traditional pint glass.

Quelquechose

Unibroue, Chambly, Québec

*This beer is really "something," as its name says. It's a huge fruit beer
meant to be warmed and drunk in a mug. It's made with almost as many cherries
as it has malt, giving it a bright red color and obvious cherry aroma and flavor. It is not
a sour, lambic-style beer, but instead a tart, fruit-flavored, strong ale.*

Original gravity: 1085 • **Final gravity: 1022** • **8% abv** • **20 IBU**

Heat 3 gallons (11 L) water to 164°F (73°C). Crush:
- **5 lb. (2.3 kg) pale malt**
- **3 lb. (1.4 kg) malted wheat**
- **8 oz. (227 g) medium (50°L) crystal malt**

Add to liquor and steep at 152°F (67°C) for 90 minutes. Sparge with
3¾ gallons (14.2 L) water at 168°F (76°C). Add to runnings:
- **4 lb. (1.8 kg) unhopped, pale dry malt extract (DME)**

Bring to a boil, then add:
- **5 AAUs Brewer's Gold hops**

Boil 90 minutes, then remove from heat. Cool, then top up to 5¼ gallons
(20 L) with chilled, preboiled water. Cool to 68°F (20°C), then pitch:
- **Belgian strong ale yeast (recultured Unibroue, Wyeast
  1388, or equivalent)**

Ferment at 68°F (20°C) for 2 weeks, then transfer to secondary fermenter onto:
- **6 lb. (2.7 kg) sour cherries**

Condition cool (50–55°F [10–13°C]) for 3 to 4 weeks. Rack to a clean
carboy for 2 weeks to clarify. Prime with:
- **⅔ cup (158 ml) pale dry malt extract**

Bottle and age at 55–60°F (13–16°C) for 3 weeks.

Alternate Methods

All-extract: Steep 1½ lb.
(680 g) pale malt, 1 lb.
(454 g) malted wheat, and
the crystal malt as in main
recipe in 2½ gallons (9.5 L)
water at 150°F (66°C) for
45 minutes. Increase DME
to 8 lb. (3.6 kg). Follow
directions from beginning
of boil.

All-grain: Mash 10 lb.
(4.5 kg) pale malt, 4 lb.
(1.8 kg) malted wheat, and
the crystal malt as in main
recipe in 11¾ gallons
(6.6 L) water at 152°F
(67°C). Sparge with 5 gallons (18.9 L) water. Omit
first DME and proceed as
in main recipe, reducing
wort volume to 5¼ gallons
(20 L) or less.

 Serve at 160°F (71°C) in a ceramic mug.

St. Ambroise Stout

McAuslan Brewery, Montréal, Québec

They call it a "bière noire," or black beer. What it is is one of the most respected and award-winning oatmeal stouts in North America. It is full bodied, full flavored, creamy, and delicious. Every note, every flavor, every hint of color and aroma is perfectly in place and in balance.

Original gravity: 1058   •   Final gravity: 1015   •   5.5% abv   •   30 IBU

Heat 2¼ gallons (8.5 L) water to 164°F (73°C). Crush:

3 lb. (1.4 kg) pale malt
1 lb. (454 g) flaked oats
8 oz. (227 g) Munich malt
4 oz. (113 g) Belgian Special B malt
8 oz. (227 g) roasted barley

Add to liquor and steep at 152°F (67°C) for 90 minutes. Sparge with 3 gallons (11 L) water at 168°F (76°C). Add to runnings:

3½ lb. (1.6 kg) unhopped, dark dry malt extract (DME)

Bring to a boil, then add:

6 AAUs Bullion hops

Boil 75 minutes, then add:

4 AAUs Willamette hops

Boil 15 minutes, then remove from heat. Cool, then top up to 5¼ gallons (20 L) with chilled, preboiled water. Cool to 68°F (20°C), then pitch:

English ale yeast (Wyeast 1098 or equivalent)

Ferment at 68°F (20°C) for 2 weeks, then transfer to secondary fermenter and condition cool (50–55°F [10–13°C]) for 3 to 4 weeks. Prime with:

1 cup (237 ml) pale dry malt extract

Bottle and age at 50°F (10°C) for 3 weeks.

Alternate Methods

All-extract: Steep the oats, Munich and Belgian Special B malts, and roasted barley as in main recipe in 2½ gallons (9.5 L) water at 150°F (66°C) for 45 minutes. Omit pale malt and increase DME to 5½ lb. (2½ kg). Follow directions from beginning of boil.

All-grain: Mash 8 lb. (3.6 kg) pale malt and the oats, Munich and Special B malts, and roasted barley as in main recipe in 2½ gallons (9.5 L) water at 152°F (67°C). Sparge with 3 gallons (11 L) water. Omit first DME and proceed as in main recipe, reducing wort volume to 5¼ gallons (20 L) or less.

 Serve at 50°F (10°C) in a traditional pint glass.

Seigneuriale Réserve

Brasserie Seigneuriale, Boucherville, Québec

A vaguely Belgian-style country ale, this beer is strong and complex with caramel and fruity notes balanced by yeasty and alcoholic aromas. Smooth and medium bodied, this is a beer to savor.

Original gravity: 1075 • **Final gravity: 1017** • **7.5% abv** • **35–40 IBU**

Heat 2¼ gallons (8.5 L) water to 164°F (73°C). Crush:

4 lb. (1.8 kg) Belgian pale malt
1 lb. (454 g) medium (50°L) crystal malt
8 oz. (227 g) Belgian Special B malt
8 oz. (227 g) caramunich malt
8 oz. (227 g) malted wheat

Add to liquor and steep at 152°F (67°C) for 90 minutes. Sparge with 3 gallons (11 L) water at 168°F (76°C). Add to runnings:

4 lb. (1.8 kg) unhopped, pale dry malt extract (DME)

Bring to a boil, then add:

6 AAUs Brewer's Gold hops

Boil 30 minutes, then add:

4 AAUs Saaz hops

Boil 30 minutes, then remove from heat. Cool, then top up to 5¼ gallons (20 L) with chilled, preboiled water. Cool to 68°F (20°C), then pitch:

Recultured Seigneuriale yeast or Belgian ale (Wyeast 1214 or equivalent)

Ferment at 65°F (18°C) for 2 weeks, then transfer to secondary fermenter and condition cool (50–55°F [10–13°C]) for 3 to 4 weeks. Prime with:

¾ cup (177 ml) pale dry malt extract

Bottle and age at 50°F (10°C) for 3 weeks.

Alternate Methods

All-extract: Steep 1 lb. (454 g) Belgian pale malt and the crystal, Special B, and caramunich malts and malted wheat as in main recipe in 2½ gallons (9.5 L) water at 150°F (66°C) for 45 minutes. Increase DME to 6 lb. (2.7 kg). Follow directions from beginning of boil.

All-grain: Mash 10 lb. (4.5 kg) Belgian pale malt and the crystal, Special B, and caramunich malts and malted wheat as in main recipe in 2½ gallons (9.5 L) water at 152°F (67°C). Sparge with 3 gallons (11 L) water. Omit first DME and proceed as in main recipe, reducing wort volume to 5¼ gallons (20 L) or less.

 Serve at 50°F (10°C) in an abbey-style chalice glass.

Appendix: Beer Style Guidelines

This thumbnail sketch of beer styles is adapted from the guidelines used by the Beer Judge Certification Program in competition judging. Descriptions are supplemented with my own observations and research. Not every beer fits neatly into the style category it claims to be in, and I left out some of the more obscure styles and combined some of the closely related styles.

ALES

Ales are brewed at relatively warm temperatures using a strain of yeast that ferments at or near the top of the beer.

Style	Original Gravity	Bitterness (IBUs)	Characteristics
Light Ales			
Blond ale	1045–1060	15–30	Light in color and usually crisp and hoppy.
Cream ale	1044–55	10–22	Light in color, clean in flavor, and sometimes brewed with a lager yeast. Can include nonmalted adjunct grains.
Pale Ales			
British-style pale ale	1043–56	20–40	Deep gold to amber color; hop flavor and aroma are characteristically British.
American pale ale	1045–56	20–40	Much like British-style pale ale, but using American hops.
California Common (steam beer)	1040–55	35–45	Ale temperatures with a lager yeast gives a sour, tangy bitterness.
Bitter Ales			
Ordinary bitter	1034–39	20–40	Milder version of a British pale ale.
Best bitter	1040–46	20–40	More full-bodied version of an ordinary bitter.
Extra strong (or special) bitter	1046–60	30–50	Like best bitter, but a notch stronger and hoppier.
Scottish Ales			
Light (60/)	1030–35	9–15	The emphasis is on malt, with much less hop flavor and bitterness than British pale ales or bitters. They are labeled according to the old tax designations (in shillings), based on their original gravity.
Heavy (70/)	1035–40	10–17	
Export (80/)	1040–50	10–20	
Brown Ales			
Mild	1030–38	10–24	A light-bodied, low-alcohol session beer with a mild caramel flavor.
Southern brown ale	1040–45	15–20	On the sweet side; emphasis on malt over hops, but still balanced.

Style	Original Gravity	Bitterness (IBUs)	Characteristics
Brown Ales (continued)			
Northern brown ale	1040–50	15–30	Slightly bitter and stronger version of Southern brown ale.
American brown ale	1040–60	25–60	Bigger, fuller, more bitter version of English ales.
India Pale Ales			
English-style IPA	1050–75	30–60	Traditionally brewed in England for shipment to the colonies (India in particular); brewed a little stronger and hoppier to preserve it for the journey. Often aged in oak.
American IPA	1050–1080	35–70	Brewed and aged like English IPA, but made with American hops.
German Ales			
Kölsch	1040–48	16–30	Blond ale, fruity and crisply bitter, from the Köln (Cologne) area.
Altbier	1040–55	30–60	A light amber ale, crisp and bitter, brewed traditionally in the Düsseldorf area. There is a milder version in the Münster region.
Porters			
Robust porter	1040–58	25–40	Deep black, bitter, and hoppy.
Brown porter	1040–50	20–30	Rich brown to almost black; less bitter and more malty than robust porters.
Stouts			
Dry stout	1036–55	25–40	Traditional Irish beer style. Flavor and aroma of roasted barley dominate; big creamy head, black color, and a smooth, medium body.
Sweet stout	1038–56	15–25	Less bitter and more full bodied than dry stout.
Oatmeal stout	1038–56	15–25	Sweet stout made even smoother with the addition of oats.
Foreign/extra stout	1060–75	25–60	A big, hoppy stout brewed for export, or brewed in former colonial territories. Sometimes called "tropical" stout.
Wheat Beers			
Bavarian weizen	1045–55	8–14	Sweet to medium, golden, sometimes hazy; fruity and spicy aromas.
Bavarian dunkelweizen	1045–55	10–15	Medium-dark version of the light weizen; slightly richer in flavor and body.
American	1035–50	10–30	Lighter in body than Bavarian style, but hoppier.
Berliner weissbier	1028–32	3–12	Very light, hazy, lactic, sour wheat beer typically brewed in the Berlin area; often served sweetened with fruit syrup.
Belgian witbier	1044–50	15–25	Pale wheat ale that is hazy, spicy (coriander, bitter orange, and ginger flavors), and aromatic.

ALES (continued)

Style	Original Gravity	Bitterness (IBUs)	Characteristics
Strong Ales			
Old/Strong ale	1060–90	30–60	Catchall category for the many "special" beers that don't fit another category. These are often simply "strong" versions of other beers, such as brown ales, porters, bitters. All full bodied, high in alcohol, warming, and rich.
Scotch ale	1072–88	14–35	Big and malty beers, slightly smoky, amber to brown in color. Often lengthily aged and vintage dated.
Imperial (Russian) stout	1075–95	50–90	Originally brewed for the court of the tsar in the 19th century; a big, rich, black stout, high in alcohol and made with roasted barley. Often sweet, with burnt-sugar or molasses flavor and aroma.
Barleywine	1080–1120	50–100	Big, strong, full bodied, bittersweet, and alcoholic.
Belgian Ales			
Dubbel	1060–70	20–30	Originated in Trappist abbeys; second-strongest style the monks brewed. Often amber to brown, rich, and alcoholic.
Tripel	1075–90	25–40	Originated in Trappist abbeys; strongest style the monks brewed. Often amber to brown, rich, and alcoholic.
Strong golden ale	1060–70	20–30	Dubbel strength, but tripel flavor profile.
Strong dark ale	1070–96	25–50	Tripel strength, but dubbel flavor profile.
Bière de garde	1060–80	25–30	French-style beer strong enough to store for months; amber, malty, and spicy.
Oud Bruin/Flanders red ale	1045–55	15–25	Slightly acidic/sour, reddish brown beers from southern Belgium.
Lambic	1040–70	3–22	Sour beers based on wheat and a variety of bacteria and wild yeasts. Several different versions: blends, fruited or sweetened varieties, etc.
Saison	1048–80	20–40	Refreshing, sour, tart, summer beer; orange to amber in color.

LAGERS

Brewed colder than ales and using yeast strains that ferment at or near the bottom of the beer, lagers tend to be crisp and clean as opposed to the coarse fruitiness of ales.

Style	Original Gravity	Bitterness (IBUs)	Characteristics
Light Lagers			
Standard American light lager	1035–50	8–22	The most common style made in the United States and Canada. Loosely based on the Pilsner style, but often using a nonmalt adjunct grain.

Style	Original Gravity	Bitterness (IBUs)	Characteristics
Light Lagers (continued)			
American dark lager	1040–50	14–20	Slightly dark-colored version of a standard American light; usually colored with a nonmalt coloring agent (such as caramel).
Bohemian Pilsner	1044–56	25–40	Deceptively full bodied, rich, and hoppy (mainly Saaz hops).
Continental Pilsner	1044–50	25–45	German, Dutch, and Scandinavian versions of Bohemian Pilsner. Sweeter and less full bodied.
Dortmunder export	1050–60	23–30	A crisp, golden lager with a nice balance of malt and hops.
Munich helles	1045–55	18–25	Full-bodied and malty golden lager; more sweet than bitter.
Amber Lagers			
Vienna lager	1046–52	18–30	A malty, reddish amber lager. Most today are brewed in Mexico.
Märzenbier/Oktoberfest	1050–60	20–30	Rich, malty, hoppy, and medium to full bodied; deep gold to amber color.
Rauchbier	1048–60	20–30	Based on a Märzenbier, but with the addition of beechwood smoked malt. Amber, malty, rich, and with a distinct smoky aroma and flavor.
Steinbier	1048–55	25–30	Made by immersing superhot stones into the kettle, thus caramelizing the sugars and giving a smoky, burnt-sugar taste to amber lager.
Dark Lagers			
Munich dunkel	1050–58	16–30	Dark amber to reddish brown, malty and slightly sweet, not at all bitter.
Continental dark	1045–55	16–25	Catchall category for the dark lagers in Europe that don't fit the Munich dunkel or Schwarzbier profiles. They may vary greatly in color, bitterness, and body.
Schwarzbier	1040–52	20–35	German black lager with dry flavor from roasted malts; not burnt or bitter.
Bocks			
Traditional bock	1064–74	20–30	Strong amber to brown lager, rich in flavor and body, alcoholic and warming.
Maibock	1064–68	20–30	Lighter in color, but every bit as rich and warming as darker traditional bocks.
Doppelbock	1072–1120	17–40	Stronger than traditional bocks; rich, intense, and full bodied.

Beer Style Index

Smoked Porter, 13
Stovepipe Porter, 125

Scottish Ales
Double Eagle Scotch Ale, 98
Road Dog Ale, 33
Samuel Adams Scotch
    Ale, 70
Smuttynose Scotch-Style
    Ale, 88

Stouts
Barney Flats Oatmeal
    Stout, 16
Black 47 Stout, 83
Black Chocolate Stout, 91
Black Fly Stout, 50
Boréale Noire, 156
Boulder Stout, 28
Dempsey's Extra Stout, 142
Fat Bear Stout, 92
Gray's Imperial Stout, 143
Gray's Oatmeal Stout, 144
Heart of Darkness
    Stout, 122
Martha's Vineyard Extra
    Stout, 67
Moose Juice Stout, 148
St. Ambroise Stout, 160
Stony Man Stout, 132
Wild Goose Oatmeal
    Stout, 61

Strong Ales
Bigfoot, 17
Black Chocolate Stout, 91
Buzzards Bay Stock Ale, 62
Double Eagle Scotch Ale, 98
Fred, 103
Hampshire Special Ale, 52
Hibernation Ale, 30

Immortale, 39
Old Bawdy 1998, 135
Pranqster, 23
Private Stock Imperial
    Stout, 68
Quelquechose, 159
Seigneuriale Réserve, 161
Smuttynose Imperial Stout,
    87
Smuttynose Scotch-Style
    Ale, 88
Winter Solstice Ale, 72

Wheat Beers
Bert Grant's Hefeweizen, 134
Calusa Wheat Beer, 40
Harpoon UFO Hefeweizen,
    64
Honey Weizen, 105
Tabernash Weiss, 34

LAGERS
Amber Lagers
Abita Amber, 47
Adirondack Amber, 90
Capital Summerfest, 141
Creemore Springs Premium
    Lager, 152
DeGroen's Märzen, 57
Festbier, 112
Hammer & Nail Vienna-Style
    Lager, 37
Hübsch Märzen, 20
Point Amber, 146
Schild Brau Amber, 44

Bocks
Harpoon Spring Maibock, 63
Maifest, 79
Mercator Doppelbock, 106
Shiner Bock, 117

Stein Bock, 45
Subliminator Doppelbock, 59

Dark Lagers
Berghoff Dark, 139
Black Bavarian-Style Lager,
    140
Saranac Black Forest
    Lager, 97

Light Lagers
Acadian Pilsener, 48
Bohemian Pilsner, 41
Dominion Lager, 129
Grain Belt Premium Beer, 77
Longshore Lager, 93
Lucknow Munich-Style Lager,
    85
Moosehead Lager, 150
Pete's Signature Pilsner, 22
Phil's Pils, 82
Prima Pils, 113
Rolling Rock Beer, 114

OTHER
Crazy Ed's Original Cave
    Creek Chili Beer, 14
Hempen Ale, 58
McSorley's Black & Tan, 75
Michael Shea's Black &
    Tan, 94
Rogue XS Smoke Ale, 109
Tunbridge Sap Brew, 126
Weizen-berry, 137
Wisconsin Belgian Red, 147

Other Storey Titles You Will Enjoy

Brew Ware: How to Find, Adapt & Build Homebrewing Equipment,
by Karl F. Lutzen & Mark Stevens.
Step-by-step instructions to build tools to make brewing safer and easier.
272 pages. Paper. ISBN-13: 978-0-88266-926-7.

CloneBrews, by Tess and Mark Szamatulski.
One hundred and fifty recipes to brew beer that tastes just like
premium commercial brands.
176 pages. Paper. ISBN-13: 978-1-58017-077-2.

Dave Miller's Homebrewing Guide, by Dave Miller.
A simple yet complete overview of homebrewing that is clear enough for
the novice but thorough enough for the brewmaster.
368 pages. Paper. ISBN-13: 978-0-88266-905-2.

Homebrew Favorites, by Karl F. Lutzen & Mark Stevens.
Favorite recipes collected from homebrewers across North America, with
straightforward directions for everything from the simple to the exotic.
256 pages. Paper. ISBN-13: 978-0-88266-613-6.

The Homebrewer's Answer Book, by Ashton Lewis.
Hundreds of brewing problems solved by *Brew Your Own*
magazine's Mr. Wizard.
432 pages. Flexibind. ISBN-13: 978-1-58017-675-0.

More Homebrew Favorites, by Karl F. Lutzen & Mark Stevens.
An expansion to any homebrewer's repertoire, with more than 260 new recipes.
320 pages. Paper. ISBN-13: 978-0-88266-968-7.

The Secret Life of Beer, by Alan D. Eames.
A fun collection of cultural history, legends, lore, little-known facts, and quirky
quotes by beer drinkers from Nietzsche to Darwin.
384 pages. Paper. ISBN-13: 978-1-58017-601-9.

These and other books from Storey Publishing are available
wherever quality books are sold or by calling 1-800-441-5700.
Visit us at *www.storey.com.*